GOD'S ECSTASY

GOD'S ECSTASY

The Creation of a Self-Creating World

BEATRICE BRUTEAU

A Crossroad Book
The Crossroad Publishing Company
New York

This printing: 2019

The Crossroad Publishing Company
www.CrossroadPublishing.com

Printed in the United States of America

Library of Congress Cataloging-in-Publication Data

Bruteau, Beatrice, 1930-
    God's ecstasy : the creation of a self-creating world / Beatrice
Bruteau.
        p.   cm.
    Includes bibliographical references and index.
    ISBN 0-8245-1683-4 (pbk.)
    1. Creation. 2. Trinity. 3. Ontology.   I. Title.
BT695.B78   1997
231–dc21   97-15611

*There is no music, no worship, no love,
when we take the world's wonders
for granted.* *

There Is No Singing without God: A Prayerbook for Shabbat, Festivals, and Weekdays, edited, with translations, by Rabbi Jules Harlow (New York: Rabbinical Assembly, United Synagogue of America, 1985).

CONTENTS

PREFACE

Religion without science is lame.
— ALBERT EINSTEIN

 THIS IS A BOOK on science for Christians. It's for already religious people who are acquainted with the basic doctrines of the Trinity and the Incarnation, and especially for contemplatives. However, you don't have to be a contemplative trinitarian Christian to find its basic metaphysical argument understandable. Everyone has to face the questions of the One and the Many, the infinite and the finite. My hope is to show religious readers that scientific knowledge of the natural world (which includes people and people's cultures) is important, is part of our religious life, our practice, the way we live the divine life.

It is about how the Trinity is showing itself as world, especially with the characteristic trinitarian trait of living-together, *symbiosis,* mutual indwelling, interacting, sharing. From elementary particles in the atom, through atoms in molecules, molecules in cells, cells in organisms, organisms in societies, to social actions and even ideas — all of them being organized as *systems* — the trinitarian image, as a Many-One, as a Community, has been present and growing. "Growing" (from the inside out) is the right word; the Creativity that makes the world is built into the world as its own essence. God is creating a self-creating world.

Randomness, the pool of all possibilities, is part of how it is done. So is spontaneous order, and adaptation by natural selection. What we now call *complexity,* and recognize as doing its creative work on the very edge of chaos, is at the heart of this miraculous picture. There may not be an external Designer and a micro-managing Providence from the outside, but neither is the world devoid of divinity. The divinity is so intimately present in the world that the world can be regarded as an incarnate expression of the Trinity, as creative, as expansive, as conscious, as self-realizing and self-sharing.

I have called this creative act God's ecstasy. Ecstasy means standing outside oneself. It is kin to the *kenosis* of Philippians 2:6 — being God is not a thing to be clung to, so God empties Godself, taking the form of limitation in finitude, and is born as a universe. It is the defining divine act: self-giving, being-bestowing. Ecstasy has the connotations of extreme love and supreme joy. That is right for the creation of the universe.

Therefore, we are not to feel the universe as cold, indifferent, or alien. Nor are we ourselves strangers here, meaningless accidental products of mindless cosmic shufflings. We belong to the universe, a living universe; we are its own natural children — as the *Desiderata* says, "as much as the trees and the stars, we have a right to be here."

The cosmic complexity has supported the development of consciousness, and now we can know and understand and contemplate this beautiful and marvelous universe. We can appreciate it as the externalization — the ecstasy — of Creativity itself, of the trinitarian God: manyness so symbiotic as to be one whole living being.

The conclusion for the religious person should be that the world is God's most personal work, therefore something for us to know and admire and revere, to take part in, to contribute to creating — since it is made as a self-creating universe. This is participating in the divine life, precisely what the religious person wants to do.

So I have tried to set forth a general view of this cosmos that shows it in this light. My hope is that others will get a sense of how the universe is radiant and exciting and how we are poised right on the creative edge, right where the new action is happening. God's action, our action. A self-creating universe that is God's ecstasy, God standing — indeed, God dancing! — outside Godself, still doing the Godly things: being One, being Community, sharing being, indwelling, rejoicing, always being more.

BEATRICE BRUTEAU
Pfafftown, N.C.,
March 1997

MANY THANKS are due Jeffrey Schmitt (biochemist) and William Calvin (theoretical neurophysiologist) for reading the science chapters and to Maureen Krah, Judith Fulcher, Kent Outlaw, and Gordon Kendall for giving feedback on behalf of the expected reader. I am especially grateful to my husband, James Somerville, for reading and rereading the text and assisting with the illustrations. Grateful acknowledgment is made of permission to use the diagram of the neuron from Calvin and Ojemann, *Conversations with Neil's Brain* (Addison-Wesley, 1994). I am very pleased to have Ansgar Holmberg's gouache painting for our cover art; a Sister of St. Joseph in Minneapolis, the painter says that she "sees art as an incarnational expression of the continued birthing of Hope in our world."

Chapter One

THE CONTEMPLATIVE AND THE COSMOS

 PEOPLE WHO IDENTIFY THEMSELVES as contemplatives may shy away from science for a number of reasons. They may think that they have "no head for" numbers and the analytic kind of thing science deals with. They may feel that it's too impersonal, has no human warmth. It's too technical, too abstract, doesn't have immediate emotional appeal.

I want to suggest that we come at the question of contemplatives studying science from a different angle. Before we consider whether we are interested in the scientific study of this universe, let us ask whether God is "interested in" the universe, how it is structured, how it works, how it's developing. If we believe in a Creator-God, who is still in the act of creating this universe, how can we pretend to be interested in God, but not interested in what God is doing, in what (presumably) God is interested in? And if we were to attain our contemplative ideal of sharing in the divine life, would we not be sharing in the activity of creating the universe?

It is a curious and wonderful thing that the Godmade universe is made as a self-making universe. I think this is a very important point and has much to do with the whole idea of "sharing in" the divine life. We may say that the "divine" is that which has life in itself. John 5:26 says, "As the Father has life in himself, so he has granted the Son also to have life in himself." Now, if the Son is the Exegete, the Revealer, as John 1:18 tells us, and if the exegesis, the manifestation and revelation of the invisible God, is the cosmos, then may we not read: "As God has life in Godself, so God has made the cosmos to have life in itself"?

For me as a contemplative, the conclusion seems to be that to share in the divine life I must accept the vocation of consciously living in this self-creating universe. But consciously living in the activity of self-creating means that I need to know something about the whole thing, how it works, how it's moving, how to take my place in it, make my meaningful contribution to this general improvisation.

Joining in the creative work is really central to the whole contemplative enterprise. Cosmogenesis — the generation of the cosmos — can be seen, as Teilhard de Chardin saw it, as "Christogenesis," the growth of the "ever greater Christ."[1] This Christ has been "growing in stature and wisdom" (Luke 2:52; read "complexity and consciousness") these last dozen or so billion years and is nowhere near finished yet.

So there are two motivations for including some knowledge of science in our contemplative lives: one, we need to understand God's artistic work in order to appreciate it properly and relate lovingly to the Creator; two, we need to know something of the work in order to join it, to participate in creating the world from here on. This last is the real way of loving, that is, by joining in the life of the beloved.

But again, there is looking at it from God's point of view. If I may modify Psalm 19 slightly, I will say: "The heavens declare the glory of God and the earth manifests the divine handiwork." What Earth and the other heavenly bodies are manifesting is the glory, the overflowing creative activity, that necessarily expresses and thus images the Creator. If the Trinity-Creator so puts Its heart into the natural world, showing and revealing Itself on every side, displaying Its glory, then we certainly ought to pay attention, to learn as much as we can, and to appreciate the amazing variety, subtlety, niceness of adjustment and interrelation, beauty, capacity for development, novelty, inventiveness and creativity in its turn of this cosmos.

It is, at the very least, the artwork of God, and if you know anything about art, you know how the artist is unavoidably present in the artwork, and how important it is to the artist that the artwork draw attention and succeed in communicating. Since the divine Artist has chosen to create, we cannot love the Artist without giving our best attention to the artwork.

A Renewed Sense of the Sacred

This looking from God's point of view helps us to reassert our sense of the sacred, something we seem to have lost lately. The world has been presented to us as a great machine, something dead and in itself meaningless, something that rolls on relentlessly, ruthlessly, incapable of sensitivity or significance. It starts from a fluke of a fluctuation and thereafter operates by chance and necessity. It's not trying to accomplish anything, it has no purpose, and we human beings have no special place in it. We are simply an accident, an improbable accident, and our request for meaningfulness meets with no reply from the universe. In such a world, how could we have a sense of the sacred that would be anything other than a superstition fit only for scorn? Ever since we've had this mechanistic, accidentalistic worldview, we've been despondent, and when we're despondent, we turn to artificial stimulants such as greed and success, inventions of local meaningfulness. But, deprived of the sense of the sacred wholeness of things, our bonds are weakening. Underneath we know that we're whistling in the dark.

We dream of times gone by when there used to be a palpable sense of belonging to some great wholeness that was meaningful in itself and extended its meaningfulness to us. Keiji Nishitani describes it as a feeling that all of us, not just human beings, but all living things, were living from the same life, like leaves on a single tree. Each soul was life itself, taking some particular form, whether human, animal, or plant. This was the basis for a "sympathetic affinity" among the living, indicating a unity deeper than our everyday superficial relations.[2] The mysterious wholeness, beyond our individual selves, was the sacred, and we felt it as such. Can we not have that any more?

Somewhere deep down, we are all filled with mystical longing, longing for meaningful belonging, for profound union, longing to be securely embedded in the ultimate meaningfulness, and therefore we need to see all our world in that context. We long to feel the ultimate meaningfulness as real, all around us, concrete, real, intimate, tangible, communicating with us. To attain this in today's climate, we need a new theology of the cosmos, one that is grounded in the best science of our day. It will be a theology in which God is very present, precisely in all the dynamisms and patterns of the created order, in which God is not rendered absent by the self-organizing activities of the natural world, but in which God is actual as the one who makes and the one who is incarnate in what is made by these very self-making activities.

Can our science be seen that way? Yes, I think so, and I would like to show it to you in those terms, so that all the world turns sacred again and we truly feel our unity and our wholeness and our belonging to the all.

Living Together in Wholeness

The view of the sacred world that I am proposing says that the world consists of communication — interactions among its components or members in which they exchange matter, energy, and information. I feel that we should recognize and celebrate it as a gigantic Eucharist in which each one feeds all the others with each one's own being. Of course, this happens on various levels of organization and awareness and commitment. But they are all instances of what I call "living-together" — symbiosis — by that sharing of matter, energy, and information. And any symbiosis, sharing of life so as to make one whole being, is an image of the Trinity, the original symbiotic Unity. It is that presence of the Trinity as a pattern repeated at every scale of the cosmic order that makes the universe the manifestation of God and itself sacred and holy.

As contemplatives in the Christian tradition, we are familiar with the concept of the Mystical Body of Christ, the church, or the sacred community imaged as an organic unity, a single living organism. We have been taught to think of it as composed of a rich diversity of functions, all of them necessary and noble, contributing to the single, unified life. In fact, that very diversity is what makes for vitality, moving energy, and for unity, wholeness. Each member, making a particular contribution, draws the whole into tighter communion.

Lately there has been a willingness to extend the borders of this living Body, to consider that it really includes people who are not official members of whichever is "our" church and maybe are not even Christians. Now, keeping to this sense of organic, interlocking functional unity, expand still further. Get a feeling of a cosmic extension of shared life, shared relations, interactions making each part of the universe a significant contributor to the unity of the whole. Keep the sense of the sacred, the feeling that God is somehow resident here.

The church body is explicitly intended to be "like" the Trinity in the way that it is "one" — "that they may be one even as we are one" (John 17:22) — and this inter-living way can be extended as a model for the whole universe. Notice that it is the *actions* of the members toward one another that constitutes the unity. The Persons of the Trinity love one another to the extent of "indwelling" one another. The members of the Mystical Body are to love one another and share the various gifts of their lives. Now even the cosmos can be seen and meaningfully experienced as a vast network of interactions of all sorts, from our human interactions, through biological and chemical exchanges, all the way down to physical laws such as the gravitational attraction that governs the galaxies.

There is a sense in which it all constitutes one thing, which is why it is called a uni-verse. We need to experience it this way, feel it all as relevant to us and ourselves as relevant to it, all of us being here together, members of this one developing body with its repeated patterns of diversity, interaction, and wholeness. The universe may be said to be the original Adam, a great body of dust, organized into a system and energized by the "breath" of God so that it keeps on developing, becoming more complex — more diversified, more interactive, and therefore more unified. The universe shows the holy Oneness of Being.

This is our home. We might even say, this is who we are. All of us are this one being. We human beings are supported by everything the universe does with its various interactions that make the galaxies in their clusters and the stars with their attendant planets, some of which have the right conditions for biochemistry, which evolves to the point of self-consciousness and knowledge of all these universe interactions. When we are conscious and knowing, it's the universe that is conscious and knowing. And our consciousness and our knowing are still working in the same pattern: diversifying, interacting, unifying. We are not alien or strange or different. We are the universe's own.

What our sciences — our consciousness and knowing — are now suggesting to us is that maybe it is perfectly natural to a universe to become conscious and knowing. Maybe it's not highly improbable at all but quite to be expected. (I say "maybe" because this idea at the present time is still disputed and debated. But I am going to tell the universe story from this point of view.) In any case, our activities as human beings have the same very general form as all other activities in the universe, the form of diversified, interactive wholeness.

Moving and Growing

The wholeness I've been talking about is called, in the sciences, *system*. Systems are composed of units, or members, that move in relation to one another. Some of the movements can be quite complex. And when they are, wonderful things happen. Life is one of them. Notice that it's the moving together that makes it. The parts, separately, are not living. But when they all move in relation to one another in a certain way, then the whole group of interacting members becomes suddenly a new kind of unit, a living being. "Living" is the name of the kind of interactions, the kind of traffic, that is going on in that community. The collective behavior is greater — and different from — the mere aggregation of the parts.

The living beings keep organizing themselves, organizing the matter-energy-information around them as "inputs" or "food" for themselves, organizing these into their own beings. The particular atoms and molecules of which their bodies are composed are changing constantly — an oxygen molecule you inhale now may get built into you and stay for some time, but eventually it will be excreted in some way, its place having been taken by a new oxygen molecule. Even whole protein molecules made of thousands of atoms are often unraveled every day and then remade if they are still wanted. But through all this making and unmaking, the wholeness and the sameness of the composed beings are preserved — more or less. The whole also changes — we grow up, we grow old — and yet we feel that we are still ourselves, and we recognize that continuity in others as well. The materials and the energies flow through us, but our form is, if not absolutely constant, at least continuous.

Matter, energy, and information are being sucked into our being, our living being, that very movement being our living. They are built into us, and the matter, energy, and information that we discard are dissipated into our environment. We are "dissipative structures." The energy is degraded in the process, some of it lost as heat, but even so, most of what we dissipate can be taken up by some other system and organized into its self, its rejecta being passed on in turn to yet further systems.

The universe is not merely "running down," as we have been told, fated at long last to go completely out of business. The universe is also very significantly "building up," layer upon layer, all quite spontaneously, quite naturally. Protons and neutrons naturally clump together into atomic nuclei. Atoms spontaneously bond together to form molecules. Molecules following their own natural laws align with and adhere to and catalyze each other until living cells emerge as self-maintaining and self-reproducing units of wholeness. And so on.

New wholes are built of combinations of units from the previous level of wholeness. Dynamic combinations — it's the inter*actions* that make them combine and that therefore constitute the unity of their wholeness. Layer after layer, level upon level. Cells interact as organisms, organisms interact as communities, whether of the same species or of different species, as in an ecosystem. All this is building up. An egg dropped on the floor and broken will not spontaneously reassemble itself, but an egg left to its own devices in a supportive environment will develop into an animal that will be party to producing another egg. Building up is also natural. It's what a universe does.

Certain things have to be right in the beginning (and we will discuss this later), but if a building-up universe can get as far as making stars, some exploding and some slow-burning, it stands a good chance, perhaps a very good chance, of going on to knit up its matter-energy-information into life, and if life, then on to intelligence. This is wonderful and sacred but not miraculous. Not against nature. It's perfectly natural; it's what nature does as the image of the living, being-sharing God.

It is an awesome thing to be in the hands of the living God, we say.

A dynamic God! Have we thought of it that way? We used to think in our theology that the changeless was superior to the changing. Now we tend to think differently. Everything we know is dynamic. The world is in constant motion — motion of vibration, motion from place to place, motion from one state or condition to another, motion of combining with others to give rise to new levels of emergent wholes, motion of developing, motion of evolving. All kinds of motions, even motions of destroying, dying, and decaying, are included. They all make up the living texture of the world and are now seen as vital parts of the total picture, a moving picture. We are about to see this interplay of building and tearing down as not necessarily bad. It is part of the way a finite world images an infinite but dynamic God.

The world of self-organizing beings evolves. They experiment with ways of interacting with their environments (both living and nonliving aspects) and the better ways are able to make more copies of themselves and become more prominent in their populations. Gradually — and sometimes not so gradually — their forms change. Species acquire variations of size and shape. New species appear. Whole new branches on the tree of life develop. Some commentators on this scene, Eric Lerner, for instance, say that there is a "natural tendency of all matter, both animate and inanimate, to evolve continuously toward higher rates of energy flow, toward the capture of greater currents of energy."[3] Others, Pierre Teilhard de Chardin, for instance, believe that a trend can be discerned in favor of increasing consciousness.[4]

The interactions are complicated. Organisms have to struggle with the environment, yet the environment is what sustains them. They often fight with members of their own kind, yet they also care for their own kind, in some circumstances at the individual's considerable expense. They may be in a predator/prey relationship with other species, or again, they may be in a symbiotic relationship of mutualism, in which each helps the other. The struggles against each other usually lead to discovering better ways to succeed in the struggle, first by one side, then the other. Even better ways to *find* better ways are developed, better ways to evolve are evolved.

It is one long fascinating story of the creation of novelty. When the Bible represents God as saying, "Behold, I make all things new," it is saying something that is very true of nature. It is constantly renewing itself and constantly giving rise to forms that never existed before. And the most exciting thing about this novelty is that it is unpredictable. A theology that imagines that the whole history of the world from start to finish is already known is no longer a source of meaningfulness for us. It is not true to our experience. And the more our experience expands, the more we know about the world, the more meaningfulness for us will have to include unpredictable novelty. Not knowing what will happen will become for us not a deficiency but a sign of creativity, a far deeper sense of divinity.

Religious Metaphors

I think we can develop a deeper sense of divinity if we study the natural world (including ourselves). And it may even be that we can find in religious traditions some useful concepts and icons for grasping as a whole what the sciences are bringing to light. There are several metaphors in the religious traditions of the West that can be very helpful to us in our effort to find meaningfulness in the cosmos revealed to us by contemporary science. I will make use of three of these to develop an overall view of our cosmic knowledge. The ones I find most expressive and unifying are the Trinity, the Incarnation, and the Theotokos. They all have to do with holding together the extremes of reality as we perceive it, basically the one and the many, then the infinite and the finite, the divine and the human, and finally the spiritual and the material.

I use the term "Trinity" in two different ways, as community and as life-cycle. In the first way I point out that the prefix "tri-" in many languages means not specifically three, as 2+1, but more vaguely "more than two, several, many." Some of the older languages had three numbers in their grammatical structure: the singular, the dual, and the plural, one, two, and many. "Tri-" indicated the plural. The Trinity, with this understanding, is a representation of God, fundamental Being, as both One and Many. The many are not reduced to the one, and the one is not scattered or separated into the many. Both have to be held.

This is clearly a fine model for what we observe in the natural world. Everywhere there is multiplicity organized into unity, the unity being strongly dependent on the multiplicity and even on diversity. The refusal to let the tension collapse either way, in favor of either unity or multiplicity as being the more primitive, is what is so valuable about the Trinity. And this is exactly what we see in the world at every level or scale of organization. Galaxies, molecules, organisms, societies — they are all examples of unity supporting and implying multiplicity, and multiplicity sustaining and implying unity. It is probably the fundamental pattern of all reality.

The one/many dynamism shows especially in *symbiosis,* which I will use as a very general term for any kind of collective, cooperative, communitarian, shared organization and systemic functioning. I suggest that the Trinity, regarded as Persons who dynamically indwell one another, is the primary expression of such symbiosis, and that all other instances of it — of which the universe is full, of which in a way the universe consists — are images of this original symbiosis. Such a view enables the trinitarian contemplative to extend the sense of reverence directed to the divine Trinity to the Trinity's expression, image, reflection, projection, manifestation in the created order (including human beings) and thereby to find the world sacred and meaningful.

This basic holding of extremes in harmonious tension has more specific derivatives in other polarities. Gathering and scattering would be such a pair. The universe as building up and the universe as running down. Forming and destroying, living and dying, both absolutely essential to the overall evolutionary advance, are symbiotic with each other. Later on we will explore good and evil as dependent on point-of-view and as natural to a finite evolving world. Stability and flexibility or variation are another important pair. Self and other, inside and outside, inclusive and exclusive. Determinism and freedom, predictability and unpredictability. Randomness and order. Self-protection and self-sacrifice or self-giving. The interactions of the pairs characterize the vitality of the world.

The interaction of such pairs, especially within the basic context of unity and multiplicity, gives us *community*, and this is where the contemplative has an excellent opportunity to put everything together in a familiar and congenial way. Begin with considering that God is a community. We haven't said it plainly this way, but perhaps we do mean this, and perhaps it's a rather striking if not unique metaphor for the Holy Ground of Being. It acknowledges not only the divine Oneness, which no one questions, but, somehow in some suitably expressed way, also multiplicity — or something like multiplicity.

I believe that this is necessary if God is really to function as a Ground of Being, because all the rest of being is clearly communal, collective, systemic — dynamic unions of various sorts of manyness. If the world is made in the image of God, then such a basic fact of the world cannot be left out completely. The notion of God as Trinity may answer this need. It speaks of three "Persons" of God, existing in such close union as in no way to disturb the Oneness of God. Of course, such an idea has been quarrelled over, since it looks, on the face of it, quite contradictory, as well as unacceptable to monotheism. I am going to offer in the next chapter my attempt to ease this sense of contradiction and to urge that the oneness aspect and the manyness aspect actually imply one another, once we have looked hard at Being itself.

Contemplatives are usually deeply into a sense of the human world forming (either actually or ideally) a community. Community is probably the most important character and value at stake in the contemplative's view of humanity. If God is conceived as Community and humanity as ideally community, then it is very clear how humanity is made in the image of God. It is clear where the value lies, what we should try to achieve, where the meaning is coming from. The concern for God and the concern for neighbors unite; we see how they are like and how we practice our religious life toward both simultaneously.

Such a view protects the polarities that are so important for a just, even a viable, human collective life. Because humanity is intended to image God the Trinity, we must not attempt to reduce everyone to one single kind, nor should any of us undertake to bring all of us to be like ourselves. Diversity and variation must be preserved, nurtured. They are part of the image, part of the life. On the other hand, we must also look for and find and celebrate and feel in terms of the fundamental and pervasive unity of the human race, the real kinship, the single family. Both attitudes have to be practiced; that is the point, and this is why the Trinity (or any concept of the ultimate that would hold the one and the many together this way) is such a good model for us.

Recognizing vitality in the polarities helps us to have a more understanding and accepting and working-with-reality approach to the ups and downs of our own lives. Things build up and then fade away or are destroyed or replaced. This does not have to be seen as bad. The history of life here has included a great many such experiences and has kept right on growing and advancing. In fact, some of the most significant advances have arisen directly out of the greatest catastrophes. Creativity in the finite order seems often to work this way. Continuing to look at our lives in this context, we may get a more creative handle on the balance between self-protection as we must practice it and self-giving as we want to practice it.

Further, this human world will be much better understood when we set it in the large context of the cosmic community, when we see that its ways of working with the polarities is an outgrowth and elaboration of the general cosmic way of doing the same basic things. Much of our "good" and "evil" can be seen more realistically in this cosmic context, and I will try to give an explanation of this in chapter 9.

Finally, the great world itself is seen, in its dynamic unity and diversity, as our kin, made on the model of the Trinity. It is not alien, it is not "dead" or mechanistic or "indifferent" or any of the rejecting things that we have sometimes been prone to say about it. The cosmos is being created exactly along the same lines of oneness and manyness, symbiotic community, creative use of polarities. We are part of it. Our imaging of the Trinity as human beings is a special case of the cosmos's imaging of the Trinity. It's all of a piece. Therefore, our practice of our religion, our devotion, our spirituality, has to include the cosmos. Reverence is due it, the peace of friendship and kinship is to be extended to it, it is to be cared for. Just as we can say that when we become conscious and knowing, it is the universe that has become conscious and knowing, so we can say that when we pray and praise the Creator, the universe is praying and praising.

The Incarnation and the Theotokos

And this brings me to the other two great revelatory ideas of the Western tradition that I like to work with, the Incarnation and the Theotokos. (I will explain them at greater length, too, as we go along.) The Incarnation is the union of the infinite and the finite, the Creator and the created, the divine and the human. This is necessary, because there cannot be any separation here any more than there can be separation among the created themselves. In fact, it is more necessary here because of the bond of creation itself. But I am going to stress the great intimacy of this bond, the real presence of the Creator in and even as the created, extending the Christology familiar to trinitarians to the entire cosmos. Just as the Trinity itself is a model for the cosmos, so the Incarnation becomes a model for the cosmos. It tells how the Creator and the created are bonded and therefore what the value of the created is, that it is the "beloved child." It represents the cosmos as God taking form as the finite, God "coming down" into/as the world. This is God's act, for God's reasons, God's self-expression.

The last metaphor I will use, the Theotokos, goes in just the other direction, from the world to God. It is the union of the material and the spiritual. "Theotokos" may be a strange word to some. It is a Greek word meaning "God-bearer." It is used traditionally for the Blessed Virgin Mary. Its virtue lies in its paradox, reversal and closure. The Theotokos is a creature. It is "born from" God. But then the Theotokos becomes the Mother of God in turn. I will use this metaphor like the others, expanding the concept of the Theotokos to cosmic dimensions. The cosmos is the great Theotokos, made by God as capable of giving birth to God, bringing the creative act full circle.

This is the second way I use the model of the Trinity; I call it the Trinitarian Life Cycle and it does use "three" as two plus one. The First Person, or Poise,[5] of the Trinity is the purely transcendent aspect, the infinite, the absolute, the Creator. The Second Person, or Poise, is the

Incarnation; in my suggestion it is the transcendent divine Community becoming incarnate in the cosmos, the Creator in the created, the infinite and invisible being manifested as finite and visible (see John 1:18). The Third Person, or Poise, is the gift or emergence of Spirit from the Incarnation, or in our other image, from the Theotokos. God empties Godself and takes form in matter. The material cosmos evolves until it becomes self-conscious and realizes that it is being created by God. This is the union of matter and spirit, and the emergence of the spiritual from the interactions of the material. The self-conscious, God-conscious cosmos goes on to realize that it is being created by God precisely as an image, that is, as a self-creating cosmic community, and thus it is God's "beloved child" and delight. This realization is both the birth of God in and from matter and the uniting of the incarnate and cosmic to the Transcendent (the contemplative's goal) and completes the Cycle.

When we get deeper into how the universe is structured and how it operates, the marvel and mystery of this will appear more fully. As we study the nature of finitude, the ways of evolution, the interactions of the polarities, and especially when we look at the world as a complex adaptive system whose future is essentially unpredictable because creative, we will be moved to ask: Can a finite world be made that will express the value of the Infinite? Can God create a cosmos that will live and grow and come to consciousness of itself as an incarnation of God? Can the Creator create a universe that will more and more participate in its own creation? that will image its Creator by being creative? Can the Eternal make a world in which there will be genuine novelty, unpredictable newness? Can finite beings, which have to protect themselves in order to remain as finite beings, achieve through their finitude and mutual dependence a willingness to give themselves to one another, to conceive and to act for the good of the whole? Can God ask a question God cannot answer by supernatural foreknowledge but only by actual experiment?

This is, I believe, the sort of thing that is going on in the cosmos, in the world the contemplative, the religious person, lives in. If we think of ourselves as such persons, we shouldn't ignore or neglect or withdraw ourselves from this marvelous world where God is living and creating. We should study and strive to understand it so that we can really *live* in it, with God.

Chapter Two

GOD AS PERSON-COMMUNITY

 I SAID IN THE PREVIOUS CHAPTER that I would try to show that it is necessary that the Ground of Being be both one and many and that this need not be a contradictory idea, but rather the oneness may imply the manyness and the manyness imply the oneness. Since I am addressing (primarily) people who already think of God as Trinity, I am saying to them that this is how your idea of God can work with respect to understanding the cosmos. We can see the cosmos as made in the image of this trinitarian God if we develop certain aspects of the trinitarian theme.

I am not trying to prove that the cosmos or our science supports or favors some particular religious view. I am rather working the other way around. If you already hold a certain religious view, I would persuade you to see the cosmos from your point of view and take it seriously, study and appreciate it, make it part of your religious life.

I myself think that the trinitarian model, as I will work it out, is a rather good way of grasping the cosmos as a whole, but the mythic or theological aspects of it could be done some other way. The metaphysical aspects can be argued for more strongly. They are not dependent on any theological model but rather underlie the theological model I am using. And if you are a trinitarian Christian, you will notice that I have to develop my particular theology of the Trinity before I can apply it to a theology of the cosmos.

The particular way of looking at the trinitarian Godhead that I have been developing stresses the distinction of Persons, and the communitarian unity of the Deity. It is attentive to the "equality in majesty" of the Persons and it neglects the question of "processions," the derivation of the Second and Third Persons from the First. This question is not taken up because I do not need that aspect of the traditional theme for my concern, which is with oneness and manyness. In other contexts I have spoken of First, Second, and Third as the Transcendent, the Incarnate, and the Realized, making a Trinitarian Life Cycle, and there will be a small mention of that in the last chapter of this book. But for this chapter, I will work with a plurality of Persons who are not in any particular order.

I am going to begin by looking at what we mean by God as the ultimate Ground of Being and looking at the nature of Being itself. This already will give us the root of the argument in the discovery of the expansive, or radiant, character of Being. Then we will consider why we regard God as Person and how the radiant character of Being shows as love. This will involve explaining what a person is and what the nature of divine love is. With this background, we can understand why persons must exist in community, and we will go into some detail about the nature of the community relationships in terms of the dynamic of divine love. It is at this point that it will, I hope, become clear why both manyness and oneness are necessary and how the oneness implies the manyness and the manyness implies the oneness, because of the nature of person and the nature of love, which themselves arise out of the nature of Being and its ultimate Ground.

God as the Ultimate Ground of Being

When we say that God is the ultimate Ground of Being, what we mean is that God accounts for the existence of everything else, but God itself doesn't have to be accounted for. If we didn't say this, we would be involved in an infinite regress: A is accounted for by being referred to B, and B by being referred to C, and so on, endlessly. Something foundational has to account for all of them. It has to make them possible, be the condition on which they depend.

This is a way of saying that all these things are contingent. They depend on something else. If it is there and if it is right for them, then they can be. If it isn't there for them, then they can't be. They don't *have to* exist. But if that on which something depends itself depends on something else, then we are caught in the infinite regress again. So all contingent things must depend on something that is not contingent, something that is necessary. God is the Necessary Being. The necessary being grounds the contingent beings.

Contingent beings are dependent on the necessary being, but the necessary being is not dependent on them, is not dependent on anything. To be independent of something is to transcend it. When one thing transcends another, it has some quality that cannot be accounted for by the qualities of the one transcended. The transcendent one has something over and above all that, something new, something more. It belongs to another domain. God transcends all other beings. Anything that grounds others has to transcend them. If it were bound by the same limitations as they are, it would be as much in need of grounding as they are. God is the ultimately Transcendent Being.

This means that God is not in any way referred to something else. The meaning and being of God do not involve reference to any other. We talk about God in reference to ourselves or the world in general. But that is only to make things plain to ourselves. God in itself does not acquire meaning by being the ground of all the rest of us. God is and is "meaningful" in itself.

I have just pointed to God in terms of being not-contingent and not-transcended and not-referred. That pointing is for our benefit. God is not really defined by such relations. God is not relative. God is Absolute Being.

This has an interesting corollary. God is not to be understood by reference to other understood things. That means that either God is not to be understood at all or else God is to be understood directly in itself, by an unmediated intuition. All other understandings are referred to one another, the new being explained in terms of the old, the unknown made familiar by reference to the already known. You can't do that with God. God has to be the ground of all understandings and meanings, too. Our referred understandings are based on an unreferred understanding, something we see directly. This is why, when we do metaphysics, we have to try to begin with something which we simply see in itself. We begin by asserting what seems to us to be incontestable. We have to begin with something for which we do not require a proof or even an argument. Only pointing.

If God is absolute being, then God cannot be any particular being, cannot be one being among others. All particular beings are defined by their relations to one another. They limit one another. This one is not that one. It is different and cut off in some way. Things are in different places or made out of different materials or behave in different ways. They are bigger or more complex or more capable of certain activities. They are what they are because of their relations to the others: they eat them or make their homes in them or make things out of them or mate with them or fight them or... All sorts of relationships define the particular things. God isn't defined this way. God isn't limited this way — not by being relative, not by being different, not by being separate. Beings that are mutually defined this way are finite beings, limited and particular and embedded in a net of relations. God is not; God is Infinite Being.

However, notice a curious thing. By this very assertion, we are obliged to admit that God cannot be deprived of anything. God cannot be defined as that which is not finite. God can't be separated from or different from anything. While God cannot be limited to being one finite being among other finite beings, God may have to include all finite beings. We will deal with this further in the next chapter.

I think all this is more or less what we mean when we say that God is the ultimate Ground of Being. As such, of course God is the most real and the most meaningful and the most valuable — that's human language and indication, of course. But the point is that God is the ground of our sense of meaningfulness and value. And we have set out to see how the cosmos fits into this meaningfulness and value and thereby has meaningfulness and value of its own and is sacred and precious to us.

Now we need to say more about Being itself. There are several interesting things to be said. These are some of those assertions that we are supposed to see directly without needing proof. Proof is always reference to something else, accepted as known or true or understood. But here we are dealing with the ground, with that to which ultimately all the proofs have to be referred. Nevertheless, different people pick out different things to focus on as what they see directly and feel need no argument. Here are some things about Being that jump out for me and enable me to see the cosmos as the expression of the trinitarian God.

The first is that Being is really Be-ing; it is not really a noun but a verb. Reality is What-Is-Going-On. It is not well thought of as a Thing. If you think of it as a thing, then you have to add action. So I see Being as essentially dynamic. To-exist is dynamic, not static.

If Being is dynamic, then I feel we can say, as helps to our understanding, that it has "tendencies." These describe its dynamism. To be is to persist in being. That's basic. It can't tend to go out of being. Then, to be is to expand in being. This is the most important insight. Dynamic be-ing means more-being, being more. Endlessly more. Every kind of "more." To be is to be in every possible way. This can be elaborated and will be in just a moment. But first notice that the tendency of Being to be-more means a tendency to communicate, or give, being. To be is to be radiant, to be being-giving, to be self-diffusive. This is the note of Being that we will discuss in the next section as "love."

Now, back to being in every possible way. We have already noticed some of these ways. (I will mention only some very general ways. A glimpse of "every possible" way can be had by considering all the sorts of things, especially living things, on our one little planet.) Being tends to be both contingent and necessary, relative and absolute, finite and infinite. The very general way that I most want to point to is that Being must be both one and many. These are possible ways to be. Being tends to be in every possible way. Being is observed to be both one and many.

I think the pairing runs all the way back into the Ground itself. If it doesn't, we are going to have to derive multiplicity from unity or else unity from multiplicity, and neither of these efforts has been successful. There is always some of kind of gap between them. If Being is simply both one and many from the very Ground, then we have an explanation for the one-many that we observe and no further explanation is called for. This is why the Trinity as model for the Ground of Being is so appealing to me and why I focus on that aspect of the traditional idea, the union of unity and multiplicity.

Here is another very basic way of being: everything that is, is itself, is centered and rooted in itself and remains itself. This can be called being "en-static," standing in oneself. But Being also goes out from itself, Being gives itself out. This is "ecstatic," standing outside oneself. Being is both, and this will figure also in my treatment of the Trinity and the discussion of community as the ground-form of all Being.

There are other important ways of being, such as being conscious, being person, being free. And being creative. This is the culmination of all the others. And God as ultimate Ground of Being grounds them all. God is the ground of self-possession, self-consciousness, ecstatic self-expression and self-gift, of personhood and love, of freedom and creativity. The great doctrines of Trinity and Incarnation and Theotokos show how the cosmos (including human beings) is part of this whole reality, sharing meaningfulness and the value of the Ground.

God as Person, God as Love

Now I am going to begin to talk about the Trinity itself, and I will use for this several of the points made in the discussion on Being: the Trinity is both one and many; Being is present there as Persons; the Persons are necessary and infinite; the Persons are both enstatic and ecstatic; and the Persons are Being-communicating.

What do we mean by "person"? We ourselves are persons. How do we experience it? Person is the one who says "I." Usually we think of this "I" in terms of our descriptions: gender, race, age, relationships, work, history, personality type, cultural commitments, and so on. These give us a feeling of definiteness (which we confuse with reality) by defining how we are different from others. I am I by being not-you. I have a different description.

But these descriptions are abstractions; they tell how we can be classified and rated in comparison with others in that class. They tell about us as if we are being looked at from the outside, as an object. That is not "I." I am a subject, concretely living, experiencing being I from the inside. But in that case, I cannot be defined by those descriptions. They don't identify me, they don't capture my reality as a person. They don't tell about my lived sense of being a living subject, a real being, not a collection of classifications.

I, as person, transcend all those categories of descriptions. Take off those predicates by which I usually say "I am such and such," and what is revealed is pure I AM, unmodified, indescribable, unclassifiable, incomparable. As person, I am not defined, not finite.

All those categories of descriptions may be said to characterize our "nature" as distinct from ourselves as "persons." The natures are different from one another by "mutual negation." What one has another does not; it has something the first does not. This is how their definitions are made. But persons are not defined. So persons are not "different" from one another. Persons are absolutely unique; they are not identified by reference to another, not compared with others, not even to say that they are "different." But this does not mean that they all collapse into some undifferentiated union with one another and can't be "told apart." Persons are differentiated, but it's by another kind of differentiation, not mutual negation based on different descriptions.

Persons are beings, and Being is self-diffusive, active, and being-communicating. When we ourselves, in meditation, strip away all the descriptions and center in our bare I AM, we discover that it is a radiant energy, it goes out from itself. The same reality, the same act of be-ing, that says I AM enstatically, in the same breath pronounces the ecstatic MAY YOU BE. This is how Being is, and Person is fundamental Being. The act of being "I" is not an act of negating another but of affirming another. This act of affirming is what differentiates the persons. They are distinct not by their descriptions but by their acts. Not by the kinds of acts (that would be description again) but by the existential actuality of act-ing. And the primary act-ing is affirming the be-ing of the other. That is the essence of being a person.

Thus person is also origin of action. This action starts from the person. It is not a re-action, but a first action. It doesn't respond to some quality in its environment. It isn't caused or even provoked or motivated by something outside. It is an absolute, first act, dependent only on itself. These acts of being-communication, performed by persons, are the dynamic reality of Being.

That is what I shall mean by person, what I shall mean by the Trinity of Persons. God, as Ground of Being, is these acts of being-communication by the Persons. And there have to be "several" such Persons. For any person to express the affirmation of be-ing of another to the full, that other needs to be another person. If we relate to any other being in terms only of its descriptions, we are not truly affirming the other's be-ing. We are only cataloging, filing, rating, and ranking the outsideness of the other as object. That doesn't activate us in our reality as person. Properly to affirm another, we must affirm the other's inside, the other as subject, the other as another self, another I AM, another who is transcendent of all description. Affirmation means putting myself in the other's place, communicating MAY YOU BE in the other's own terms, coinciding with the subjective reality of that other, joining with the other's act of being-communication. Unless I do this, I am not being person, because that is what person does. It is what makes a person to be a person. Person is altogether affirmation of other persons. God, as person, has to be Persons, plural.

These acts of affirming the other's I AM=MAY YOU BE are the way Being's self-communicating tendency shows in persons. Being is be-ing when it is communicating being, and person is person when it is affirming person. This affirmation/being-communication is what we call love. In the Christian tradition it is a special kind of love called (in Greek) *agape*. It can be distinguished from another kind of love called *eros*. Eros is love in the sense of desire for some good for oneself. Eros is a love that goes out from myself toward another in the context of gaining or enjoying some benefit for myself. It seeks the good of the lover. Agape is a love that seeks the good of the beloved. It goes out from myself and does not return. It wills the welfare, the being and better being, of the beloved, that the beloved should thrive in terms of the beloved's own good. It is being-communicating; it is ecstatic. It is the characteristic act of the person. In the Christian tradition, "God is love," *ho theos ein agape* (1 John 4:16).

These acts of love are not motivated, as already said. They are completely free, uncaused. This is why they are called "grace." Grace is the free, unmerited gift of a benefit, especially an act of self-giving. Any act of agape is grace. And the paradigm of interpersonal love is the Trinity. It is God who is agape. The Persons of the Trinity give grace to one another. All other graciousness is named after this. The divine life is the activity of unmotivated self-sharing; this is how Being is dynamic, how it is radiant. It is also how it — how God — is both many and one.

The Trinity is the paradigm of grace, the paradigm of self-giving, of person-affirming. It is the dynamic reality of love. It is what God *is*. But God is the ultimate Ground of all Being. So here we can note an interesting thing. We have heard, "If you try to hoard your life, you will lose it; but if you pour out your life into another, you will not only survive but maximize your living." The interesting point is that this is the rule for all persons, and in modified form, for all beings. The paradigm of it is the Trinity itself. It is the nature of Being itself. Being is mutual being-communication.

Persons Must Exist in Community

Jack Miles, in his book *God: A Biography*,[1] has suggested that we translate the mysterious utterance from the Burning Bush to Moses not simply as "I am who am," but as "I am what I do." I agree. God, Being, is dynamic. I AM is enstatic, and that is true; MAY YOU BE is the quintessential divine do-ing and is ecstatic. The complete divine Name. The fullness of Trinitarian Life.

This is the paradox of personal life. To be a person is to be in a being-communicating relation with other persons. Personal life has to be lived in community. I will argue presently that this community has to consist of at least three persons. Certainly there can be no such thing as a single person, a solitary person. Person always implies persons, plural.

The bond of the community is love, especially agape love. But look at the dynamic of personal being even from the point of view of erotic love. Eros desires to be united with the other (as a good for oneself). Many erotic relationships begin with desire for the descriptions of the other, but if the desire runs deep, if there is strong attraction to the other as person, then an interesting thing happens. One is not satisfied with merely being intimate with the descriptive reality of the other. One wants to be close to the interior of the other, to feel the other on the inside, as the other feels. One yearns to be with the other not as the other appears to be but as the other really is from the other's own profound sense of self. How can we achieve that? We have to abandon our own point of view and strive to enter into the beloved's point of view, to see and feel as the beloved does. That means to value as the beloved does, to seek the beloved's own welfare together with the beloved. But that is agape. If you really want to fulfill yourself, you have to abandon yourself and enter another. Isn't that amazing?

I explain this urgency in the matter of love in terms of the three grammatical persons: him/her, you, and I. If we truly treat another as an object, we are engaged in an I–it relation with the other. But even if we simply talk about, think about the other as if the other is not present, is not a subjective consciousness as we ourselves are, we are engaging in an I–him/her relation. The other's descriptions are there for us but the other's living subjective presence is not there for us. Notice how different it is when we shift to saying "you." Our whole consciousness has to reorient itself. The other is now present in living actuality. The other is also a person, even as I am. The other as person transcends the other's descriptions. I am no longer relating to the descriptions but to the person, "yourself." You are present for me and I am also present for you, as I was not for "him." Each of us looks at the other. When we love the other as a person, this is what we desire to experience. There is another self there (just as I am a self), looking at me and acknowledging that I am a self. I am to this extent united with the other in this I-you relation.

But now, if the love persists and deepens, one becomes dissatisfied. The union is not thorough enough. The other is still too "other." The other is a self, even as I am. I am a deep center of selfhood, what we called our enstatic being, where we transcend all the descriptions and can no longer be called finite or particular. This is the true heart of my being. The corresponding reality must be the true heart of the other's being. If I want to be united with the other, it is with this center that I want to be united. I want to enter into the other where the other is no longer "you" for me but "I" for its own self. I want to be united with that "I." This would be an "I–I" relation.

When I enter deeply into my enstatic reality as person, I realize that this is the fulfillment of any personal love, and that my own nature, my whole nature, is to live in these terms. And to do this, as already explained, I must go out from my own point of view and coincide with the other's point of view. My enstatic reality obliges me to be ecstatic. I will to enter the other's enstatic reality. What is the other to the other (as I am to myself)? How does the other experience being enstatic? Ah! exactly as I do! By being ecstatic! What is it the other loves? Whom does the other adore? Toward whom is the other's agape intended? This is the deepest truth and reality of the other whom I love, and therefore it is there that I desire to experience union. My enstatic reality is expressed in my ecstatic love for the other, which is a will to union with the other's enstatic reality, which in turn is an ecstatic movement out to yet another.

Therefore, the way I love the other is by loving whom the other loves, that is, by joining the other in the other's own ecstatic life. Now notice carefully that it is not a matter of knowing whom the other loves, or of loving the other for loving that way, or of loving that third party because my beloved's love is extended there. None of those would be truly joining in the beloved's own subjective life, that is, doing the same thing that the beloved is doing. To do that, I must love the third party from myself, with my own agape, as my own authentic act. It must not be motivated by my desire to be united with my beloved, because that would keep the love from being true agape, which has no motive. Paradox upon paradox and more and more curious. To be united with my beloved, I not only have to abandon myself, I have to abandon my beloved! I have to transcend that love. My love for the third party has to be independent of any other consideration, or it will not be agape. And, of course, my love for the third party has to be ecstatic, has to go out from myself toward an other.

I know this sounds a little involved. And it *is* involuted. It has to be, because it is going to make an absolutely tight union out of this perfectly differentiated plurality. Albert Einstein said, "A theory should be as simple as possible — but no simpler."[2] I believe this is about as simple as we can make an argument that passes from "God is love" to "God is Trinity" and shows why both oneness and manyness have to be present and balanced, not being reduced in either direction, why the enstatic and ecstatic realities of the Persons imply one another, and why there have to be at least three Persons.

I will say just a word more on this last point. Sometimes people wonder why my beloved can't just love me back, why there has to be this "third party." It is for this reason: my love has to be ecstatic. If I am united with my beloved by loving whom my beloved loves, and that turns out to be myself, then I would be called upon to love myself with an ecstatic love, which is a contradiction. My beloved will no doubt also love me, but for my love for my beloved to be fully expressed, displayed, verified, I have to be willing to love whom my beloved loves, from myself, ecstatically, and that can be manifested only in the case of loving still someone else, not myself. It will be true that when my beloved loves me, all this dynamism will run in the opposite direction: to love me fully, my beloved must love someone further whom I love and thus fulfill the enstatic union with me by joining in my ecstatic movement — joining by exercising his or her own authentic ecstatic movement. It can be remarked that the most intense and intimate of human loves, the spousal relation, achieves its fulfillment typically by the joined loves of the parents for their children. Friendship loves are expressed in common love for great values. The saints love each other by all loving God.

The Self-Creating Community

Bear in mind that we are discussing the ideal nature of things in themselves. Our everyday loves aren't fully up to this standard, but they are sufficient pointers for us to intuit the nature of love in its perfection. And when we have worked out the dynamics and the interrelational bonds of the divine level of Being, we will have a paradigm for the cosmos. This shared being, shared life, will be the pattern repeated on all the levels to various degrees. There will always be unity and multiplicity, enstasis and ecstasis, symbiosis, and community. I want us to see it first in God, and then see it in the universe — see it in the universe, realizing that it is God's image we're seeing. Then the universe will come alive for us and be meaningful and sacred.

So let us move ahead with this dynamic model of the Ground of Being and see where it leads us. The enstatic Persons in their ecstatic Being-communicating acts constitute the divine Community. It is a community because it consists of persons differentiated from one another by their ecstatic loves for one another and united with one another by being present in each one's enstatic reality. It is only agape that achieves this. Usually one needs one principle to explain diversity and another to explain unity. But agape does both out of the very same activity. Love both implies differentiation and creates union. But each union engenders further differentiation, which intends further union. This network of interactions is called "community" because it is a moving balance of differentiation and union. It does not settle in either way, as many or as one. It is always both.

In this circle of differentiation and union there is no starting point. In this model of the trinitarian Godhead, there is no "First Person" from whom further Persons are derived in an asymmetric fashion. Every Person is "derived" from other Persons. There are plural Persons, all equal, none in a privileged position. No one is special or singular or different from the others. This is not intended as an alternative to theologies of procession. Great theological motifs are susceptible of many lines of interpretation, some of which seem to say quite different things from one another. But, like the complementarity of wave and particle in physics, a variety of theologies which say contradictory things can nevertheless help us by enabling us to cover all the things we need or want to say. So I am simply leaving aside for the moment the question of an order of processions, taking only the idea of Being-communicating acts and relations and the consequent "equality in majesty," so that we can see the Ground of Being as symmetrical and edgeless.

So: no starting point, no ending point, no privileged positions, but perfect symmetry. Symmetry means that if you plunge into the network at any point and engage in the activity, you will realize the same pattern as if you entered at any other point. Dante, in his vision of the Trinity, sees a perfect sphere. That's the idea. No point on the sphere is privileged or special. You can turn the sphere and look at it from any point of view, and it is always the same. In the case of our Persons, if you begin to trace the process of enstatic/ecstatic activity from any one Person in the Community, the dynamic will look exactly the same. Any Person can be called the "First Person" who is communicating Being to a "Second Person" and finds that this implies commitment to a "Third Person." Any two love each other by joining in loving a third.

And the Community is edgeless. Again this is like the surface of a sphere. Whichever way you move, you stay on the surface; you never come to an edge and fall off. In the Community, you always stay in the Community, no matter how many Persons you love. You never come to the "last Person."

This brings up an interesting idea. We are used to thinking of the Trinity as just three Persons. But this is only the minimum for real community, due to the nature of love. There is nothing to say that there couldn't be more. There is even the suggestion, again from the dynamic of love and nature of Being as expansive, that there might be an uncountable multitude of Persons. An innumerable infinity. In any case, persons as such can't be "counted." Things that can be counted have to be quite separate from one another so that they can be lined up with numbers, and we have to have a way of knowing whether we've already counted any one. Persons aren't like that at all because they don't have descriptions.

Paul Quenon has a wonderful poem, of which I am very fond, called "In the Womb of Angels,"[3] in which this uncountability and being-giving dynamic are evoked. Angels give birth to angels, angelic relations have angel offspring. The angelic domain grows and expands without limit, without holding still. And then they intertwine and interlock and interact in all sorts of complex ways, and the whole community throbs with angelic life. This is the sort of vision I am proposing. Hold on to it at least tentatively, because it is going to be very meaningful when we begin to describe its images in the created universe.

This poetic vision of angels begins to give us a sense of the next important thing I want to say about the Trinity as Ground of Being: it is self-creating. Daniel Walsh, whose philosophy of the Person is ancestral to this view, said an amazing and daring thing: "Love is so intense that it expresses itself as the Trinity. The Trinity is not God; the Trinity is the first expression of Love, who is God."[4] In the language I have just used, it is the dynamism of the intersubjectivity, the communication of Being, that is God, and the Community emerges from it.

This is an interesting and fruitful proposal if we are trying to see God as a paradigm for the cosmos, a God in whose image this world is made. For here what I am going to say about the universe itself—that it is self-organizing, self-making, self-creating—shows in its original context. It is not unheard of to call God self-creating; *causa sui* (cause of itself) is a familiar epithet for the Ground of Being. But with this discussion of the dynamic of love, we can believe that perhaps we have some insight into just how this works. Of course, we mustn't take any of this too literally. Words and ideas used of God mustn't have hard denotations. They have to be soft and pliant and suggestive. They have to whisper hints, nudge us gently and nod, "Something on that order may be how it is."

The divine Community is "self-making." The love-acts intend to give Being; this is their definition; this is what love is, what makes these to be acts of agape. In this sense, each Person who loves another Person intends to give Being to that Person. We have already spoken of this as "grace," the paradigm of all graces. Orthodox theologies of the Trinity say that the Father generates the Son and breathes forth the Spirit. The Western church says that the Father and the Son together breathe forth the Spirit. All these dynamisms are love-acts that "make" the Persons. The Persons are said to be the very relations between them. And the relations are the love-acts. The love-acts "make" the Persons to be the Persons they are. Even the Father is "made" to be "a Father" by the act of loving the Son and being loved as Father by the Son. The acts of loving thus establish the Persons in their dynamic relations with one another, each Person precisely its act of loving and being loved, without which it cannot be. And the Persons in their dynamic relations constitute a kind of network, what I am calling the Community, and this is the Trinity.

The Persons of the Trinity are said to live in one another, to "indwell" one another. Mutual indwelling is their characteristic. "The Father is in me, and I am in the Father" (John 14:10). This is a way of expressing the perfection of love as both differentiation and union. Each Person claims the other's life as one's own. "I have given myself totally to the other." "I am nothing but the other living in me." These extravagances strive to convey what we mean but cannot well say. "We are one" perhaps captures it best.

But think what an odd thing that is to say. "We" are "one." But that is what "we" means. Extraordinary — apparently impossible — idea. It comes from this mutual indwelling. Even when we ourselves say "we," we are able to do so only because of a certain degree of mutual indwelling and intersubjectivity. Plurality of the first (grammatical) person, the subject! Being "subject" together! Acting as one, looking out from the same point of view, not regarding one another as (grammatical) objects. This is what is achieved by the trinitarian life. Not a bare "I," not a collection of "I's," but a "we"!

And this relates to the theme of self-creating, for the trinitarian "we," as the *wholeness* of the community of Persons in their interlocking, intersubjective, dynamic relations with one another, can be said to "emerge" from the interactions of the Persons. It is a wholeness that is neither pure unity nor an extrinsically gathered manyness. It is unity that is the intersubjectivity of the many.

The emergent wholeness is a oneness. A community is not a collection. It is truly one being. It has internal differentiation, but it is one. I want to argue that it is more truly — and more valuably — one through such wholeness than it would be through mere singularity. A singular being can have only extrinsic relations with anything else. This does not satisfy the divine quest for union — and if God is love, then God must be a "quest for union," for oneness. The love-relations must be intrinsic to the oneness, must be total self-givings that are mutual indwellings, drawing all into a vital, a living oneness. Love is like that: it has to differentiate into plurality in order to be ecstatic, to give; and it has to draw into perfect oneness. So the only oneness that satisfies it is this complex oneness of wholeness. This internally differentiated oneness, this dynamic oneness, the oneness made of the acts of loving. A self-created Wholeness-Oneness.

This is the special focus on the Trinity that seems to me to be meaningfully paradigmatic for our understanding and appreciation of the cosmos. We are now going to build on it as we pass to a consideration of the next great traditional theme, the Incarnation. It will be a continuation of the basic dynamism of Being, that tendency to communicate Being and to be in every possible way.

Chapter Three

THE INCARNATION AND THE NATURE OF FINITUDE

 THE BASIC DYNAMISM OF BEING, I said, is the tendency to communicate Being and to be in every possible way. The Trinity itself is a constant gracious communication of Being — agape — that constitutes the Godhead as a Wholeness-Oneness. Now, the next step is that the communication of Being overflows the infinitude of the Trinity because the tendency of Being is to be in every possible way, and this has to include being finite. But the agape pressure of God also means that God will be present in this finite being. I propose to describe and discuss this presence in terms of the familiar theological concept of "Incarnation."

The traditional understanding of the Incarnation is that the Person of Christ subsists in two natures, a divine nature and a human nature. But Christ is only one Person, the divine Person called "the Word." The human nature is assumed by the divine Person, who becomes incarnate in it. The Person unites the human nature and the divine nature. What would seem to be the antipodes of Being are held together in the intimate union of a single Person. Without ceasing to be God, the Word becomes human. And without ceasing to be incarnate as a human being, this Person is divine.

It seems impossible, but this is what Christians claim we believe. Such a marvelous thing has to be expressed by us in terms that are meaningful to us on some deep level or it would be totally meaningless. Indeed, we could never have proposed such a thought to ourselves if we had not sensed its reality in ourselves. We do not pretend to understand the Incarnation in an analytical abstract way. We rather understand it in an experiential way. We know what it means because we resonate with it in our own being. Whatever meaning it has for us comes from the deepest level of our sense of our own reality.

We experience ourselves as indescribable beings who are nevertheless expressed and manifested and concretized in a great variety of descriptions. We the indescribable show ourselves in terms of these descriptions. We extend our reality to them. They incarnate us. Without ceasing to be unique, we become particular. We can't explain it in some formal way, but we know perfectly well what it is. It is the way we are.

My proposal is to extend this understanding to the cosmos as a whole, and to say that the cosmos is an externalized and manifested expression of the indescribable Reality that is God, that is the Trinity.

The Theocosmic Exegete

This is where you pick up a little Greek if you don't already know it. "Theo-" is God. "Cosmic" you know — the ordered universe. And "exegete" means one who interprets or manifests or reveals. The manifester is the God-universe. Or, what "unpacks" the meaningfulness of God is the cosmos. Or, what the full Incarnation is, is God manifesting Godself as cosmos and cosmos expressing God. There is a hint that God isn't thoroughly "said" until the cosmos is fully deployed.

John 1:18 reads: "No one has ever seen God; the only begotten God, who is in the interior of the Father, That One exegetes." Some notes help. No one "sees" God because God is not "seeable"; God is formless, infinite. Nevertheless, there is the "only begotten God," the *monogenes theos*, who is in the *kolpon* (literally, "hollow") of the Father. It is this One who "exegetes." That is the actual Greek word, *exegesato*. It means to interpret sacred mysteries, but the root meaning is to "devise" ways to accomplish something. So the Formless God is interpreted by the Exegeting God who is embedded in the Infinite One. This Exegete "devises" ways to make the invisible visible, and this amounts to a revelation of the hidden sacred mysteries. We may perhaps say that the cosmos is the "devised ways," or that the cosmos itself is the Exegete, and as such bears a relation to the Invisible God that is described as "singly generated" and as being in the "pocket." Both in the pocket and displaying the secrets, inside and outside. And from this coincidence of insideness and outsideness arises meaningfulness. That is just what we want to experience: the coincidence of insideness and outsideness as a satisfying grasp of meaningfulness. And it arises because the full power of the generating one is poured into this single offspring. The Invisible is present in the visible. Really present.

This is the same basic movement of Being as affirmed of the Persons within the Trinity, the movement of agape, of MAY YOU BE. The Parent is in the Child as the agape movement is satisfied with union with the beloved. And the note of "joining" takes a new form. Just as the loving Person abandons self-concern in favor of concern for the other and joins the other in authentic love for still a third, the parenting lover experiences self-abandonment in generating the offspring, thereby giving the offspring the power to have offspring in turn. The element of risk is present in self-abandoning love. This is where insideness turns into outsideness, where one relinquishes control. One gives being but one does not control how it is expressed, one does not know what form it will take, what will happen next, how it will all turn out. To pass on the gift of life is to pass on the ability to give the gift of life, and what happens past that point is out of one's hands. That is what makes it truly a gift of love.

This is what I am calling "ecstasy," the insideness turning into outsideness. It can also be called exegesis, manifestation, revelation, showing, phenomenalization. It has been likened to speech, to "uttering" what has been "hidden" (Ps. 78:2 quoted in Matt. 13:35). I myself like best to liken it to dancing, because the dance is precisely the dancer, in the act of dancing. The dance movements and gestures are outsideness for the dancer; they are phenomena, things shown. But they are revelatory of the dancer. They are contingent upon the dancer and the dancer transcends them all, but the dancer is really present in and as them. The dancer's inside turns into the outsideness of the dance when the dancer dances. This turning inside out is ecstasy. I am suggesting that this is God's relation to the cosmos. The cosmos is a kind of dancing revelation of God. It is a kind of offspring of God. It is a kind of speech of God. It is a kind of phenomenalization of God. It is a kind of incarnation of God. God creates the world as an act of agape-ecstasy.

This is not (from the point of view I am taking) a diminishment or contraction of the divine Being, but a natural and fulfilling act of the divine Be-ing, like unfurling or blossoming, like celebrating. The Eternal appears as process; the Formless takes on form. And process and form will have ways of be-ing of their own, ways in which the communication of being takes place. MAY YOU BE always means "May you give Be-ing in the way that you do it." Agape is passing on the power to communicate being. Eternal, Formless Being will not specify and control the process of the forms, but It will be thoroughly present in them. It can no more be separated from them than the dancer can be separated from the dance. It cannot be separated from them because they exist as an act of agape, which means that the lover is united with the beloved. Just as the Trinity had this holding together of the One and the Many, so the Incarnation expresses the holding together of the Infinite and the Finite. They are different, but they are one. And the process of forms, the phenomenalization is to be honored just as the Eternal Infinite is. To dishonor the world is to dishonor the God expressed in it (John 5:23).

We are trying to gain a sense of the sacredness of the world, a direct sense of the numinous in nature, of the divine and the holy in the everyday, of the meaningful in the large picture made up of the little pictures, many of which will not be meaningful in our local and temporal terms. It is my suggestion that understanding Being as agape and seeing that the union of one and many, of infinite and finite, of inside and outside, are necessary and natural to it is basic to achieving this sense. The further understanding that risk — the commitment to the unknown — is also a built-in factor in agape will help us to relax our demand that the future be controlled by supernatural power for our benefit. Unknowability, uncontrollability, do not imply meaninglessness. They come with agape, with self-giving, self-abandoning love. But they also indicate creativity, improvisation, novelty, adventure, life at the fullest.

The world as improvising, as moving ahead in ways that cannot be foreseen, is imaging its Creator by being creative. Its creative activities actually make itself, as we are going to see in detail, starting with the next chapter. This is what happens when "having life in oneself" is passed on. This is part of what makes the universe holy.

We ourselves are embedded in this movement, we are improvising from moment to moment in our own lives, just as nature as a whole is doing. We are engaged in creative activity, making our contribution to creating the world. This is part of our holiness. We are not doing our thing as separate from, or different from, or against nature. We are doing nature's own thing. It is one dance, one Exegete, the only-begotten, the *monogenes*. And this is just as holy as the Invisible God is. This is where we are situated, what we are doing, what our meaningfulness and value are.

The Exegete, like agape itself, does two things: it establishes distinction, or "severalization," and it unites by interactivity; it makes different, and it makes one. This is how a finite world is constructed. The Theocosmic Exegete, God exegeting Godself by making the world, does the characteristic Godlike thing: being many who are one. Both the "unpacking," the spreading out in variety of the unlimited potentialities of Being, and the gathering together so as to make still more different kinds of things, and gathering them yet again and again until all is one universe composed of an enormous number of interacting distinct and various beings — both the scattering and the gathering are acts of the Exegete. Both of them manifest and utter what was hidden in the Formless. Make different, bring together by means of the interactions of the different — that's the rule. You can make atoms, molecules, living beings of all sorts and their communities and cultures and artworks and ideas by such a repeated means. All these (so far; no one knows what is yet to come) reveal the "inside" of the Invisible One who is also Many.

The Child of the Trinity

I have told this story before, but it's an important story for me, so I'm going to tell it again. Edward Fredkin, an early computer genius, has said that the universe looks to him like a great computer with a program running in it.[1] This being so, he says, two questions arise: What is the algorithm (repeated rule of operation) for the program? and, What is the question whose answer the program is supposed to compute? Reading this and thinking to make a clever retort, I said to myself, Why, the answer to both questions can be found in the beginning of the Bible. The rule of operation is "Be fruitful and multiply," or more generally, Be more! Communicate being and be in every possible way! And the question to be answered by running the program is the interrogative form of "Let us make human beings in our own image": Can God make an image of Godself? One that really images the Creator by being self-possessed, self-giving, conscious, and creative in its turn? One that knows itself as Child of the enstatic/ecstatic Trinity? Fredkin didn't say (at least in the piece I read) what he thought the algorithm and the question were, but he did say another very interesting thing: that the program is so complex that there is no way to shorten it and jump to the final answer. The only way to find out the answer is to let the program run in real time. The only way for God to find out whether the image of God is fully possible is to try it and see.

This appeals to my imagination as one way to put what is going on in the universe, what we are caught up in. It "explains" why we don't know any more than we do, and what we are trying to accomplish, and by what means we are working. The value of the whole enterprise shows too, for both the question to be answered and the algorithm are essentially divine.

And here the metaphor can shift over from program-in-computer-answering-question to the Parent/Child model. A parent engendering a child passes on to the child the genes that program the parent's own life. (Overlook for the moment the differences between sexual and asexual reproduction and recombination and mutation and other refinements.) But genes never run anything unaided and uncontested. They have to be "expressed," "development" has to take place, and environment and historical accident have to play their parts and be taken into consideration. The "program" has to be left to "run its course" in these new terms. You can't predict how it will turn out. The child is thus a new being, and may be quite different from the parent, and yet the parent (in the form of the genes) will be "reincarnated" in the child, present in the child. The child (in general) will be the kind of being the parent is and be able to do what the parent does, including being a parent.

Notice, by the way, that as the program runs, unpredictably — due to complexity, expression, development, accident, adaptation, selection, etc. — the initial stage of the creation process has surrendered control over the process. The parent, in engendering the child, has made an independent being. When the insideness of the Creator — and here we may also think of an artist — ecstatically is expressed as outsideness in some medium, duality becomes present. But, as the running program produces the answer, as the child grows, as the artwork is manifest, the initiator, the creator, is united with this created other — by having the answer in the same mind that asked the question, by having the genes of one's own life active in another and again another, by having the inside of one's artistic being expressed outside in sound or shape, whence one can again perceptively assimilate it inside. This is nonduality. And the duality and the nonduality themselves are united. They do not conflict; they imply one another. The duality is for the sake of the nonduality and the nonduality for the sake of the duality. As Bruno Barnhart says of the gathering of all things into Christ, the more the diverse beings of the world become one in him, the more the fullness of the One becomes present in them and the more creation and diversity can thrive and join together in ever more intimate unions.[2]

The universe itself, as Child of the Trinity, expresses both diversity and unity in itself, still under the driving force of Being. It is Being itself that tends to be everything that can be, that tends to actualize every potentiality. Paul Davies speaks of this under the title "The Principle of Plenitude" as a basic principle of the universe: "That which is possible in nature tends to become realized.... Few rules or processes...fail to be instantiated somewhere.... If there is no impediment to the formation of life, life will form."[3] And life, as we are going to see shortly in detail is exactly the union of diversity and unity, which is exactly the image of the Trinity.

Akin to the conjunction of diversity and unity is the balance of variation and stability. If there is not enough variation in the universe-process, nothing of interest will happen; there will be no development. On the other hand, if there is too much variation and not enough stability, the whole operation will become chaotic and formless. To have developing, creative forms, both these factors have to be present and be capable of being adjusted. This is another way of imaging the enstatic/ecstatic Trinity.

In the theology of the Trinity there is something called *circuminsession*. It means the mutual immanence or coexistence of the divine Persons in one another, mutual indwelling. My version of it showed in the discussion of "joining" as the fulfillment of agape in the "I–I" relation of persons. It is a kind of interaction, and this interaction is essential to the unity of the community that is thereby formed. Now, in the universe this same sort of thing is absolutely central to the whole structure. The diverse beings of the universe exist in terms of one another, in terms of their relations to one another, of their interactions with one another. They constitute mutual support systems and systems of such systems. Each one is able to be what it is only in the context of what it is doing for the others to which it is related. Self-being and for-others-being arise together.[4] In the natural world, there are many activities and processes. But it is the interactions,[5] the relations of several processes to one another, that make the universe-process, that build up the structure and the operation of the various levels of wholes that the cosmos is. These processes "mutually indwell" one another, so dependent are they upon all the others in order to be themselves. But this is just the way enstasis and ecstasis are related and united in the Trinity.

Just as in the Trinity there is no such thing as a single Person, so in the universe there is no such thing as a single being. All beings exist in coacting communities or systems of many beings. And it is from the collective, cooperative, interactions of the beings in the systems that whole new levels of being emerge.[6] This fundamental feature of the natural universe is significant for the view I am proposing of the cosmos as a kind of "incarnation" of the Trinity. It can't be done by any single cosmic being. It can be done only by the whole cosmos, in its multitude of ordered and creative interactions.

This helps us to see a last point about the universe imaging the Trinity, being its "child." This imaging is done by the whole universe, together. There is no privileged center. Earth-people have believed that our planet, our species, our nation, our hero, our story is the axis about which all created reality turns, and only gradually have we given up first one, then another, of these too narrow views. The Trinity (as I have focused on it, setting aside for this purpose the order of processions of Persons) shows us equality, mutual indwelling, no starting point, no ending point, symmetry, no privilege. This is what we will be seeing in the natural world.

For all these reasons, I say, the world is dear. It is dear to God as God's Child, and it should be dear to us. It is God's own offspring, self-expression, fulfillment. The highest, best, most perfect way to be a Creator is to create a self-creating world. This most satisfyingly fulfills the Creator because it most thoroughly incarnates the self-givingness of the Creator. To stop short of making the creature self-creative would be an imperfection.

A self-organizing, or self-creating, world and a creative God do not conflict or exclude one another. In fact, they go very well together. A self-organizing world is precisely the kind of world you would expect a creative God to make. Therefore, this self-organizing world of ours is not deprived of sacred meaning but, rather, filled to the brim with sacred meaning, filled with the intentionality and the creative power of God, as like the divine Being as finitude can get. And the dynamic universe is not "finished," and may never be finished, and so may be expected to become more and more "like."

My point, addressed to those who feel that modern science has stolen their God or made God unnecessary, is that this is not so at all. Our sciences are revealing God, showing "how God does it." And it all has to be done under the conditions of finitude, to which we will now turn. These will include both randomness and determinism, which religious people often yearn to reject. But these should not dismay us. Randomness and determinism are two of the ways you get creativity in the conditions of finitude. They provide for novelty and stability. Apparently unconscious and meaningless in themselves, out of their intricate interactions (and several other factors), what we recognize as consciousness and meaning will emerge. These values will grow out of these principles of finitude, grow from the inside out. The universe will grow as a Child of the Trinity, in whom God takes great delight.

The Nature of Finitude

When we were discussing the Persons of the Trinity and ourselves as persons, I stressed that persons are not defined, do not have descriptions, cannot be limited and particularized, are essentially formless, and so on (see above pp. 27–29). Especially, I pointed out, they do not relate to one another in terms of mutual negation, "I am I by being not-you," "My characteristics are different from yours." Now we are going to deal with the kind of being that *is* defined, does have description, is limited and particular, possesses form, and relates in terms of mutual negation. The cosmos is the Child of God but it is also the Exegete of God, the one who unpacks and spreads out in detail and shows in a multitude of ways. We have to take into consideration the conditions of "showing."

I likened the universe to God dancing, being a sequence of gestures in an improvising, self-expressive, artistic way. But such movements have to flow into one another according to their own rules. Artistic improvisation does not escape rules altogether; rather, it is the creative use of the rules that makes the work art. The universe has such strictures, such terms within which the work develops: space and time, the laws of nature, the great parameters, the laws of complex development. And in back even of these general contexts is the notion of what it means to be finite at all.

Take a sheet of blank paper. Draw any sort of closed figure on it, such as a circle. This is the basic idea. The figure divides the space into the inside of the figure and the outside. The originally unbounded, undefined space of the blank paper is now severed into two meanings, related to, but excluding one another. G. Spencer-Brown, a mathematician who has studied the consequences of this initial act, says some striking things about how this simple but fateful act projects our world:

> By tracing the way we represent such a severance, we can begin to reconstruct, with an accuracy and coverage that appear almost uncanny, the basic forms underlying linguistic, mathematical, physical, and biological science, and can begin to see how the familiar laws of our own experience follow inexorably from the original act of severance,... our first attempt to distinguish different things in a world where, in the first place, the boundaries can be drawn anywhere we please.... Although all forms, and thus all universes, are possible, and any particular form is mutable, it becomes evident that the laws relating such forms are the same in any universe.

The general theory of forms and their relations reveals "a reality which is independent of how the universe actually appears," but it also gives the rules for appearing, for phenomenalizing, as such. This is the work of mathematics, and "in common with other art forms, [it] can lead us beyond ordinary existence, and can show us something of the structure in which all creation hangs together."[7]

Although not all universes will actually *work*, in the sense of developing into a highly diversified and organized whole that attains to embodied consciousness, and although randomness and unpredictability are important parts of our picture, the mathematics of finite relations will make certain very general things inevitable, and this will be of significant interest to us as contemplatives and religious people. Self-organization is the main one of these inevitables, leading to life and other subsequent emergents. We will come to these topics in time. But from our special point of view, we may also notice that what we say here about finitude will be fundamental to what we say later about the "evolution of evil," and that some of our familiar stories and metaphors from religious tradition may seem to resonate with the points now being made.

For instance, the *Exsultet*, a liturgical song used in some celebrations of the Easter Vigil, speaks of the *Felix culpa*, "happy fault," and the "truly necessary sin of Adam," which made possible all the rest of spiritual history. We might see this original severance in such terms. Severance is where development starts, and "sin" finds its first ground in finitude and separation. Together, these remarks say that if you're going to have a finite universe as an embodied expression of divine life, this is how it has to be done — starting from severance and repeating severance in various ways — and that inevitably involves hurt and failure, but overall, despite, and more often *by means of* hurts and failures, the whole process grows and becomes more an image of the Trinity.

Now let's go back to the figure you drew on the paper, severing the paper into inside the figure and outside the figure. Notice that the figure has a boundary. The boundary defines it, separates the inside from the outside. The closed boundary makes the figure contain its insideness. This is the beginning of selfhood in the finite order. Also, we might think of the boundary as drawing the space together inside itself; it makes a spot, a body, a corpuscle, in the space. There is a togetherness inside the boundary that there is not outside. The figure is "discrete," set off, separated. This is the beginning of the universe's general tendency to "clump." To be discrete and then to clump, that's the basic way of making a universe. When you have drawn several (from "severed") discrete bodies, you can have various clumping patterns, and you're on your way to variety and creativity. The discrete bodies, and the discrete clumps of discrete bodies, will be "different" from one another in various ways, initially just by being severed from one another, but then by being in different clump patterns. Of course, there will be clumps of clumps and patterns of clumps of clumps and patterns of patterns of clumps.

Do you get the feeling that somehow there is more unity in a patterned clump than there is in just a single bounded figure? And more unity somehow even than there was on the unmarked paper before you drew the severing line? Isn't that interesting? This is the exegesis of the invisible in terms of finitude. If we had left the paper undivided, if the universe were just an evenly distributed homogeneous continuum of energy, there would be no structure: no differences, and hence no creative unions. This is an important point to bear in mind. It's the point the author of the *Exsultet* was making. The great marvel, the great beauty, the great delight of the creative unions to come are dependent on these strange requirements of severance. These creative unions in the finite are incarnations of the sort of union of many in one that is the Trinity. They unpack and display what was hidden before the foundation of the world. The world is made to "radiate" externally, that is, to "glorify" God.

Relations among Discrete Beings

But having severed, discrete, and clumping beings, we can now have relations among them, and the diversity, type of union, and interest goes up enormously. The first relation, and a continuing one, is that between the figure and the ground — the paper on which the figure is drawn. This will develop into relations between natural beings and their "environments," what surrounds and supports them. The next relation is that between different discrete beings. Just being different, severed, is the first relation, but then there is being in the same clump or being in another, a "different" clump. Notice that severing and clumping start all over again with the clumps themselves. They will be mutually discrete, related, united, and so on. Relations between first beings in different clumps will be dependent on the relations between their respective clumps. And the clumps, we said, will have patterns. There will be relations according to different patterns and relations between patterns.

What kinds of relations? Endless variety. Mutual definition is a basic one. The outsideness of the others, that they are outside "my" boundary, is part of what defines "me." If they are in my clump, that's another defining relation, or in another clump, a different relation. I have a relation of dependence on them for these aspects of my definition. In the natural order, I will have relations of dependence on them for my continued existence with whatever characteristics I have. All finite beings are in this way contingent upon the presence of their ground and the other finite beings. None of them is self-sufficient, self-defining. Definition, whether we mean our speaking about something or mean the thing's actual existence in a definite way, is always a matter of relations with other beings. Mutual reference.

In the natural world, beings will have relations of position in space and time, relations of movement with respect to other beings; some of these movements will be operations that affect the clumping and the patterning, and the clumping and patterning will limit the kinds of movements that can take place. We find ourselves in a universe of three spatial dimensions and one dimension of time. That's not arbitrary. Together with the laws of nature, that's the kind of universe that works, that is, that develops in interesting ways, that can *be more* without running into a dead end at some point.

Other relations are specified by the great parameters, certain fixed numbers, constants, that characterize how gravity works or electromagnetism, or nuclear energy, or how light relates to matter, very basic things. There are several of these numbers and ratios, all independent of one another, and if they did not have the values they have — weren't just those numbers or very close to them — this universe couldn't exist. Later relations in a finite material universe depend heavily on these fundamental relations, relations arising from the very natures of space, time, energy, and matter themselves. I'll give examples in the next chapter.

Then there are relations of process and change that govern how further severing and uniting take place, take place more or less continuously as ongoing processes. Accreting and radiating, feeding, growing, reproducing, mixing, mutating, dying, disintegrating — all these are relations of finitude with inevitable consequences for all the further developments as the universe builds us, organizes itself, and gradually becomes sensitive and conscious and religious!

Individuals, Interactions, and Emergents

Finite beings occur as individuals, that is, whatever one we are speaking of, that one cannot be divided. The boundary that defines it in its relevant space contains it, holds it together as the one that has that particular definition. If the boundary is broken and another boundary formed, then we no longer have that "individual," but something else with its own proper boundary and definition.

However, individuals can belong to classes, clumps of individuals that all have some characteristic in common. For, although finite beings are different from one another, they are not totally different from every other; they share most of their qualities with many others, while differing from them in some other respect. In relating to one another, finite beings take advantage of this fact and relate to all those of a common class in a common way. Because this is so, we are able to discern universal laws of nature, and because this is so we have various sorts of class-consciousness and social prejudice. Both things that have high value for us and things that have low value for us can be traced to certain features of finitude itself.

Individuals that are not the same as one another can also clump together and by their process relations with one another compose a new kind of individual. This is called an "emergent." It exists precisely as the group of interacting individuals. It is not their product as something separate from them; it is themselves, interacting. One might think of it as the "clumping" of those interactions. A molecule formed of atoms is a good example, or a living cell formed of nonliving molecules. The emergent is a new individual. It cannot be divided and still be itself, be present. It has its own boundary now in a space that is "outside" it, while the beings that constitute it are "inside," are parts of itself. And notice that it does have its own "selfhood." It is a whole, it has its own oneness; it is distinguishable from others.

This wholeness can be seen to govern the activities that take place within the new emergent, can be seen as its principle of internal unity. And when the emergent, as an individual, as a unit wholeness, relates and interacts with other beings outside it, it does so as a single unified being, in terms of its characteristics as a wholeness — characteristics which do not apply to any of its constituents singly — but only to the whole set of their interactions. The new characteristics now become the players in a whole new level of interactions among the constituted beings of this new class of finite things. Trinitarians may remember that their theology says that although there are relations among the divine Persons within the Trinity, whenever God acts "on the outside" — toward creation — the Trinity acts as a whole, as one single reality. The finite beings are imaging in their finite way the life of the Trinity.

Once this sort of clumping starts, unlimited diversity and development lie ahead. All sorts of new interactions become possible. "Eating," for example, is something that a whole set of intricately organized molecules do to another well-organized set of molecules, but single molecules don't do it to one another. But also some things now become impossible. Wood will burn in air, which contains oxygen, but not under water, which is composed in part of oxygen. The clumping interactions, forming emergents, have opened up new interactions and blocked others. And most interesting of all, they have made some developments — under appropriate conditions — inevitable. Once you have clumping and patterning (combinations and permutations), possibility and impossibility (probability and branching development), in limited populations, certain things will spontaneously happen. Some of these will come right out of the nature of finitude itself, the laws of form, that is, from the mathematics, which would be the same in any universe. This is how the self-organizing, or "self-creating," feature of the universe comes into being. This will be explained further in succeeding chapters.

Akin to possibility and impossibility is need. Emergents will form when the conditions for them are right, but once formed, they need those conditions in order to continue. And since Being always presses to be, to continue in being and to be yet more, "need" becomes a significant category for further development. And the first need we have, in order to have clumping and interaction, is for multiplicity and diversity. But the sheer multiplicity of the universe is itself finite, and the availability of any particular kind of being locally is always finite. This is an important condition, which we will discuss next. But the need for "many" is fundamental, and "many" in large numbers are required for the self-developing features to appear.

Diversity is even more important. Interesting interactions happen between diverse beings and create still more diverse beings. Diversity breeds diversity. This can become disadvantageous to self-organization. One can have too much. If there is too much diversity, too many interactions will be possible, and the boundaries of beings will be destroyed as fast as they are formed. To have a universe, a cosmos, something ordered and organized, there must be a certain amount of stability, of protection against disruption of organized sets of interactions. Selfhood must be maintained.

But, on the other hand, a great deal of diversity is required in order to have a high chance of getting useful interactions. Notice that the number of ways of putting pieces together is always much greater than the number of pieces themselves. And when you include the patterning of the arrangement, as well as the mere combination, then the diversity is greater still. If there is a certain probability of a particular interaction occurring, and if there is sufficient multiplicity and diversity, the probability of that interaction actually happening a significant number of times will approach inevitability, even if the probability in any single encounter was quite low. The chance may be one in a million, but if you've got a million, you should get one. And since there may be more than one way of getting a desired effect, the diversity will improve the chances as well.

This sort of thing will be very much to the fore when we consider how life may have gotten started, and it will continue to be the fundamental issue as we watch the various living beings finding places to live and ways to maintain and reproduce themselves. The diversity of the environment, the multiplicity of other beings around, will help them find the "niches" into which they can fit and fulfill their needs. And we will also discover that every niche tends to be filled sooner or later. It represents a certain set of interactions with the environment, and there will usually be found some creature that can live by those interactions.

Scarcity and Competition

The subject of need now brings up an important area of discussion: scarcity and competition. Go back to the formation of "emergents." These are clumps, groups, sets of interacting units of diverse sorts. In order to get the emergent feature, the new wholeness, every one of those interacting units has to be present and functioning. If one should be lost or damaged, the whole will fall apart, cease to be a "self." So the formation of such a whole is clearly dependent on gaining the needed components from the environment. If one set of units, on the way to forming an emergent, succeeds in attracting a needed component, and there is a limited number of such components in the reachable neighborhood, then any other set of units that might have been in the process of making up that same kind of emergent will be deprived of the needed material. When all the available material has been used up, no more emergents of that kind can be assembled. This is a fact of finitude and figures very significantly in the way the universe develops. The failure to assemble and the stopping of the assembling are among the things that are "inevitable" in a finite world.

But we said that Being always tends to continue being and to be yet more. Therefore, there will be assemblies and assemblies of assemblies, and they will always have their needs for certain materials and conditions in the environment. When repeated self-assembly has appeared on the scene, we may begin to be justified in speaking (softly at first) of these compounded beings as "striving" to attain what they need to stay in business. In any case, those that succeed in satisfying their needs will be able to repeat their self-assembly, and those that do not obtain what they need will not be able to do so. In a finite space of limited resources, not all will succeed. Some will be deprived, will fail to continue, will die. That is a fact of finitude. And it will push the assemblies of beings to more and more complex, diverse, self-controlling, and environment-controlling levels of organization.

So the self-assembling beings will compete with one another for the conditions of continued and expanded being. In the beginning, the most simple units will gather into the first emergents. But then, we said, there will be assemblies of assemblies, compounding. Self-assembling beings will take in as raw material subassemblies of themselves, already assembled subunits. This is the beginning of "eating." Again, the beings will compete with one another for such needed subunits. This is destruction of the autonomy of the subunit as in itself a self-whole, but it is enhancement and growth and success for the greater whole, for the "eater."

So we see that finitude inevitably creates what we may call points of view. Advantages and disadvantages with respect to assembling appear. And what is advantageous to one being may very well be disadvantageous to another. The eater is pleased to eat; the eaten feels very differently about it. Notice that it is the same event, seen in two different ways. If we want to style it "good" or "evil," we have to specify the point of view; we have to refer it to the being for whom it is good or bad. This will get much more complicated as the universe gets more complex and consciousness begins to develop in it, but this is where it starts. There is a natural history for even human moral concerns.

Meanwhile, we can note that self-reference has come on the scene and the distinction between self and other. That is to say, the compound assembly being can tell the difference between itself, parts of itself, needed materials for itself, and competitors for those materials. Various interactions will therefore develop to help preserve oneself and to give one better standing in the securing of materials and in succeeding against competitors. The latter may include destroying competitors, as well as simply getting there first. And, of course, those beings that are apt to be regarded by others as raw material would rapidly disappear unless they developed some safeguards, protections, and ways to fight back. Among these devices, disguise and deception will be found especially useful, so falsehood will appear in the world.

Competition and the effort to stay in existence mean that there is preference. Any being prefers to be and to be more, rather than to be destroyed. This means that there is something like an "observer," one who takes the point of view and acts in terms of it. The competing beings make something like judgments; certain acts are performed rather than others. There are acts in response to others' acts and in response to conditions in the environment. Those beings that are able to "judge" accurately what is to their advantage and disadvantage will continue in their being; those who make mistakes will be less likely to maintain themselves. This is the origin of value and of inequality. Even among those things that are preferred, some are preferred more than others. Some are more needed or give a greater advantage. This, too, is an inevitable effect of the working out of finite interactions among diverse clumping beings.

But judging means that something like knowledge of the other is needed, some way to have information of the being of something that is not oneself, enough information to determine an action with respect to that being in terms of possible advantage to oneself. Sensitivity becomes valuable, and the more varied, the more far-ranging, the more delicate to subvariations and quantities, the better. Being able to detect what is disadvantageous, what kind of disadvantageous, how badly disadvantageous, is clearly an advantage. Being able to feel pain is good. Being able to feel pleasure is also good. Being able to tell the difference is crucial. That's why sensitivity takes the form of being a kind of internal "badness" or "goodness" for the self.

But all that would be of no help if a response could not be produced that was relevant. Relevant means that the interaction initiated by the sensing being must have an effect on the outside that the sensing being can again sense and evaluate. In the evaluation, if mistakes can be detected and not repeated, that is an advantage. If more or less successful actions can be compared, that helps even more. If a diversity of actions is available to the sensing being, that is a great advantage. If control of the repetition is a power of the being — that is, if it has a "memory" that can renew the judgment and can start or stop the actions — then the being is in a very advantageous position. When the memory is able to run two or more versions of judgments and can compare them in a "memory" way, without external action yet, what we call choice makes its appearance. When there is sensing of memory, that may be what we recognize as consciousness. And when there is sensing of remembering the remembering, perhaps that is self-consciousness.

I have described the beings as vying among themselves for needed resources and discovering advantageous ways to manage in their environments. One of the necessary advantageous ways is by cooperation with all the other beings of the environment. "Co-operation" means initially just that, operating together, which they must do since they are all in the same environment, since they in fact constitute "environment" for one another. There's no choice about that. If your mode of operation is too uncongenial to those of your fellows, you won't last long. But some optional ways of cooperating in the sense of positively helping one another soon appear. Sometimes there is a trade-off; cooperating beings have to lose a little in one way in order to gain more in another way. Experience shows whether it pays off. Succeeding ways repeat. Some striving against, some cooperating with — variety and diversity of ways of operating together. We call this flexibility. But even cooperation is inevitable in an interacting community.

All this, with its many elaborations, developments, and consequences, comes from the very nature of finitude itself. We will see these developments as we go along. We are going to study self-organization, evolution, adaptation, selection, randomness, and historical development. But underneath it all will be the very basic, very general lawfulness that makes all the rest possible: the *mathematics,* the "laws of form," which are "the same in any universe," eternal and necessary. Any universe is an "incarnation" of the mathematics. This is a wonderful thought to grasp. If mathematics — being thought-forms that are eternal and necessary — can be said to be an aspect of "the mind of God," then mathematics may be regarded as the "mediator" of the creation, the Word, the Exegete, that incarnates as the cosmos.

The Value of the Finite

Now I want to pause before we start considering the actual matter of the sciences to review and clarify the relation between the infinite and the finite. The very first thing we must say is the simplistic and tautological "Being is." But there are a few things we can say about *how* Being is. It is, most importantly, Being-communicating. It is from this principle that I developed the whole theology of agape and the Trinity. But it will also be behind everything said in the cosmology. Then, if Being is Being-communicating, it must be one/many, enstatic/ecstatic, interactive, and wholistic.

Two corollaries to being Being-communicating are: Being tends to be more, and Being tends to be in every possible way. From these we see that Being must be both infinite (formless, unlimited, undefined) and finite (with form, limited, defined). Any particular finite being is contingent on the conditions that enable it to be, but that Being should occur as finite is necessary. It comes out of the very nature of Being.

Finite being will again be Being-communicating, therefore one/many, enstatic/ecstatic, interactive, and wholistic. But it will have something infinite being does not. It will have difference and change. These will be possible and necessary because it can be said of a finite being (as it cannot of the infinite) what it is *not*. "Not-being" will play a major role in everything about finite being, whereas infinite being is the "fullness of Being" and nothing can be denied of it. This characteristic of not-being means that finite beings will be different from one another: one will have features another does not. This contributes to their ability to define and limit one another. They will thus occur in *kinds;* classes of features and new kinds will be endlessly possible. Because the finite beings are-not some things, they are able to interact with one another to constitute and produce new things, different from all the interactors. This is the basis of change. (Let this include change of position in space and time, considered as an active relation to space and time that results in a new location.)

Notice that all this is necessary. If Being is Being-communicating, it has to be finite, which means it has to be severed and interactive and novelty-creating. And these same characteristics will again be present in the new beings, which will in their turn interact, creating further novelty.

Nobody "causes" these things to happen. This is how Being is. I have suggested that infinite being, as the paradigm of Being in general, can be said to "incarnate" itself in the finite, to express its invisible potentialities there. The "fullness of Being" includes the necessity for finite being, so that finite being is a kind of "unpacking" of what is implied in Being as such. There is no "choice" about whether this will be done. Nor does the Infinite "design" the forms of the finite. The forms of the finite arise from fundamental necessary relations in finitude itself.

Part of this necessity is going to be randomness and accident and seizing on the nearest best alternative, so don't think of some locked-in, mechanistic determinism. When, following out the necessity to be more and to be in every possible way, the compounded interactive wholes have reached a certain richness of complexity, true choice will appear. The amazing thing about the finite is that out of these very simple rules about how it has to be there come eventually consciousness and choice and creativity, morality and art. This is what I point to under the mythic icon of the Theotokos.

This leads to the next point, which may be difficult and repugnant to some religious people: the Infinite does not "intervene" in the finite. The Infinite as a whole is "exegeted" in the whole of the finite, but the Infinite cannot be a participant in any interaction among the finite beings because that would finitize it. Only finite beings can be agents in finite interactions. The Infinite can be "present" in and even as the whole finite world, but it cannot be some particular part of the finite world or control some particular interaction in the finite world. All finite interactions are defined from particular points of view, and the Infinite cannot take one point of view rather than another. While this may be disappointing, it also relieves us of otherwise intractable problems, especially questions about why the Infinite doesn't intervene in ways we (from our point of view) would like it to do.

Here an interesting possibility presents itself. If we were to mean by the name "God" both the Infinite and finite — perhaps even refer to the whole reality as "the Incarnation" — then we might be able to say in a religious context some of the things we are used to saying and like to say. The world would become the "body" of God, a very old idea, and everything that happens in the world would be the "doing" of God. But the doing has to include everything — no picking and choosing — everything, what in our eyes is good, bad, and indifferent. This is the same principle as the Infinite relating to the finite as a whole, not to selected parts or points of view within it. The reason it has to be this way is that if the Infinite is selective, it becomes finite and can no longer be the impartial Ground for all being. This necessity has to be constantly borne in mind, because failure to acknowledge it lies at the root of most theological tangles.

When we begin correctly to appreciate the nature of the Infinite and the distinction between it and the finite, we may have to give up expecting (requiring?) God to take our part every time we are involved in an interaction that is apt to prove disadvantageous to us. (For popular religion, this is close to being the main item in the job description for God.) But God is "perfect" (literally, doing thoroughly), that is, whole, not partial, sending sun and rain on both the good and evil, the just and unjust (Matt. 5:45; cf. Deut. 10:17). Many people do not like this; they want a re-active God who operates in terms of the same comparative scales they themselves use (and so protest paying all the vineyard workers the same for different hours, Matt. 20:1–16).

And if there is no intervention, what about miracles? Miracles do occur! Wonderful things happen indeed, and many of them we cannot yet explain. But our failure (so far) to explain them does not mean that they are outside the laws of nature, the forms of the finite. The movements of the planets, the eclipses of the sun and moon, were once marvels, mysterious, frightening. Volcanic eruptions, earthquakes, storms, floods, droughts, blights, plagues — even simple things such as fire and the different forms of water — were once miraculous. We can sympathize with how supernatural all these must have appeared before we understood what naturally caused them. Originally they were all — as some of them still are for insurance companies — "acts of God."

Generation, the birth of human beings, was once magical and still arouses awe. The healing of wounds, disease and recovering from disease, were baffling and so were referred to deities. They are now sufficiently explained that we no longer categorize them as miraculous, unless they happen when we do not expect them. But this only shows that our expectations are not sufficiently refined. Even these unexpected events are complex but perfectly natural interactions of the finite.

This pattern of the unexplained being explained — and for that matter, of the "impossible" being done — has repeated itself so many times in our remembered history, that we ought by now to have more confidence in it. We have been appealing to our various gods to control the world in our favor, but little by little we have been doing it ourselves. In fact, at the moment we are in danger of doing it too much, upsetting other creatures, the common environment, and perhaps important interactions we do not yet know about. So it is essential that we continue to learn, and to appreciate and value, and therefore to act in ways that permit the great finite interactive Whole to go on.

For it is great. It is marvelous. If we wanted to call anything "miraculous," we should call the existence and operation of the whole finite cosmos miraculous. That out of such a few simple principles it brings by repeated interactions all this complexity and creativity into being, culminating (here, at present) in beings such as ourselves who can begin to understand the whole thing and to value it and to try to cooperate in it and with it, is the supreme marvel of all our experience.

I am not saying that this was done by an outside Designer "on purpose." I am only saying that this in fact is the case. This is what is actually going on. We are now looking for patterns of understanding in it, and we can see some, some necessary ones. Let me say again: nothing mechanistic, no railroad tracks. It is "necessary" that there be contingency and randomness and chance and accident and choice. Nobody causes this; nobody "gives" it to somebody else. It is the nature of finite being, which is Being-communicating and pressing to be in every possible way.

Well, does finite being "add" anything to infinite being? This is a trick question, of course, because nothing can be "added" to the infinite. Is infinite plus finite being "better" than infinite being alone? If infinite is the "fullness of Being," then of course nothing can be "better." Nevertheless, we know what we are trying to ask in these paradoxical ways, and I am going to answer "yes" to this unstated question. I shall put it this way: Being *has* to be both infinite and finite, and if it were not, it would not be complete and true and real Being. This double nature of Being is what I am pointing to by using the familiar notion of the Incarnation.

Chapter Four

THE SELF-CREATING UNIVERSE: PATHWAY TO THE STARS

 WITH THE BACKGROUND we have thus developed, we are now going to survey the various levels of cosmic organization. This is obviously a huge task, because we are overwhelmed with both the wealth of detail on our world and the plethora of theories about it. Fortunately, there is no lack of excellent books for the general reader, some of them taking broad views of the forest, others close-ups of the trees.* My main ambition in this book is to persuade my particular audience — religious people who shy away from science — to read such books without fear that our basic spirituality will be completely undercut. I admit that we may have to rearrange some of our ideas (particularly about such things as supernatural design and intervention), but I argue that a deeper spirituality emerges and that a more satisfactory theology is suggested.

The deeper spirituality comes from referring back to the fundamental principles of Being, which I hope to show manifesting themselves in all these levels of cosmic organization that we are now going to examine. In particular, I hope to bring out how the most fundamental themes — "Be more," "Be in every possible way," "Communicate Being," and "Be a new whole by interaction" — govern everything that we know. The trinitarian character of combining one and many, enstasy and ecstasy, by engaging in Being-communicating, will be imaged on every level. This is what I am calling symbiosis, "living together," generalizing the term beyond what it strictly means in biology. And the divine character of creating will be imaged by the self-activating and novelty-producing behaviors of the increasingly complex organizations of the developing natural world.

---

*In the notes for this chapter (see pp. 182ff.), you will find brief descriptions of some recent popular books. Please read the notes as you go along, because some of them give additional information, explaining things further for nonscientists or giving extra details for those who want more.

58

The more satisfactory theology will come, I think, through a more thorough application of the theological idea of incarnation, which will have three advantages. (1) God will be intimately present in the world without intervening in it in a supernatural way; thus, even if everything about the behavior of the world is explained in worldly terms, in natural ways, this will not "eliminate" God. Science will not be a threat to spirituality, for the more it displays a self-running, self-creating, self-explaining universe, the more the religious person can feel content that the universe is exhibiting the glory of God. (2) The problem of "evil" — how can a good and powerful God allow it without becoming morally responsible for it — will receive an answer of sorts, which I will set forth in chapter 9. It will make more sense after we have gone through all the ways in which the universe organizes itself and communicates within itself. (3) The nonintervention and the not-knowing the future will be seen as derivative from incarnation and creativity themselves. A greater God will be revealed than the rather simple magician who knows everything and can do anything, which has been such an unsatisfactory idea of God.

The benefit to the religious person of studying the cosmos in the context of a sound metaphysics is to realize that we are much closer to a more realistic God. Some problems and anxieties will be removed, I believe. Meaningfulness will be enhanced and thus energy for pushing ahead in generous ways with the creation of the world will be released and joy in life will be secured at a level where it cannot so easily be attacked by the unpredictable twists and turns of this world, which does its creative thing right on the edge of chaos.

Living on the edge of chaos means that the patterns of behavior in this world are complex. When we start to study them, we are tempted to feel that it is all too complicated, too hard to understand. If we are contemplatives, we may feel that it is not our style, that we tend more to get a global sense of things being valuable. We may prefer to have the world process described for us in poetic images rather than in scientific analysis. But I want to lay it before you in some detail of scientific analysis so that you see the wonder of *how* all this is going on and you find out that you can understand it. It will take a little effort. You can't read a science book the way you read a novel. Rereading is to be expected. (That's why you have a *book* and not just a conversation.) But your sense of appreciation of the Reality in which we "live and move and have our being" will so increase that you will agree that it was worth it.

Problems of the Origin

The difficulties we confront when we ask how the universe got started can be remarked on whimsically by a story. A mysterious time-traveler from an ancient time appears at a lecture on modern cosmology. The oldtimer catches the lecturer afterward and gently corrects this complicated science. The world, says this sage, is supported by a giant elephant. "What supports the elephant?" inquires the lecturer, humoring the ancient one. "The elephant stands on the back of an enormous turtle." "Ah! And what supports the turtle?" "An even bigger turtle, of course." "Oh! And the even bigger turtle?" "Now, just hold on," says the one out of time; "I can see how you're headed, and I can tell you right now, it's turtles all the way down."

Our attempts at explaining the origin are something like this. Where did this come from? Why did that happen? Always a reference to a predecessor or a more basic level of explanation. Is there no ultimate turtle? The trouble with beginnings is that either they are the same kind of event as all those that follow them — in which case they themselves stand in the same need of explanation or cause — or else they are totally different from these followers, in which case we know nothing about them. Unless, of course, we ourselves somehow straddle the two kinds of being. It is for the sake of trying to do something about this difficulty that I proposed looking more closely at the idea of the Incarnation.

The physicists have not given up, however; they have made several suggestions. The one I am going to tell about is a modification of the Big Bang theory called "inflation." It is a way of explaining our present observable universe as the result of a very rapid expansion of an originally tiny quantum field which, fluctuating the way quantum fields do, produces energy from which all our matter and radiation are descended. A further development of this basic idea (which, beyond a brief mention toward the end of the inflation story, I won't go into) is "chaotic inflation," in which many different "universes" appear, expanding at different rates and with different characteristics.

Aside from the chain of "why?" questions, is there anything physical that makes us think there must be at least a local beginning to our present universe? Yes, there is. For one, our universe seems to be expanding. The galaxies are moving away from each other. We can measure how fast it is happening (there is some dispute about what the actual number is). But if they are moving apart now, that means that in the past they must have been closer together. In the far past they must have been very close together. In fact, there is a limit to how close together they can get. That point is the "beginning."[1]

Another reason for thinking there must have been a beginning is the way energy is transferred. An everyday observation is that heat passes from a hotter body to a cooler, not the other way. If molecules in an enclosed space bump into each other enough, they will transfer their energy from the more energetic to the less until it all averages out, each molecule having about the same energy. Everybody having the same or the average energy is the most probable state. It is called equilibrium — "thermal equilibrium," to be exact. It is so balanced that there is no tendency to go one way rather than another. The motion of the molecules is completely random.[2]

But there is also a trend from randomness to order, arrangement, and self-control: atoms, molecules, cells, organisms, societies — compounded organizations made of simpler organizations. How do they come about, if there is this universal tendency to reduce everything to a "most probable" state? Well, curiously enough, these complexities do come about precisely by means of the tendency to go to the most probable condition. But it's going to take a good bit of explaining to show that, and we have to take it one step at a time. Meanwhile, we can notice that both of these movements, toward the random and away from the random, indicate that time runs in only one direction; and so, observing how things are now, we can retrace the path and conclude that there was at least a local beginning.

Both of these movements are going to give us problems. We can observe that the universe is in (almost perfect) "thermal equilibrium" now. But the standard Big Bang cosmology couldn't account for it adequately. "Inflation," which I'm going to tell about, does. That's one reason why the scientists like it. But then we have the opposite problem: if the whole universe is in "thermal equilibrium," how do we come to have all these different objects? Stars in galaxies, stars with planets, planets with life, and all the rest of it? Well, the equilibrium wasn't quite perfect. There was a little bit of difference left, and all the rest of this has grown from that. We'll talk about that, too.

But see an interesting thing here at the outset: both *sameness* and *difference* play major roles. Like the One and the Many, they will be with us through the whole development. Protons are all alike, but put different numbers of them together, and you get completely different substances. Or, take a certain number of carbon atoms, a number of hydrogens, oxygens, and nitrogens, and, without varying the numbers of each, just put them together in different arrangements, and again you'll get very different substances. And when these chemicals are made up into living beings, the same chemicals will be used again and again, but so differently functioning that all the marvelous diversity of the natural world appears as if by magic.

I might observe here that one of the reasons we think the universe is so miraculous that it must be controlled directly by an outside Designer is that we look only at the finished products, the complex assemblies. We don't see the detail of how these intricate structures and operations are built up of the multitudinous interactions of a simple and necessary sort. But when we trace these interactions down and look at them close up, we begin to see how really marvelous the universe is. It doesn't have to be "tinkered with" at each stage. It can grow itself, from the inside out, step by interactive step, following the fundamental rules of Being: be more, be in every possible way, communicate Being, interact, be both one and many.

Aren't the rules in our universe more particular than that? Yes, they are, and they're called "laws of nature." They are presumed to be the same everywhere in our observable universe, and so far that presupposition has checked out. Examples are the law of gravitation, the laws governing the nuclear forces and the electromagnetic interactions. They are all interactions, and from this mutuality come the further organizations of the cosmos. But where did the laws themselves come from? Why does our universe behave this way and not some other way?

The answer to that is that if you changed any of them very much — or even very little — you wouldn't be able to build this universe, the one we're in. In fact, you wouldn't even be able to build stars. Stars seem to be the crucial step.

If you can get as far as stars, you can probably go on to people. Other universes (supposing that there are other universes) with other versions of the natural laws, won't develop this way. So we observe our universe to be the way it is because it's the kind of universe that can have people in it. This statement is called the Weak Anthropic Principle.[3] It is a constraint on what kind of laws our universe can have: they have to be such as to make people possible.

And, of course, the laws all have to be congenial among themselves. We are now looking for one single law, a Theory of Everything, of which all these separate laws would be just special cases. From such a foundation, all the further structures and events follow. Not just anything can happen. Complex arrangements and operations don't start from pure randomness. They start from what has happened up to this point, and they proceed according to the rules. Each thing that happens is the foundation on which the next things have to build. Each relation that develops grounds further relations. Yet, in this way, novel things will emerge.

Think of a painter using a palette of a dozen colors, a two-dimensional canvas, and working with the laws governing perspective, shadows, warm and cool colors, and so on. A few basic materials, restrictive conditions and rules, and yet what masterpieces of imagination and beauty result! The same way with music: a few tones, limited array of timbres and volumes, but the combinations within those restrictions, and because of those restrictions, produce the soul-stirring compositions we so enjoy.

It's the same way with our universe. Complicated things can build up from few, simple, and restricted ones. And the most amazing thing is that they will *have* to build up, precisely because of these basic laws and the derived relations. When the conditions are right, the interactions will happen. That's the magic of the self-creating universe.

The Cosmic Parameters

But the conditions do have to be just right. This is, apparently, a rather special kind of universe. When we start to look into the ways in which our world might be special, we find all sorts of very interesting and amazing things. The first is that there are some special numbers that describe the characteristics and behaviors we observe. They are called "parameters" (not to be confused, as is now popularly done, with "perimeters"). They figure in equations as constants, but their values are adjustable and have to be discovered by observation. There are about fifteen basic ones.[4] Some of them are simply the sizes of elemental things, such as the mass of the electron, the mass of the proton, the charge on the electron, the velocity of light. Others are like the gravitational constant, which modifies the way the force of gravity is proportional to the product of the masses of the attracting bodies (and inversely proportional to the square of the distance between them). There are similar parameters for the "strong" and "weak" nuclear forces.

Then there is the "constant of least action," Planck's constant, h — very small, as many of these numbers are. And there are some others. None of them can be derived from the others, but all of them have to be congenial with one another; none can "contradict" another. Among them, they control a lot about this universe.

For instance, consider the parameter that governs the intensity of the strong nuclear force, which holds the protons and neutrons together in the atomic nucleus. If it were a little larger, these nucleons would stick together so tightly that there would be no free protons, no hydrogen (whose nucleus is a single proton), so no water, so no life. Decrease it a little, and you can't get any of the nucleons to stick together, so there would be nothing *but* hydrogen — no oxygen, for instance, so again no water and no life.

Now add electrons to properly balanced nuclei and see how the parameter for the electromagnetic force (properly called an interaction) controls chemistry. If it's too strong, attracting the negatively charged electrons to the positive nucleus very securely, it will take a lot of energy to rearrange the electrons and get them to share with other atoms in making chemical compounds. Shifting rapidly from one compound to another, one reaction following another in a useful pathway, would be out of the question. But that's what life is, so no life. Weaken the attraction slightly, and you won't get bonding at all — same conclusion, no life.

Try the gravitational constant. If we weaken it, the stars won't form, won't be attracted to clump together. They won't become so dense inside that the pressure and temperature cause the nuclear reactions to start so that the star "shines" and later on, it won't collapse still further under gravity, make heavy nuclei for elements beyond hydrogen and helium, and scatter them abroad by exploding, providing raw material for other stars and planets. If we make gravity too strong, the stars will go into overdrive and burn up so rapidly that they can't provide nice gentle continuous sunshine for planets who need a few peaceful billion years to get their lifeforms, with their delicate chemistry, going.

Yes, billions of years. How do we arrange for that? The density of the universe has to be just right. Too dense, and gravity will crush the poor thing promptly. Not dense enough, and the bits of matter won't be close enough to attract one another and form stars. Forming stars is the essential thing. Long-lasting second- or third-generation stars that have some heavy atoms to share with their peripheral planets, things like carbon and nitrogen and oxygen, all of which have to be cooked in the nuclear furnaces in the hearts of stars and then bequeathed to new stars and maybe cooked yet again to make still heavier elements like iron. Very critical density. We've got it.[5] It buys us time in which to go through all the stages of organization and superorganization by which we build up atoms, molecules, fancy chemistry, cells, and all the life forms with increasing ability to sense their environments and relate adaptively to them (including changing them), becoming more sensitive, more aware, and finally producing a creature that can look at the universe and figure out that all these conditions had to be just right in order for the creature to be there and look.

So why do we observe the universe to have just these perfect conditions, these special values for its basic parameters? We observe it so because only in a universe that has these conditions could we possibly be here to observe it. The universe is fifteen billion years old now because it took fifteen billion years to assemble/evolve a creature that could calculate the age of the universe. Doesn't that look as if this universe was rather specially planned and designed with a view to getting us at the end of the line? Not necessarily. So far it's really just a tautology. It only amounts to saying that we can't observe a universe in which we can't exist. So naturally the universe we see is the universe in which the conditions for our existence are being met. They are such very special conditions, surely quite improbable. But we don't really know that. We don't yet have the Theory of Everything. Maybe they're not all that improbable. And besides, if the multiple-universes view is adopted, then all sorts of values for the parameters are being tried in all sorts of combinations. ("Be in every possible way!") In that multitude, this combination of these values would be bound to come up, and there we would be. Not improbable at all, rather inevitable.

While we wait to see what the theorists will come up with, I will merely call attention to the fact that all these conditions and these great parameters have to be in "community" with one another to produce a universe. They are interacting with one another, and increasingly organized wholes are emerging. This is what I am calling "symbiosis," living together, and pointing out to religious people as a way of seeing an image of God deeply embedded in the world. If Being-communicating is the Ground, then we are certainly seeing Being-communicating exemplified — exegeted — in the cosmos. These fundamental interactions produce diversity and manyness, and they also produce union and wholeness. The two conditions together — the same and the different, the one and the many — make possible development and novelty, creativity. Image of the Creator, incarnation of the Trinity.

The Big Bang

But now let us look at the most widely held view of the early universe. P. J. E. Peebles (Princeton), in his *Principles of Physical Cosmology*, remarks that the name "Big Bang" is unfortunate because "it suggests we are identifying an event that triggered the expansion of the universe, and it may also suggest the event was an explosion localized in space. Both are wrong."[6]

There is no evidence for a preferred center; the universe looks the same in every direction. What cosmology studies is the universe as it now is and as far back in time as we can trace it. There is a good bit of evidence to go on, and there is a lot of interesting speculation. There are many puzzles, and it is possible that considerable revision may be required in the future; it is a very active field of study.

The basic Big Bang view is that the universe is expanding, that is, the clusters of galaxies are moving away from each other at a rate that depends on how far apart they already are and what the value of the Hubble parameter is at that point in time. The Hubble parameter, H, is expressed as a velocity divided by a distance, so it is the reciprocal of the elapsed time $(H = \frac{d}{t} \times \frac{1}{d} = \frac{1}{t})$.[7] This means that as t gets larger, H gets smaller. But when t was small, H was larger. When the universe was very young, the expansion rate was enormous, explosive. That's why this early era is called the Big Bang.

This relation of H to time also means that if we know the value of H, we know the age of the universe. We don't know exactly the value of H now, but it is somewhere between fifteen and thirty kilometers per second for every million light-years (distance light travels in a year). That gives the age of the universe as between ten and twenty billion years, so most people say fifteen billion years old.

But we must also consider that gravity is acting on the galaxies. Gravity attracts bodies according to their massiveness and according to the distance between them. How much mass have we got? And how densely is it distributed?

We already know that there must be a deceleration force acting on the universe sufficient to slow the expansion because here we are, fifteen billion years later, still going along nicely. We've not blown apart nor have we collapsed. If we hadn't had a density almost exactly the "critical density" for balancing, one or the other would have happened long before now. To have remained so close to the crucial value for such a long time means that the initial expansion rate and the other conditions had to be "just right" to within very small tolerances. If the universe expands too fast, gravity can't gather matter together to make stars, and of course if it expands too slowly, it will be caught by gravity and collapse. The universe we are in is one that "hovers" between these two disasters by continuing to expand but slowing down as it goes.[8]

This is the basic idea of the Big Bang origin of our universe. It is not pure speculation; it has some strong lines of evidence. Besides the expansion itself, as just explained, there is the cosmic background radiation, which we can measure. Its temperature is 2.726 Kelvin (that's above absolute zero, in Celsius-size degrees). This is considered to be a relic of the original explosion, radiation that is coming to us from a great distance, and therefore from a long time ago. The interesting thing about it is that it is almost perfectly isotropic — the same, no matter where you look. There are only very small variations, about one part in a hundred thousand.

This radiation is mostly in the microwave range, peaking at a wavelength of about one millimeter. NASA's Cosmic Background Explorer (COBE) satellite measured the whole spectrum from space in 1989 and found it showed the characteristic variation of intensity with wavelength that indicates that the radiation comes from heat alone. This is called "blackbody" (for perfect absorption without reflection) radiation. As the wavelength shortens, the intensity (brightness) first climbs rapidly, then falls off more gradually, with a long tail, somewhat like one side of a normal distribution curve. John Barrow says: "It was the most perfect blackbody spectrum ever seen in nature, and a striking confirmation that the universe was once hundreds of thousands of degrees hotter than it is today."[9]

The only way to understand this extraordinary unity is to suppose an origin in the early universe, when everything was highly compressed and very hot — that is, in close thermal communication. Energy could be shared and communicated among all parts of the universe and thus the whole could come to the same temperature. But this is going to raise a serious question for the Big Bang theory.

Problems and Proposals

The Big Bang is a good basic theory, but it leaves a number of questions. The first one is called the horizon problem. The horizon marks the limit of what is observable. Since light travels at a finite speed, the cosmic horizon for any observer is the distance light can have traveled since the expansion began. Given more time, more light will arrive. We ourselves are seeing about ten new galaxies every year, just because their light is only now arriving.[10]

At this point we need to make a distinction when we speak of "the universe." I've been saying carefully "our" universe, just in case there should be others. Ours is the one with the characteristics that make it possible for us to be here. But now we must restrict our concern further and speak of the "observable" universe, because after all, this is the only thing we actually know anything about. So the rest of our discussion will be limited to the observable universe, until we get to "chaotic" inflation and the speculations about other universes. The observable universe is bounded by this finite-speed-of-light horizon. And that's where the standard Big Bang theory has a problem.

The "horizon problem" is a dilemma because, on the one hand, distant points of the sky must have been in communication with one another in the past, and on the other hand, they can't have been. We were just saying that the COBE measurement shows that the whole sky is the same temperature (with tiny exceptions), and that the only way all the matter could have come to the same average temperature was by exchanging heat-energies, being in "thermal communication." The fastest way they could conduct this communication was by radiation, at the speed of light. All bodies would have to be able to reach each other by radiation. That means they would have to be within each other's "horizon."

But the remote galaxies that we can see now, looking at opposite sides of the sky, certainly aren't within each other's horizon because they're twice as far from each other as they are from us, and they are just barely within *our* horizon, their radiations only now reaching us. When the universe was younger, of course the galaxies were closer together and one might think that *then* radiation could have passed from one side of the universe to the other. But when the universe was younger, there hadn't yet been enough *time* for this journey to be completed. When the Big Bang theory calculates the distances at various ages of the universe — even very long ago, near "the beginning" — the distance always comes out far too great for radiation to have traveled from one side of the universe to the other in the time available since the beginning. So, the most distant points on either side of the sky can't have been in communication with each other at any time. They weren't within the same horizon — according to the unmodified Big Bang Theory.[11]

That's the horizon problem, and the "inflation" proposal is going to solve it. We need to understand the problems that inflation solves so that we can appreciate the value of the inflation scenario, and the inflation scenario is of interest to us because it seems to show the universe literally "creating itself."

The second problem is called the "flatness" problem, but it really has to do with the density of the universe. It's called the flatness problem because of the effect the density has on the geometry of the universe. This comes from general relativity, Einstein's gravitational theory. According to this theory, if the density is great, space curves "inward," as if to form a sphere; if density is low, it curves "outward," as if to make a saddle shape (hyperboloid). If the density is a certain critical value, space doesn't curve at all but is "flat."

We have already remarked (when we were talking about the Hubble parameter) that there is a critical density. If the actual density is less than that, the universe flies apart without making stars; if it is more, gravity causes it to collapse, again without making stars. The ratio of the actual density to the critical density is called Omega, written Ω. Recent studies with the Infrared Astronomical Satellite (IRAS) have determined that the actual average density of the universe is high, close to the critical density.[12] But this seems very fortuitous, a delicate balance, requiring most fine tuning. How are we to account for this by intrinsic physical explanations? Inflation may have the answer.

Another problem is the ratio of photons (radiation particles) to baryons (roughly, matter particles; strictly, particles that react to the strong nuclear force, such as protons and neutrons). The measured ratio is about two billion photons for every baryon. Why? And where did the matter itself come from and how?[13]

And a last question: if the universe is so homogeneous, how did it manage to get started making clumps? Clumps that could turn into stars and galaxies and clusters of galaxies and superclusters? This is an important one, and we have some recent observational evidence that supports the inflationary hypothesis explanation of this phenomenon.

So what is this "inflation" that is supposed to answer all our questions? Briefly, it is the proposal that the infant universe (aged 10^{-35} second*) underwent a very short period (until 10^{-32} second) of very rapid expansion powered by a force of cosmic repulsion, at the end of which all the matter and energy we have here today had come into existence from the vacuum. Alan Guth was the first (1981) to offer a model based on this idea, but any number of people have worked on it since then. Many details remain unresolved, but the basic concept seems to have widespread favor among theorists, and now the observational support is beginning to come in, so there is a good bit of confidence that we may be on the right track.

The Inflation Scenario

The inflation scenario works out of two great areas of twentieth-century physics, relativity and quantum mechanics. Two important things happen in the inflation, the extremely rapid expansion and the production of matter and radiation. The expansion comes out of relativity considerations, and the matter/radiation production from quantum mechanics. Both of these are necessary in order to resolve the problems of the Big Bang, and they work together.

The basic thing is that two energies will be kept in balance: gravitational energy (which is going to be negative) and nongravitational

---

*10^{35} means 1 followed by 35 zeros. 10^{-35} means 1 divided by 10^{35}.

energy (which will be positive). The negative gravitational energy will produce the inflation, and the positive nongravitational energy will produce matter and radiation (our observable universe). Since the positive and negative energies just cancel each other out, both of them can increase a great deal without violating the conservation of energy law, and the net effect will be a big universe containing matter and radiation!

Gravity, as we are familiar with it, is an attractive force between masses. When Einstein developed his theory of general relativity to describe the way the universe operates under the force of gravity, he put into his equations an extra factor called the "cosmological constant." This represented a repulsive force and was intended to keep the universe from simply collapsing in on itself under gravitational attraction. This was before Hubble alerted us to the observation that the universe is in fact expanding; Einstein at that time assumed that it was stationary.

Various people then made models for the universe based on the Einstein equations, giving different values to the constants to see how they would work out, what kind of universe you'd get. One of these people was Willem de Sitter, and one of the models he considered was one in which there was practically no mass to be positively attractive and the universe was run on the cosmological constant alone, the repulsive force. This naturally made the universe expand. And indeed, Hubble shortly thereafter observed that it does expand. But if you track the de Sitter universe through all its possibilities, you find a state in which the expansion is very, very rapid. The expansion velocity itself increases exponentially and exceeds the speed of light. But that is not forbidden by relativity, because empty space is not a "thing" and there is no restriction on the growth rate of space![14]

But is there a cosmological constant to cause this expansion? Well, there is something like it available from the quantum particle physicists. The de Sitter universe is operating in a vacuum — little or no matter. But a vacuum from a quantum mechanical point of view may be full of energy and activity. The fundamental idea in quantum mechanics is that events are "quantized," that is, they occur in discrete packages of a finite amount. In our money, for instance, a penny is (so far, 1997!) the least unit of exchange. In quantum mechanics, a quantum of "action" is the least unit of energy exchange. This is Planck's constant (discovered by Max Planck in 1900), called h, and its value is 6.625×10^{-27} erg-second. That's energy multiplied by time.

One consequence of this is that we can't measure smaller than this least quantity. If we try to measure both energy and time, we lose in accuracy on one what we gain on the other. This is one form of Heisenberg's Uncertainty Principle. This means, say the QM physicists, that if the time interval is perfectly measured, then nothing is known about the energy, and all sorts of energy may have come into existence during that interval — and gone back out again. The energy appears as matched pairs of "virtual particles," matter and antimatter, such as an electron and a positron (just like the electron but positively charged instead of negatively). Being antiparticles, they then mutually annihilate and disappear.

So the empty space could be full of energy. The inflation scenario takes advantage of this and supposes that there is a field — we'll call it an "inflaton" — filling all space homogeneously and consisting of both kinetic and potential energy. (Kinetic energy is energy actually expressed as motion; potential energy is unexpressed as yet, but invisibly stored, capable of expression.) What is "potential" in the inflaton is actual mass, matter particles. But that is to anticipate.

Now we want to see how this field acts like the cosmological constant and exerts a repulsive gravitational force. First we remember that for Einstein energy and mass are equivalent, so the energy in our "inflaton" will be subject to gravity just as ordinary massive objects are. The next thing to know is that the gravitational force is figured in terms of both density and pressure. This is because mass can also be thought of as inertia, that is, how much force it takes to start something moving or to change the speed or direction of its motion.

There is sitting-still, or just-being, inertia, and there is moving inertia. Density measures the just-being inertia, and pressure measures the moving inertia. So both of them contribute to the gravitational force. The formula for gravitational force consists of a density term and a pressure term, and if the pressure is high, the pressure term will control the outcome (see Fig. 1). It's this pressure term that is going to do the trick, give us the repulsion.

The final point to learn is that the pressure term itself is a combination of positive kinetic energy and negative potential energy. But our "inflaton" is almost entirely potential energy, so its negative term is going to dominate the pressure, which will consequently be very negative. And that's what makes the gravitational force be negative, repulsive. Under this repulsive force the universe inflates rapidly.[15] It goes from being much smaller than a proton to being maybe 10^{50} times that size.[16]

During the inflation, the potential energy of the field starts to convert to actual (what is usually called "kinetic") energy. But in this case it doesn't really turn into motion but into the "rest mass" of particles. Rest mass is the mass of a body at rest — not moving, therefore not really "kinetic" energy. This is the sitting-still, or just-being, mass that

Gravitational force equals $\left\{\begin{array}{l}\text{density (measure of resting inertia)}\\ +\\ \text{pressure (measure of moving inertia)}\end{array}\right.$ $\left\{\begin{array}{l}\text{sum of kinetic energy (+)}\\ \text{and potential energy (-)}\end{array}\right.$

If the field is mostly potential energy, there will be little density, and the gravitational force will be determined by the pressure.

If the pressure is mostly potential energy, its sign will be negative and, added to a negligible positive density, will make the gravitational force negative, repulsive.

As the potential energy turns to rest mass, the (positive) density term gains, and when the potential energy has been completely converted, the gravitation returns to positive, attractive.

Figure 1

we mentioned above. And as this conversion of potential energy into actual energy takes place, getting faster as it goes along (a lot of it becoming radiation, too), the store of potential energy is used up. When all of the potential energy has converted, the pressure term will no longer be negative and the gravitational force will no longer be repulsive. The inflation will have come to an end. Gravity is back to positive (attractive), and the universe is back to the regular Hubble expansion. But the universe is very much bigger, and effectively all of our present matter and radiation have been created.[17]

The Phase Transitions

Starting from the observed Hubble expansion and running the clock backward, we understand the very early universe as very compact and very hot. As it expanded and cooled, it underwent changes that we call "phase transitions." A "phase" is a certain state of affairs, to put it most generally. Familiar phases are the "states of matter": solid, liquid, gas. We know that when a gas cools sufficiently, it liquifies (condenses), and when a liquid cools, it solidifies (freezes, crystallizes). These changes are "phase transitions." In tracing the history of our universe, we meet a number of phase transitions. In fact, it may be that the idea of phase transition is an excellent way to see the whole picture: the universe evolves and "self-creates" by passing through a series of phase transitions. Of course they aren't all cases of condensing or freezing. The appearances of the composed unions, such as atoms, molecules, and living cells, constitute phase transitions. And the first second of our universe may have seen some interesting phase transitions.

An attractive, but so far insufficiently substantiated, picture of the very early universe supposes that there was so much energy exchange that all the fundamental forces — gravity, strong nuclear, weak nuclear, electromagnetic — were of equal strength and effectively constituted a single unified force. (There is a way of seeing the weak and the electromagnetic as two versions of a single force, called "electroweak," and there are some good tries at getting a Grand Unified Force that includes the strong — called "electronuclear" — but gravity is so far a holdout.) Insofar as this unified condition prevailed in the first second, we say that there was a state of total "symmetry." It means no differences, everything equivalent, interchangeable, no particular order or pattern. When the phase transitions happen, this symmetry breaks.

These transitions work a little like the water transitions we're used to in that they are brought on by falling temperature. The forces separate, one by one, and these events are sometimes called "freezing out." The timetable runs like this: at 10^{-43} second, gravity, if it was united with the electronuclear, is so no longer. Between 10^{-35} and 10^{-32} second the strong force separates from the electroweak (this is our inflation epoch). At 10^{-10} second the weak and electromagnetic are no longer combined. Later on there will come times when the nuclei of atoms form and then capture electrons; these will also be phase transitions.

These early phase transitions are examples of symmetry-breaking, and it is the falling temperature that brings them about. If the temperature had remained constant, the various particles or forces could have continued to be interchangeable. But take the case of our inflation event. In the end the potential energy converts to rest mass of matter particles and to massless radiation particles through the mediation of some huge-energy particles of the type called "mesons." The potential energy first turns into the mesons and then the mesons decay into ordinary matter and radiation.

Particles that now have mass (and therefore can no longer travel with the speed of light) are matter particles, and particles that do not receive mass in this distribution (and some don't, in particular the photon) are radiation. The mass-bearing particles are governed by the strong interaction and the radiation particles by the electroweak. This is the way the Grand Unified symmetry breaks down. When the electroweak in turn splits into weak and electromagnetic, the weak particles will acquire small masses, while the photon (the particle of electromagnetism) will remain massless.

This meson decay comes about because the energy relations of the universe are no longer in equilibrium, meaning the daughter particles resulting from the splits don't have enough energy to reconstitute the parent particles.[18] Not being able to run the reaction equally in both directions indicates that the symmetry is no longer present, and it is not present because there is not enough energy for it because of the falling temperature. We will see several examples of this sort of thing as the universe evolves.

Here we can see how one of our four troublesome problems with the standard Big Bang is resolved, the question of why the ratio of photons (radiation particles) to baryons (matter particles) is what it is and where the matter came from. Where the matter is from and why has already been answered as well as it can be, but there is a little more to tell about the ratio and about why we are in a matter-universe rather than an antimatter one.

Those big mesons into which our "inflaton's" potential energy is converted are called "X particles," and they occur as both X and anti-X in equal numbers. It is from them that the baryons are made, for the X particles decay into quarks and the baryons are made up of quarks (*very* small ultimate matter particles). Quarks and baryons — such as the proton and neutron — are particles that respond to the strong nuclear force.

When the equilibrium fails, the decay *rates* of the X and the anti-X are found to be different, so that slightly more quarks are formed than are antiquarks. This excess of quarks over antiquarks carries over to an excess of (for instance) protons (made of quarks) over antiprotons (made of antiquarks). The baryons and antibaryons annihilate one another, but there are a few baryons left over.

The annihilations produce photons (radiation particles). The ratio of baryons to photons is now known to lie between 0.2 and 0.7 parts per billion, or putting it the other way around, about two billion photons to one baryon. Suppose a billion protons annihilated with a billion antiprotons, producing two billion photons. But there was one extra proton for every billion proton-antiproton pair. That's why we observe the ratio we do.[19]

The phase transition to the matter and radiation universe governed in different ways by the now distinct forces is completed as the matter particles descended from the X mesons begin to interact among themselves. The rest mass energies of the mesons have been further converted into true kinetic energies of the daughters, moving energies which translate as heat. This reheats the universe, whose temperature had fallen drastically during the tremendous expansion of the inflation.[20]

The universe then picks up where it left off and continues with its normal Hubble expansion. It is 10^{50} times bigger and all the matter and radiation of our observable universe have been created out of the "magically" — but naturally — acquired energy of the inflaton. Leon Lederman (evoking the image of the youngster who declares at his Bar

Mitzvah, "Today I am a man") says: "The universe is confirmed at the age of 10^{-33} seconds. 'Today I am a universe.' "[21] And Alan Guth says, in equal awe, "If the inflationary model is correct, it is fair to say that the universe is the ultimate free lunch."[22]

The Free Lunch

Having all this free matter and radiation is just what we needed to solve some of our problems. In particular, we needed an explanation of why we seem to have just the critical density we need to keep expanding gently but slowing down, neither exploding nor crunching. Omega, the ratio of the actual density to the critical density, needs to be one. Keeping the density right on 1 would ordinarily be very difficult; it would be unstable, and once it became either smaller or greater, it would continue in that direction rapidly.

But the inflation creates density to precisely match the expansion itself. So, whatever the ratio was before inflation and the conversion of the "inflaton's" potential into matter and radiation, the ratio became 1 during the inflation epoch. And once it becomes 1, it will remain 1.[23]

How about the horizon problem? The difficulty was that simply running the Big Bang backward gave us an observable universe that was, even in very early times, still too big for all the parts to come to thermal equilibrium in the time that had passed since the beginning. The Big Bang backward calculation didn't let the universe shrink fast enough to get inside a single observation horizon. Or, running it forward, it didn't let the universe expand fast enough. The inflation scenario does that. It permits an initial region small enough to have acquired thermal equilibrium before inflation sets in; inflation then preserves this (nearly) uniform temperature and stretches the very small region. What we see now as the cosmic background radiation from every direction originated in sources that were once in close contact. So there is no longer any mystery about the homogeneity.[24]

But what of the related problem, the inhomogeneity? After all, we have definite structures in our universe now, in which the density is enormously greater than the average density of the universe. The density of our Milky Way, for instance, is about a million times greater than the average. "Gravitational instability" (as it's technically called) will make any little clump grow into a bigger clump by attracting more matter into its thereby increasing gravitational field. But how to get the little clumps to start with?

These little clumps originated in the "inflaton" itself. The field that was inflating under negative gravity was subject to random quantum fluctuations. That's where the energy came from, in accordance with the Heisenberg Uncertainty that allows energy to appear from nowhere. Energy appearing, energy disappearing, different amounts of energy. Those are "fluctuations." Any random distribution, just because it is random, fails to be homogeneous, has clumps in it. So our "inflaton" was naturally clumpy. Then the mesons that were produced by the phase transition carried these irregularities, and the inflation itself amplified them to the present large scale. The irregularities that appeared in the radiation from that epoch are what we now observe as the small "ripples" in the cosmic background radiation. And the inflation model predicts just the spread in temperatures that the COBE measurement actually found.[25]

Some scientists (including Stephen Hawking, who predicted the COBE spectrum from inflation theory) believe that the ripples prove that the inflation scenario is correct; others, for instance Michael Rowan-Robinson, feel that such a judgment is premature, but may eventually turn out to be right.[26]

One modification that has been proposed, by Andrei Linde, is called "chaotic inflation." It says that the primordial universe — *all* space-time-matter-energy — would probably have inflated at different times and rates in different parts of itself. Various "bubbles" of inflation would have appeared in a random or chaotic way and evolved quite independently of other such domains.

This would have two interesting consequences. One, the "special-ness" of our particular universe, which seems precisely designed just for us, becomes just one among innumerable others and therefore no more special than any other. And two, there wouldn't necessarily have to be any beginning to the whole process, because universes could appear as "bubbles" growing out of other universes, and this (perhaps) could be continued indefinitely into the past and into the future. Maybe the universe *is* turtles all the way down!

In any case, here we are in our particular bubble. It has its particular characteristics. It makes stars, especially long-lasting stars and stars that make ninety-two different kinds of elements and stars that have planets, planets that have people. But that's not so odd, say the theorists. If the whole universe is physically unlimited, every combination of characteristics will appear in *some* bubble. Our universe, no matter how improbable, will be inevitable.[27]

I find these ideas beguiling, not only because they are so clever in their own field, but because they can be viewed with a certain amount of complacency from the standpoint of the metaphysics/theology I have proposed. Expansion of any sort, of course, is a fulfillment of the metaphysical principle "Be more." The energy exchanges of high temperatures and of the phase transitions during cooling are versions of "communicating Being." A universe in which the variety produced by symmetry-breaking "hides" the underlying unity and symmetry of the cosmos manifests the basic one/many character of Being.

If the symmetry-breaking results in a world that makes possible intelligent observers, and we wish to avoid attributing this special result to very specific initial conditions, we can suppose that actually a chaotic set of universes was produced, and we happen (necessarily) to be in one that is capable of evolving and supporting us. This could be interpreted as an instance of the injunction "Be in every possible way." And when the energy of the vacuum in the "inflaton" is externalized as matter and radiation, we may be reminded of "enstasy" and "ecstasy." Whatever the Reality is that manifests itself as the universe, it seems to turn itself inside out in doing it.

On to the Stars!

We are almost through the first second of our local universe time now, and well on our way to the stars, because not nearly so much happens after this. Nevertheless, a few significant milestones should be pointed out.

At 10^{-5} second, the quarks combine into protons and neutrons, and I would like to show a little detail on this, because it is an example of the generalized "symbiosis" we can see at all stages of the cosmic evolution. The quarks that make up protons and neutrons are called "up" and "down." They have different electric charges, measured in the same unit as the charge on the electron. The up quark is 2/3 and the down quark -1/3. Two ups and one down make a proton, with charge +1, and two downs and one up make a neutron, charge 0. From this time on, they "live together" as these particles; we see no free quarks.[28] This is the beginning of a long series of combinations of relatively elemental units into new wholes with new properties.

At one ten-thousandth of a second, there are no more proton-antiproton annihilations, but we still have photons turning into electron-positron pairs, and vice versa. At one second (temperature ten billion degrees), the photons no longer have the energy to turn into pairs. The existing pairs annihilate, but again, for every billion pairs, one electron is left over. We now have as many electrons as protons, and originally we had as many neutrons as protons. But neutrons at this early stage disintegrate in a matter of minutes. Protons and electrons had been combining to make new ones, so neutrons were forming and decaying at equal rates. But when most of the electrons were annihilated at time one second (and no new ones created from photons), protons could not find enough electrons to make many new neutrons. After the first second, there were only two neutrons to every ten protons, and you can probably foresee that that is why the universe is mostly hydrogen, whose nucleus requires no neutrons.

The next milestone is at one minute, when the universe begins making atomic nuclei. The simplest, as just said, is hydrogen, one lone proton. (The neutron alone doesn't work as a nucleus because of its instability.) The next simplest is one proton plus one neutron, held together by the strong force, but only tenuously. Energetic photons can break this bond, and these deuterons ("twosomes") come apart as rapidly as they are formed. But once again, as usual in this cosmic process, all we have to do is wait. The universe expands, cools, interacts less. At time 100 seconds the photons no longer have the energy to break the deuterium bond, and we can start adding on to the couple. Pick up another proton and you've got helium-3; add another neutron, helium-4, good stable nucleus. So stable that if one collides with another proton (that would make lithium-5) or another helium (which would be beryllium-8), the newcomers are shortly cast off. Helium is happy the way it is. The time is now three minutes. The universe is 75 percent hydrogen and 25 percent helium, and nothing more happens for a while.

Not for three hundred thousand *years*. All this time, in spite of the expansion and the declining energy, the thicket of particles — mostly free electrons — has been too dense for photons to pass through. And because they are still colliding with electrons, they bump them from any liaison they might tentatively form with a nucleus. But at this point the falling temperature again makes a big difference. The photons lose their power to prevent electrons from adhering to the nuclei, and atoms are formed by the intercession of the electromagnetic force, the attraction between the positive nuclei and the negative electrons. Nuclei pick up an electron for every proton and matter becomes electrically neutral. With the free electrons now bound in atoms, the photons can move without impediment and the universe, previously opaque, becomes transparent. The photons' frequency is that of yellow light. If we had been there then, we would have seen sunshine everywhere.

This decoupling of matter and radiation had a further effect. It opened the way for the formation of galaxies and stars. These have to form under the influence of gravity, the weakest of the four forces, and all the frenetic activity up till now had prevented it from getting anything together and keeping it together. Now gravity has its opportunity,

and very slowly matter, and maybe radiation with it, starts to draw together, nucleated by the original density fluctuations, or irregularities. At
this point we don't know exactly what happened.

There are two basic possibilities for the generation of the large structures, and it isn't yet clear which one was followed. One way is to
start with the largest structures and work down to smaller ones. Thus
we would begin with the superclusters and progress by fragmentation
to clusters, local groups, galaxies, and stars. The other way is just the
opposite. Start with stars and work up to large-scale structures which
gather by gravitational attraction.[29]

Either way, this operation proceeds very slowly, but by one billion
years we can say that galaxies are forming. Sometimes they merge with
one another or one "swallows" another. Joseph Silk, who has done
a lot of work in this area, tells us that at age one billion merging
of dwarf galaxy-mass clouds was a frequent phenomenon, precursor
to large galaxies surrounded by dwarfs. "Our own Local Group is
such an aggregation, dominated by the Milky Way and the Andromeda
Galaxy, accompanied by a handful of dim dwarfs." He suggests that
dwarfs are the building blocks and that "dim nearby galaxies...barely
discernible...are most likely the failed counterparts of today's bright
galaxies." "Nature," he goes on to say, "most likely fails many times
before it succeeds, and dim dwarfs and giants may be testimony to this
process."[30]

The process goes slowly. In the initial stages of aggregation, the matter is held loosely and the fringes drift away with the general expansion.
But once the density in surrounding regions has fallen to half that inside
the clump, self-gravity draws the material into a strong concentration.[31]

The galactic cloud fragments into hundreds of billions of small
clouds as it collapses and these in turn concentrate by gravitational self-
attraction. They are spheres of hydrogen and helium. As they become
denser (more than 160 times as dense as water), the temperature in their
interiors goes up (tens of millions of degrees). High temperature means
vigorous collisions. Both the strong and the weak forces are at work.
The weak force enables some of the protons to emit positrons, thus los-
ing their positive charge, and to turn into neutrons; and the strong force
enables the protons and the new neutrons to stick together. Two protons
and two neutrons make helium-4 and a lot of extra energy. The energy
radiates. One by one the stars are turning on.

The first generation of stars made helium from hydrogen. When a
star's hydrogen was used up, the energy-generating production stopped,
and there was no longer a pressure from the inside outward to balance
the gravitational tendency to collapse. The star would contract, grow

much denser, much hotter, develop conditions under which it could fuse helium into carbon. It can't get two helium nuclei to stick together well, but three will! Two protons and two neutrons in each of three heliums make six protons and six neutrons in a carbon. Add one more helium, and you have oxygen: eight protons and eight neutrons.[32] And, of course, these fusion reactions release a great deal of energy. Furthermore, we now have the makings of hydrocarbons, the building blocks of life.

If the star is massive enough (at least four solar masses), the synthesis of still heavier elements can follow: sodium, magnesium, silicon, sulfur — what land masses of planets are made of. The next stage, using silicon, produces sulfur, argon, and other heavier elements. This sort of thing continues until iron (twenty-six protons) has been made, the most stable nucleus of all. Central "burning" reactions stop here, but still heavier elements can be made in the outer atmosphere of the star. Neutrons streaming out from the core under high energy are captured by the above synthesized nuclei, adding to their weight but not to their charge, thus making the various "isotopes" of any given element. But sometimes such a nucleus is very unstable, and one of its neutrons will turn into a proton by emitting an electron. This changes the nucleus into an element of higher number. In this way elements beyond iron can also be made.

At this stage, the outer regions of the star may fall in on the hot core and bounce out again, effectively "exploding." This may happen more than once. In this way the heavy elements are scattered abroad and are swept up by any new star-clouds in the neighborhood. The second-generation stars form in this way with a head start on heavy elements, producing an even richer soup of various nuclei, scattered in their turn. Released to the interstellar medium in this way, the heavy nuclei are subject to collisions. The collisions may knock off chips that are configurations of protons and neutrons that couldn't be made by nucleosynthesis, such as lithium, beryllium, and boron. So even these otherwise unavailable elements are provided for! By the time we get to third-generation stars, we may have a little of all the ninety-two natural elements.[33]

The time is now about ten and a half billion years. There may have been more than three generations of stars. Some of them burn out quickly; others last a long time with a steady production of light and warmth. There are not only atoms around; there are even a good many kinds of molecules, too. They are on interstellar dust grains, bits of silicon, oxygen, magnesium, and iron, covered by a thin layer of ice. In this environment, all sorts of combinations of atoms were tried, with up to as many as thirteen atoms in a molecule. About a hundred molecules have been discovered by radio telescopes, including carbon monoxide, water, methane, and ammonia. The favorite combinations are of carbon, hydrogen, oxygen, and nitrogen, the very elements that make up almost all of living bodies.[34]

Molecules are instances of symbiosis, different atoms "living together," sharing energies, making a unity out of their erstwhile many-ness. They are also putting together their diversities and getting something new, a new whole with new properties. A lot of new wholes of various sorts. Variety is already making a strong showing — "Be in every possible way." Nature is clearly displaying the metaphysical principles we outlined and revealing itself as very creative.

Chapter Five

THE COSMOS
AS GOD'S ECSTASY

 THE ASTROPHYSICISTS, with the help of their colleagues in particle physics, have shown us a universe that creates itself out of nothing. Virtual particles and antiparticles are constantly being created and destroyed as quantum fluctuations. In particular, they appear when the universe expands rapidly in the inflationary epoch, balancing the negative gravitational energy of the expanding space with the positive nongravitational energy of the cosmic field. Structure emerges from the original homogeneity of symmetry by symmetry-breaking, introducing difference. All of this happens without having to start from special conditions. Recent theories, especially, suggest that we are in a universe that is a member of a "multiverse," many different universes, with different values for the physical parameters. We, obviously, are in one that has the conditions for evolving us (the Weak Anthropic Principle). Very likely, most of the others didn't get very far.[1]

Steven Weinberg points out that "an important implication" of this view "is that there wasn't a beginning." There were a variety of Big Bangs in the past, and the multiverse goes on into the future forever. "One doesn't have to grapple with the question of it before the bang. The [multiverse] has just been here all along."[2]

The "quantum factor" in this development not only permits particles to appear out of nowhere without prior causation, but, says Paul Davies, "when the quantum theory is extended to gravity, it involves the behaviour of spacetime itself." Space and time become endowed "with the same sort of fuzzy unpredictability that characterizes quantum matter." This "would allow spacetime to be created and destroyed spontaneously and uncaused in the same way that particles are. Thus spacetime could pop out of nothingness as the result of a causeless quantum transition."[3]

Michael Green says that "in a theory of gravity you can't really separate the structure of space and time from the particles which are associated with the force of gravity" and grants that these all "become interwoven in some very subtle way."[4] And Steven Weinberg thinks that "space and time coordinates are just four out of the many degrees of freedom [independent variables] that have to be put together to make a consistent theory. Their geometric significance will arrive *after* the fact [after the theory has been found and shown to be adequate], rather than [as] something that appears in the fundamental principle."[5]

All these speculations and conjectures and theories are saying that there is a fundamental symmetry to the created order. Things that seem to be different are really aspects of something more fundamental that is unified, that is one. The universe — or "multiverse" — develops by breaking these symmetries and letting the differences interact. But the most fundamental symmetry of all would seem to be that between Something and Nothing. What we would ordinarily consider to be the fundamental context in terms of which other things happen — a context consisting of space and time, laws of nature, fundamental forces and particles — may itself be the expression of possible aspects of something more fundamental still, something as yet nameless. Perhaps even the vacuum is one aspect of the true fundamental. Something coming out of nothing would then be regarded as no more miraculous than something going into nothing (i.e., nothing "coming out of" something).

It is interesting to notice at this point that a Jewish (Kabbalistic) schema for the emergence of the cosmos from the Infinite One puts Nothing in the position of first emanation. Gershom Scholem, setting forth the "basic ideas" in his book *Kabbalah,* says: "God Who is called *Ein-Sof* [without end, infinite] in respect of Himself is called *Ayin* [nothingness] in respect of His first self-revelation." As a result, he continues, the formula *creatio ex nihilo* may thus be "interpreted as creation from within God Himself.... The emergence of all things from the absolute nothingness of God."

David ben Abraham ha-Lavan (thirteenth century) is quoted as saying that *ayin* has "more being than any other being in the world, but since it is simple, and all other simple things are complex when compared with its simplicity, so in comparison it is called 'nothing.'" And Scholem has also found that "it is said that 'if all the powers returned to nothingness, the Primeval One who is the cause of all would remain in equal oneness (or: unity without distinctions) in the depths of nothingness.'"[6]

We have here at least three distinct senses of "nothing" — metaphysical, epistemological, and physical — but they are parallel enough to be suggestive. There is an unbroken symmetry of the Unmanifest (Nothing) prior to — underlying — the broken symmetries of the Manifest (Something). The Unmanifest transcends the Manifest, yet is perfectly present in it and as it.

The true nothingness from which all was created manifests itself in the transition from *Ein-Sof* to the first *Sefirah* [emanated attribute or Name of God], nor is there in reality any jump or discontinuity in the structure of being. The creation from nothingness is a manifestation of the divine wisdom where human thought reaches its limit, or of that nothingness which is the first emanation, *Keter* [primordial divine will, "source of all life"].[7] In those systems where *Ein-Sof* was identified with the *Keter,* it was *Ein-Sof* itself that became the divine Nothingness in which all has its source. Such views left room for the belief that God, who is one with *Ein-Sof,* comprehends much more than what proceeds from Him in the emanative and creative processes but that He encompasses the latter within Himself as well.[8]

My own suggestion is that we try looking at our situation in terms of God's ecstasy. Ecstasy covers the emanative and creative processes. It indicates how, on the one hand, original symmetry is broken by emanation and creation, and how, on the other hand, there is unity between the original and the subsequent states. Original symmetry can be pointed to with the notion of metaphysical nothingness. Nothingness means no quality, no attribute, no particular direction, no preference — that is, symmetry. Epistemological nothingness, or symmetry, is present also. There is no adequate concept for the Original, the Underlying. All distinction among concepts breaks down at this point. Again, there is no direction, no polarity, no particularity. It is like the breakdown of mathematical representation at a singularity. There is no way to say it, no way to think it. We may say, in terms of the schema offered in chapter 2 on the Trinity, that this is the enstatic state of the God Community as a whole. Its ecstatic motion, then, breaks this symmetry by moving out from itself. Something comes from this Nothing.

The ecstatic movement outside the God Community happens (is going on) for the same reason that it is going on inside the God Community: it is the nature of the God Community to behave so. Theistic theology calls this agape, self-giving love, and metaphysics can call it the natural pressure of Being to expand, to be more and to give Being, to be in every possible way.

The multiverse idea is congenial to this. It would seem to be the ultimate of "be in every possible way." It is, on its own level, also a movement from nothing to something and a symmetry with initially no preferred direction. Quantum fluctuations oscillate between physical nothingness and somethingness, appearance and annihilation. There is no physical cause. In the metaphysical ecstasy there is no cause. In the theistic ecstasy there is no motive. We are dealing with the bottom turtle. Perhaps it may be seen as a turtle that extends its limbs (head and tail) and withdraws them. The cosmic turtle which the metaphysical turtle supports is its action of extending. When the cosmic turtle in turn "extends" its limbs, physical nothing fluctuates into physical something: energy (positive and negative), then matter and radiation.

Just as there are (according to the proposed schema) both enstasy and ecstasy within the God Community, so there are both enstasy and ecstasy of the God Community considered as a whole. As unmanifest, it is enstatic; as manifest, it is ecstatic. Its "inside" becomes "outside." But just as the enstatic reality of a divine Person is its ecstatic urgency to give itself to another Person — which amounts to joining the other in that other's enstatic reality, which in turn is that other's ecstatic activity, so the God Community as enstatic is also a drive to be ecstatic and to be really present in its ecstatic aspect. There is such a union here that the "inside" and the "outside" can be regarded as two aspects of one reality. One can see an ultimate "symmetry" between the Unmanifest and the Manifest. The whole reality is what we must consider to be the absolute and ultimate Being. If the Unmanifest is regarded as the Parent of the Manifest, then the Unmanifest "gives its name" to the Manifest, its Child. Although the Unmanifest clearly transcends the Manifest, it is also the case that the Whole is only One Being.

For the universe to be a symmetry of nothing and something, for the something to arise from the nothing without cause, does not indicate that there is no connection to a metaphysical Ground. What it indicates is the nature of that connection. If the universe is an externalized version of the God Community, then it will do in a finite and physical way what the God Community does in a Personal way. It will show enstatic reality moving into ecstatic activity without cause. It will expand, it will exchange Being-energies, it will be a whole (or a series of wholes) by its internal interactions.

The randomness, the chaos of the foundational state of the universe is the symmetry of no preference. It is the expression of being in every possible way. This is not an indication of no meaning, but the expression of the fullness of Being, the ultimate in meaningfulness on the physical level. Out of this original richness of possibilities, there has come at least one universe with enormous wealth of interactions forming successively more complex wholes. There are interactions of energies on each organizational level (atomic, molecular, cellular, etc.) and there are creative interactions of symmetric (random, chaotic, no-preference) states with preference arrangements, directions, particularity.

Looking for God from the perspective of the physical cosmos is not a question of looking for a cause. "Cause" is just a certain way of lining up a unified, wholistic physical process. It will always be a member of the physical order. Of course the universe has no "cause." Of course it is a "free lunch." People who are looking for God aren't looking for a cause of the universe. They're looking for meaning. They're looking for a larger context within which to view the universe. Not having a context is not having a meaning. When you've run out of contexts, then indeed the whole thing seems pointless. "Point" comes from context. We are living in a universe in which we are able to continue generating contexts. The search for the Theory of Everything is a particular example of this. Our own human cognitive drive keeps pushing, expressing, I would say, the pressure of Being to be more, to be ever more interactive and more inclusive — to keep on creating contexts, meanings. The interesting question is, therefore, what kind of being does this? This compounded stardust, fluctuated out of physical nothingness, that goes about asking for Meaning? What goes on here? is the search for or the creation of meanings itself meaningful? or absurd? or somehow the wrong question?

What I am doing is offering to religious people, or contemplatives who aren't "religious," a suggestion of a way to put even the most seemingly threatening views of cosmic reality in a context that gives meaning, better meaning, I hope, than some of the views which the new physics is upsetting. The suggestion is presented in terms familiar to some people (Trinity, Incarnation, Theotokos), but it can also be read, in strictly metaphysical terms, as the expansive pressure of Being. I call it seeing the cosmos as God's ecstasy.

Chapter Six

THE SELF-CREATING UNIVERSE: PATHWAY TO LIFE

 WE LEFT THE UNIVERSE swirling into galaxies everywhere, galaxies in clusters and superclusters. The cooler galaxies developed as fairly flat, with spiral arms. Such is the Milky Way. We are located on the edge of one of the spiral arms. There are a lot of interstellar gas and dust grains here. Debris from previously exploded stars is here, and new stars are forming.

Sometimes what gets a new star started is the explosion of an older star nearby. Perhaps this is what got our solar system started. The time is now about ten billion years out; we are into at least the third generation of stars. A gas and dust cloud of hydrogen, helium, and a little bit of everything else, about two-thirds of the way from the center of the Milky Way to its edge, begins to contract and rotate. Most of the material draws together in the center, but some floats around the rim and separates, like the rings around Saturn. The denser spots in the rings attract more matter and gradually roll up into rocks, drawn by the motion and the gravity into the flat plane through the middle of the central sphere that is turning into a star.

Tens of millions of years pass. The rocks and gases accrete more material and grow until all the rings but one have swept up their respective materials into single large bodies, with perhaps smaller satellites. One ring of small rocks remains (what we call the asteroid belt — unless that resulted from explosion or collision). The two inner planets have no satellites. The third has one comparatively large one — and a fantastic destiny.

Earth began its "individual" life in a thoroughly molten state (the core is molten to this day) and the heat boiled off the helium and most of the hydrogen that had not bonded to minerals. The planet was mostly minerals — iron, oxygen, silicon, magnesium, with lesser amounts of sulfur, nickel, calcium, aluminum. Some of the hydrogen united with oxygen to form water vapor in the atmosphere; the silicon and aluminum floated on the surface (and became eventually the stone we stand

87

on), while the iron and nickel sank toward the center. Stray pieces from the asteroid belt pelted the Earth. This went on for several hundred million years.

During this time Earth was rotating once every five hours. But its companion planet, the moon, exerted gravitational influence that gradually slowed it. At present its rotation has stretched to twenty-four hours, but it is still lengthening (about thirty seconds every hundred years).

By the time the sun was one billion years old (and the universe eleven billion), Earth had cooled enough that continents were forming as condensed masses floating on a sea of lava. The cooling lava emitted gases in huge quantities, giving the young planet an atmosphere a hundred times thicker than our present one, composed of hydrogen, ammonia, methane, water vapor, and carbon dioxide. With further cooling, the water vapor condensed and the first rains fell. They collected in the hollows of the rocky surfaces and became oceans.

In the atmosphere, encouraged by ultraviolet radiation, collisions, and electrical discharges, all sorts of molecules were forming. In this thick medium, many more combinations could be tried than had been possible in the interstellar medium because chance encounters occurred much more often. Many of these molecules were organic compounds (based on carbon), and they fell with the rain into the new oceans. The water was very receptive, it could dissolve almost anything, and its depths protected delicate chemical bonds from the shocks of solar radiation. It was the ideal breeding ground for more and more complex chemical arrangements.

Symbiotic Chemistry

Chemistry is the study of molecules. And here at the outset, it is important to call attention to a rather obvious fact: molecules are "compounds," that is, they are made by *putting together* simpler units, namely, atoms. Simple units, put together, result in a *new kind* of being. This is the main principle on which all the rest of the "self-creation" of the universe is based.

Two more basic things need to be said. One is that such a union results in something genuinely new. It manifests properties not possessed by the units of which it is composed. It manifests properties that never existed before.

The other basic thing to be said is that the new properties come from what constitutes the union itself, the interaction of the constituents.

All physical realities are in motion and in relation. The relations among these motions show as the new properties. The relationships, the interactions, are what make the union and what appear as the new properties. If the union is disassembled, the constituents separated so that they cannot interact, then the new properties disappear. They are the properties of the assemblage. But they are real and are in themselves integral units of character and behavior. They characterize the assemblage as a *whole*. Thus from the interaction of the constituents, a new being, this whole, has *emerged* as a new level unit. It is called, in this context, an "emergent."

In my metaphysics, I am saying that it is the nature of Being to do this, to interact and thus to form new relations, new wholes, new beings, new levels. To be is to communicate Being. To be is to be both one and many. Compound units are both one and many. The interaction of the many to compose a one I call "symbiosis," living together. This is a foundational principle for all of the universe. Each succeeding level of compounded interaction will do basically this same thing.

And each time there is advance to a further level of compounding — putting together the units made by the previous compounding — it will happen because the properties that emerged on the earlier level naturally interact in their characteristic way with other whole units of the same level. No intervention from outside the natural system is necessary, no designer or purposive agent is required. Thus the universe continues, from level to level of compounding, to create itself by successive unions and the emergence of new properties of new wholes.

This is what we are seeing now with the atoms forming molecules. The atoms themselves had been formed by the interactive unions of protons, neutrons, and electrons. These units, now acting as wholes in their own right, interact with each other, atoms with atoms, and the result is molecules, the next level of compounded wholeness.

Chemical interaction uses only the electromagnetic force, which is also responsible for the negatively charged electrons being attracted to the positive nucleus. The atom is electrically neutral when it has one electron for every proton in its nucleus. But the electrons repel one another. They are spaced out around the nucleus in a pattern of shells. This part of the atom's structure is described in terms of quantum numbers and gets rather complicated, so I am going to mention only what we need in order to grasp in a general way how atoms give and take and share and thereby form molecules.[1]

Bond Formation

Molecules are made by atoms forming bonds between themselves. A simple type of bond is the ionic bond. (An ion is an atom that carries an electric charge because it has either lost or picked up electrons.) Ionic bonds are the give-and-take variety. They are called ionic because they can be regarded as the union of two ions, one charged negatively and the other positively. The atom that "gives" electrons to the union acts as the positive ion, the one that "receives" as the negative one (it has more negative charge now). But when they bond as the molecule, the electrons lost to one atom are gained by the other, and this act of giving/receiving is what bonds the two atoms together. An example of this bond is sodium chloride, ordinary table salt. Sodium has an electron to give and chlorine needs one, so they make a strong bond.

In what sense, though, does sodium have an electron to "give"? Doesn't it need all its electrons to balance its protons? Yes, but this has to do with another consideration, how the electrons are disposed in those shells around the nucleus. The electrons will always try to occupy positions of the lowest energy. As these are filled, they will go into higher energy positions. Only so many electrons can be accommodated at each energy level. But the significant thing for us is that the outermost electrons, the ones that will be interacting with other atoms, are limited to the number of eight.

When these eight positions are filled, the atom is very stable. It is for the sake of this high-stability, low-energy state that atoms are attracted to bonding to one another. So, an atom such as chlorine, with seven outer electrons, could attain this state by receiving an electron, and an atom such as sodium, with an electron to give, would share in the stability by being thus bonded.

Another type of bonding is called "covalent," in which the outermost ("valence") electrons are shared among the participating atoms. This interaction forms a very strong bond. Familiar examples are water and carbon dioxide. Water is H_2O: oxygen has two valence electrons, and each of the two hydrogens has one. Carbon dioxide is CO_2: carbon has four valence electrons, but since each oxygen has only two, it takes two oxygen atoms to balance the carbon. In methane, CH_4, the carbon atom is surrounded by four hydrogens, each of which contributes one electron.

There are many ways of gaining variation in molecules. The basic one, of course, is by how many of which type of atoms are put together. Methane, for instance, is the simplest combination of carbon and hydrogen, but the next easiest is ethane: two carbons, side by side, with hydrogens on every available side. And then three carbons in a row, and so on (see Fig. 2).

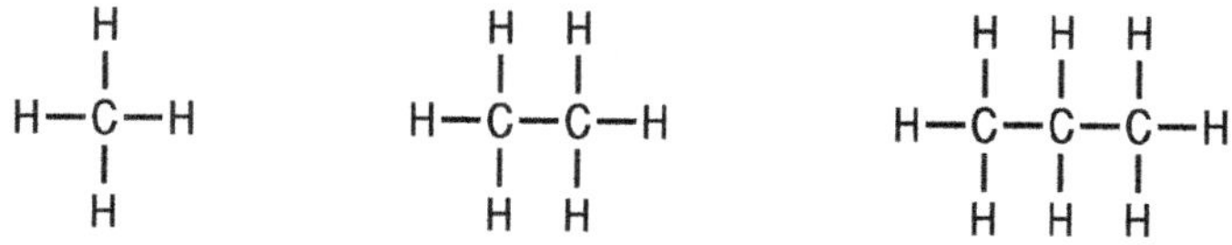

$$H-\underset{\underset{H}{|}}{\overset{\overset{H}{|}}{C}}-H \qquad H-\underset{\underset{H}{|}}{\overset{\overset{H}{|}}{C}}-\underset{\underset{H}{|}}{\overset{\overset{H}{|}}{C}}-H \qquad H-\underset{\underset{H}{|}}{\overset{\overset{H}{|}}{C}}-\underset{\underset{H}{|}}{\overset{\overset{H}{|}}{C}}-\underset{\underset{H}{|}}{\overset{\overset{H}{|}}{C}}-H$$

Methane CH_4 Ethane C_2H_6 Propane C_3H_8

Figure 2

When we come to four carbons in a row, a different type of variation becomes possible. Although the numbers of atoms remains the same, the arrangement can be different (see Fig. 3).

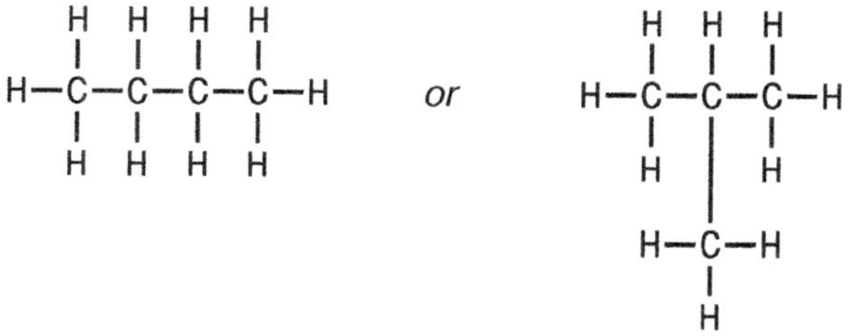

Normal butane   or   Iso butane

Figure 3

Different arrangement means different properties. An important arrangement for carbon molecules is the one in which the carbons are not stretched out in a line but formed into a ring, or cycle. Cycles may be made of three or more carbons. When other atoms are attached to such a ring, they may be considered to be either "above" or "below" it, if we think of the ring lying flat in a horizontal position. A second addition thus may be either on the "same" side as the first or on the "other" side. The arrangement will make a difference in the properties of the molecule. Another variation in arrangement is the mirror image that is not symmetrical with its original — as you can't put a left glove on your right hand. All these ways of differing may be exercised in any molecule. It multiplies the variety considerably. Nature tends to "be in every possible way."

Nature also strongly favors interaction. Especially remarkable are those interactions that are most analogous to our theological speculations about the Trinity and to the metaphysical affirmation of basic Being as a community of sharing that is thereby one. Now look at these carbon rings, which share their electrons in a mode called "delocalization." It means that the shared electrons are no longer localized to their "atoms of origin." They don't belong to the atom that they came from. They are mutually shared among all the carbons. Or, we may say that their electronic charge is spread continuously over the whole molecule.[2] This stabilizes the molecule and forms a network so strong that the ring remains intact through almost all the reactions to which it is party (see Fig. 4).

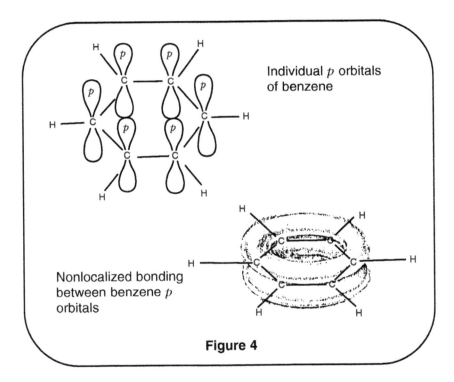

Individual *p* orbitals of benzene

Nonlocalized bonding between benzene *p* orbitals

Figure 4

Molecules for Life: Sugars, Nucleic Acids, and Proteins

Ring molecules that are of particular interest because of their significance for life are the sugars. The simplest sugars are monosaccharides, the units (or "monomers") from which polysaccharides are made — otherwise known as carbohydrates (carbon and water). Carbohydrates are the most abundant organic compounds on Earth, annual production being something like 10^{11} tons, virtually all done by green plants through photosynthesis. Photosynthesis is a living process, and we haven't got to life yet, but let's look quickly at the chemical structure of sugar. See how simple it is, yet by stringing simple forms together, more complex ones (and more different ones) can be made.

The basic formula for sugar is $(CH_2O)_x$, where x is a number by which each type of atom is multiplied — for instance, $C_6H_{12}O_6$. There are many variations, but a familiar sugar is glucose, the one our cells use for energy.

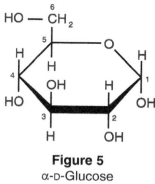

Figure 5
α-D-Glucose

Figure 5 shows a carbon ring. The six corners of the hexagon are understood to represent carbon atoms, bonded as described above, except for an oxygen at one apex rather than a carbon. And there are other small groups attached above and below the ring-plane. Glucose is the monomer from which cellulose is constructed by linking the glucose molecules together in long chains. This makes wood. Plants use glucose for structure as well as for energy. But see how far back our kinship with other forms of life goes! Glucose chemistry is fundamental.

Another important sugar is ribose, based on a five-member ring with a replacement oxygen at one apex (see Fig. 6). This sugar is important

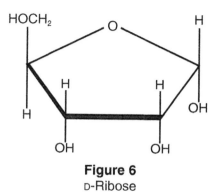

Figure 6
D-Ribose

because it is the foundation of ribonucleic acid, RNA, one of the coding molecules (together with DNA) for making the other molecules of which living bodies are composed. The key to life is the relationship between the nucleic acids and the proteins, so we need to go into this a little more deeply. It's going to be a mutual dependence relation and another opportunity to see "self-creating" taking place right before your eyes. First, we need to attach two other molecular groups to the foundational ribose (see Fig. 7).

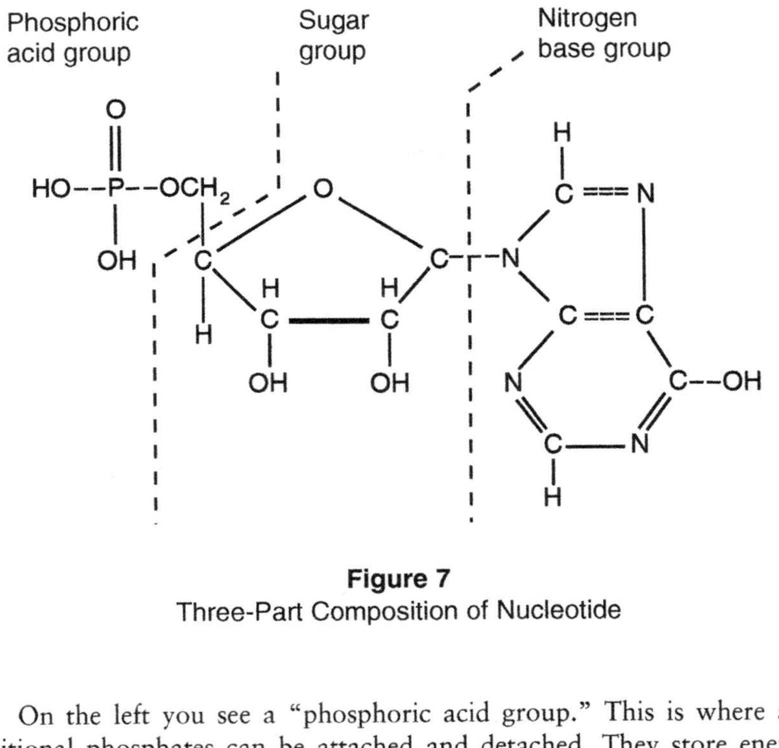

Figure 7
Three-Part Composition of Nucleotide

On the left you see a "phosphoric acid group." This is where additional phosphates can be attached and detached. They store energy when attached and liberate it when detached. This will come up again later, but that's why that molecular group is important. Then, on the right there is a more complicated structure called a "nitrogen base group." ("Base" is the opposite of "acid." Baking soda is a base; so is laundry bleach.) This is the structure that will be important for the coding function of the nucleic acid. (DNA is a modification of this three-part molecule and holds the code in long-term storage, whereas RNA is active in the complex operations that result in assembling proteins in accordance with the code. In the modern cell, RNA mediates between DNA and the structures responsible for protein assembly.)

The three-part molecule diagrammed in Figure 7, called a "nucleotide," is the "monomer" (compositional unit) for the chain that is properly called RNA. Just as glucose chains to make cellulose, so nucleotides chain to make ribonucleic acid. I will say more about the code presently, but now let us turn to the protein side of the life picture.

Proteins are chains of amino acids. Amino acids are comparatively simple and small molecules, composed of carbon, hydrogen, oxygen, sulfur, and nitrogen in different arrangements. (Notice again how complexity arises easily from simplicity just by changing the arrangement.) There are about twenty of them that combine with each other to form the more than one hundred thousand different kinds of proteins found in the human body.

Among the proteins is an important subclass, enzymes. Enzymes have a special and remarkable property: they can enter into a reaction in such a way as to enable the reaction to take place much faster than it otherwise would have done, and then they emerge from the reaction themselves unchanged! A molecule that can do this is called a *catalyst*. Catalysts are important to chemical reactions, and enzymes especially are very important to the chemistry of living beings. They can speed up reactions amazingly. An extreme example is the decomposition of H_2O_2 (hydrogen peroxide, in your bathroom cabinet) into H_2O and O. An inorganic catalyst, powdered platinum, can make the reaction go twenty-six thousand times faster, but the enzyme catalase can increase it by a factor of 10^{11}!

Enzymes are vital to the present-day cooperation between nucleic acids and proteins on which life depends. Both nucleic acids and proteins are immensely complex molecules, long chains of units put together in particular orders. Yet each of them is dependent on the other. DNA and RNA are assembled by enzymes (which are proteins), and on the other hand, the information for making the proteins is stored in the sequence of the nucleotides of the nucleic acid. Neither can be made without the other. Once more, chemistry is intensely symbiotic.

Looking at the chemical universe, we see a great variety of compounded materials, most of them engaged in vigorous interaction with one another. These interactions are made possible by the atoms and molecules being close enough together to affect one another by their electromagnetic energies and by such conditions as temperature and pressure being right for certain reactions. When these conditions are present, the reactions will take place of themselves, moving always to more favorable status, more stability, lower energy demands.

We see the incredible complexity of a huge molecule and we see how conveniently it performs some highly specialized feat. It looks as if it must have been deliberately and brilliantly designed. But if we look at something very simple, such as methane made from the attraction of carbon's four valence electrons for four hydrogens to complete them, we are more inclined to feel that this is merely natural, running from the fixed rules of impersonal processes. The mystery is in the *emergence* of the new wholeness when many of these small simple processes are arranged together into one concerted operation. Acting *together,* acting on one another, interacting, is what does it. The Many and the Diverse, in intimate processes whereby they affect one another, create new unified beings, things that never existed before, but which are now able to act as integral units in themselves.

We do not understand their way of being adequately by taking the complex units apart to see what they are made of, nor by trying to retroject the new whole into the combining parts as a goal toward which they strive. It is the interactive unions of the parts, the sharing of their beings, their energies, that actually constitutes the new whole. This is easily seen in the chemical universe, and this is why I call it a kind of symbiosis and, in a theological context, point out that it can be regarded as an expressed image of the trinitarian (many-one) God-Community. Each new whole is a community whose members' mutual "ecstasy" — giving themselves to one another, sharing their energies — makes them to be one.

Self-Assembly and Autocatalysis

Mutual self-gift is now going to enable small molecules to link together into giant macro-molecules, and these large molecules will interact with one another to enhance their respective formations. A circle of mutual help will emerge as a whole being in its own right and will begin to display new properties.

The first level of self-assembly is the formation of *polymers* (many parts) by repetition of simple units, monomers. We saw already how methane, ethane, and propane, are simply more units of a basic hydrocarbon (carbon with hydrogens attached on all sides) added to make a chain. Chains can be of various lengths. "Octane," for instance, is a chain of eight carbons. With, say, twenty-two carbons, we have a heavy oil to use as a lubricant — the longer the chain, the heavier the oil. These chains "self-assemble" because the carbons are attracted to one another and bond in the ways we have already described. Whenever the molecules are close enough together and other conditions are right, they will join spontaneously and make characteristic patterns and display characteristic properties, new and different from one another.

But not all molecules are attracted to one another, and this also is important and will be useful for life. Look at oil and water. Water is an utterly magical molecule and has many unique properties, mostly due to its spatial arrangement, the way its two hydrogens are joined to its single oxygen with a 120° angle between them. This puts the hydrogens on, so to speak, "one side of" the oxygen. And since the oxygen is so much bigger than the hydrogens, the community of electrons (six from the oxygen and one each from the two hydrogens) drawn by the positive charge of the eight-proton oxygen nucleus, tend to spend more time around the oxygen than around the hydrogen single protons. The result is that the "oxygen end" of the molecule has more negative charge than the "hydrogen end," which is thus left relatively positive. Consequently, other molecules that are charged one way or the other will be attracted to their respective opposite charges at different ends of the water molecule. When molecules of a certain substance are attracted to water in this way, we say that they are "dissolved" in the water. The solute (what is dissolved) fits right in among the water molecules and becomes so attached that it doesn't settle out or in any way separate from the water. Many substances dissolve in water.

But that is just for charged molecules. Oil is neutral. It doesn't dissolve in water. Now we can understand why applying water to oil won't remove it (for instance, from our hands). What is needed for that job is a molecule that is neutral like oil on one end and charged like water on its other end. That's what soap is: a highly charged acid group on one end and a hydrocarbon on the other end. Handwashing isn't all it's good for, though. Molecules like this will eventually form the cell membrane, all lined up together with their oily ends on the inside and their acid ends outside.

Before we get to cells, however, we must assemble other kinds of polymers. First we will see how proteins can self-assemble. Then we will see how nucleic acids can self-assemble. And finally we will see how proteins and nucleic acids assemble one another. I said above that proteins are assembled following the coded information of RNA. But in the days of the early Earth (this would be about three and a half billion years ago), there may have been other ways of making primitive proteins. It has been found in the laboratory that heating mixed amino acids to-gether until they are quite dry will induce them to link together. The sequence in which they are chained is not random but is determined by the proportions of the particular amino acids involved and by other conditions.[3]

Suppose there were shallow pools of water in depressions of warm lava, the just forming crust of the planet. There were plenty of organic molecules around already in the water, because conditions for their for-mation had been present ever since the dust and gas clouds of interstellar space were formed. Heat from the cooling lava could evaporate the water from the shallow pools, heat and dry the amino acids until they linked, and there would be "proteinoids." Rain could then wash the new molecules back into the deeper water, where they would be ready for further adventures.

These reactions can take place without catalysts, but there will be more chaining if phosphates are added. When the phosphate bonds with the amino acid, the latter is said to be "activated." Phosphate bonds carry a lot of energy. Activated amino acids easily bond to each other with the help of this energy. But now suppose that some of these short stretches of linked amino acids, called "peptides" (forerunners of the more specialized proteins), also have catalytic abilities.

If so, then some of the peptides might catalyze the "activation" of the amino acids and thus hasten their chaining to one another. This, of course, makes more peptides. And some of these might be the very peptides that served as the catalysts for this operation. This is how self-assembly can be done.

Meanwhile, similar steps are being taken among the nucleotides. Probably RNA was formed before DNA, so we will speculate on what that history may have been. Again the chaining is done by phos-phate bonds. Go back to the diagram of a typical nucleotide (Fig. 7, p. 94). The one pictured is actually adenosine monophosphate, AMP. If it had two more phosphates on it, it would be adenosine triphos-phate, ATP, which you may have heard of. It's the energy-storing and energy-releasing molecule that keeps all our systems going. But other nucleotides are possible. In addition to adenosine, we have guanine, cy-tosine, and uracil monophosphates: GMP, CMP, UMP. If they have extra phosphates, they can be diphosphates, for instance guanine diphosphate, GDP, or triphosphates, for instance cytosine triphosphate, CTP.

The chaining comes about because of the triphosphates' ability to cut off two of their phosphates and bond the remaining molecule to another triphosphate. For instance, ATP (a triphosphate) might drop two of its phosphates, becoming a monophosphate (AMP); then it might pick up, say, guanine triphosphate (GTP), to produce a two-link chain: AMP-GTP. The "tri-" link repeats the procedure: GTP drops two phosphates, becomes GMP, and attaches any other handy triphosphate, say UTP. Further chaining can be done on the same principle, adding triphosphates in any order. Such a chain is chemically RNA, and this is how it can put itself together. But it doesn't yet have a code in it for making a particular protein.

Having seen both RNA and proteins through their respective self-assemblies to their proper polymer (chained) status, we must now relate them to one another with an autocatalytic ability that will enable them to promote each other's self-assembly. When that circle has been achieved, we will have life.

The Magic Circle

We now have polymers consisting of random sequences of AMP, GMP, CMP, and UMP. And here a bit of serendipity appears. These are all rather flat molecules, so they can be thought of as like pieces of a jigsaw puzzle. Their shapes are important. And the interesting thing is that they fit together. The bases are so configured that A and U can match, and so can G and C. This is what, we will see, permits copying.

If a stretch of RNA has, for instance, the sequence C-U-G-A, it might attract another bit of RNA consisting of only G-A, which would attach to its C-U, producing the double strand:

C—U—G—A
| |
G—A

Suppose that then another sequence C-U-G happened by and was caught, matching up with the remaining G-A on the original strand, but leaving the final G of the new piece hanging out by itself:

C—U—G—A
| | | |
G—A—C—U—G

That G would attract its matching C, to which other links might be attached:

C—U—G—A—C—G—A—U
| | | |
G—A—C—U—G

The new links would in turn attract appropriate partners. You can see how a double strand would grow, adding to first one side, then the other.

If the two strands now split, they will each attract the pieces for building another strand like the one from which they had split, thus *replicating one another*. This mutual assistance — my broadly interpreted "symbiosis" — would make this particular sequence pair become more abundant than sequences that had not yet got into the matching business. And the successful sequence would be a new whole and could be distinguished from other chains.

Other sequence-pairs would also form, and some would replicate faster than others, forming a larger fraction of the total population than their fellows. Some would hold together better than others; that also would affect their "market share." Obviously, if there is anything about the environment in which these events take place that affects the rate of replication or the stability of the sequences, those sequences that do better with those aspects of the environment will accumulate in larger numbers. If, for instance, there are minor changes in a given sequence that give such an advantage, they will gradually edge out their predecessors. In this quite inevitable way, better "fits" to the environment will appear. We have seen proteins self-assemble and RNA self-assemble. Now we want to put the two together, RNA-assembling protein and protein-assembling RNA.

Among all these RNA sequences there must have been some that could interact with amino acids (the building blocks of proteins) by linking them to the ribose sections (see Fig. 7 on page 94 again) of their nucleotides. As Christian de Duve points out in *Vital Dust,* it isn't as though the primitive RNA molecule "intended" to go into business as a protein assembler. It just worked out that way by means of the simple inevitabilities of the various interactions — the way the atoms interact to make molecules and the way shapes fit together geometrically and the way the energy investment is lower and the stability is greater. RNAs carrying amino acids found it advantageous.

In any case, once there were RNAs carrying amino acids, these couples started to interact with each other. When they came close, the amino acid of one joined with the amino acid of the other to form a peptide.

Another amino acid could be picked up in a similar way, so that there were now three amino acids in the peptide, and this could be repeated until a polypeptide chain was made. Nowadays the process is much more complicated and is carried out at a work station in the cell called a "ribosome," but this may be the way the basic operation of RNA-dependent protein synthesis got started.[4]

From here it is easy enough to see what the next step would be. Proteins are apt to be enzymes. Enzymes are catalysts. Catalysts make reactions go faster. But in the early days the more general amino acid chain, the peptide, may have acted as a catalyst. Suppose some RNA sequence acts as a "template," or guide, to help put together a peptide that is a catalyst that makes the self-assembly of that very RNA sequence go faster. More of those particular RNAs will be made; that is to say that more of that particular *sequence* of nucleotides (the template) will be made. And that particular sequence is what determines the particular sequence of amino acids that makes that particular peptide, which peptide is the catalyst for that particular RNA sequence.

Thus the movement goes round in a helping, assembling circle. The peptide is a catalyst for the RNA, and the RNA is a catalyst for the peptide. We have an "autocatalytic circle." This is *symbiosis,* living together, mutual assistance, mutual enhancement. It is a circle that now has an identity as a particular circle. It can be distinguished from other circles and can compete with other such circles for needed resources (the atoms out of which the RNA and the peptide are made).

But the cycles can also interact with one another in symbiotic ways. One cycle can help make part of another cycle and perhaps the latter helps still another and so on until the helping comes back to the first cycle, like bread cast upon the waters. We will examine this in more detail after we have the code relation between RNA and protein, but here we can say that the idea of how "life" emerges from chemistry is in this cycle of cycles, a hypercycle.

This is the magic moment, the moment when life is self-created. It is this *mutuality* that is the heart of what we recognize as "living." Life is not an extra, something secret imposed on or inserted into nonliving matter that turns it living. It is the activities, the interactivities of the chemical assemblies that already exist, acting according to their natural dispositions as chemical agents (dispositions in turn dependent on physical forces, the electrostatic attractions and repulsions of the atoms of which the molecules are made) — it is these activities already in place *in relation to one another* that does it.

Life "emerges" from the network of these interactivities. It is a "phase transition," a new pattern of structured behavior, a new unit of wholeness with its own characteristic properties. The wholes will now relate to one another on their own proper level of unification, not molecule to molecule but mutual-circle to circle. There will now be new rules governing the circles as circles in their relations to one another, just as there were rules governing the molecules in their relations to other molecules. And it was the molecular rules that enabled the new circles to arise. It is not imposition from the outside, but neither is it just an accident, the work of raw chance.

Biochemists Michael Crawford and David Marsh write that once the "happy union" of nucleic acids with their phosphate-bond energy and proteins began to

> co-ordinate their activities, something that was recognisable as living matter had appeared. With the appearance of those systems the corner from chemical to biological evolution had been turned. The corner had not been turned by the principles of the casino, it had been turned by the inevitability of chemistry.[5]

Nobel Laureate Christian de Duve, observing that what we are witnessing is "authentic Darwinian evolution at the molecular level," urges that "the important point is that this result is achieved without any design or foresight."[6]

The inescapable laws of chemistry, doing — when the conditions are right — what they universally do, have enabled these molecules to assemble themselves, to constitute populations, and to replicate selectively, thus evolving. So sure is this process that we can say that if these same materials and same conditions prevail elsewhere in the universe, something very similar will result. And once you get to stars and the formation of more complex atoms, with their various valences and energies of combination, you have a fine chance of having these materials and these conditions. Life is not a stranger in the universe, but a natural child of the universe, or the universe itself in a further development.

Stuart Kauffman presses this view strongly:

> If there is some reason to believe that life is probable, then we are not mysteries in the exploding cosmos, we are natural parts of it.... [Deeper even than A-T, G-C pairing and template replication, as above], life is a natural property of complex chemical systems.... When the number of different kinds of molecules in a chemical soup passes a certain threshold, a self-sustaining network of reactions — an autocatalytic metabolism — will suddenly appear. Life emerged... complex and whole... thanks to the simple, profound transformation of dead molecules into an organization in which each molecule's formation is catalyzed by some other molecule in the organization. The secret of life... is... collective catalytic closure. Life emerges as a natural phase transition in complex chemical systems.[7]

There, as I promised, is the "phase transition" again, in which the interactions of the components of a system cause the system as a whole to assume a new state and produce new behaviors. Also note the verb "emerge." An important word, which we will meet again and again. For instance, Ronald Fox, in *Energy and the Evolution of Life,* says

> The tetravalency and relative stability of carbon bonds are responsible for the vast array of organic compounds....However,... many of the observed characteristics of the living state *cannot be predicted from first principles....* The living state is...highlighted by emergent properties....The emergent properties of nonlinear, driven, dissipative systems appear in at least three distinct ways: self-assembly, autocatalysis, and self-organization.[8]

We need some footnotes right in the text here for four interesting words. "Systems" are new wholes composed of various interactive components, all of which both make inputs to others in the system and are affected by the others' outputs. Because there are so many influences on how any variable behaves, and those influences are themselves changing in response to still others, if you express the behavior of one component in terms of the others by an equation and then graph the equation, it won't come out a straight line. Hence "nonlinear." "Driven" just means that you have to keep putting fresh energy into the system from outside the system. "Dissipative" means that the system takes materials and energy into itself, rearranges the materials into its own processes, and then ejects, scatters, "dissipates" waste products and heat. In spite of this constant movement of materials through the system, the distinctive form of the system remains the same, recognizable and operating as a unit being. And the "unit being" for us at this stage is the cell.

The Code and the Cell

We now have a peptide assembling itself on the side of an RNA chain. We have speculated — even supposed — that this peptide will act as an enzyme catalyst to facilitate the assembly of its helper, the RNA sequence. Each helping each, we said. This means that the "self"-assembly is now taking an indirect route, passing through another "self." An ecstatic element has entered into the enstatic process of the macromolecule. But it prospers. More RNA is made by RNAs that make peptides that catalyze RNA-assembly than by RNAs that don't. And similarly with the peptides: those that foster RNA-assembly are themselves advantaged by the assistance that the RNA gives to their self-assembly. The enstatic/ecstatic cycle creates a greater whole, the collective catalytic closed system.

So we next have to consider how these new systems relate to one another. There are two new levels of wholeness to be discussed: (1) the sequence orders for a particular RNA/peptide combination and (2) the collection of a group of such autocatalytic cycles. The new features that appear on the first level are the gene and the genetic code, and the new feature on the second level is the cell. We will talk about the code first, because it makes possible the more inclusive wholeness of the cell.

Some of the RNA/peptide combinations replicated faster and survived longer than others. Why? How? Better cooperation between the RNA and the peptide? Better ways of improving? Yes, a way developed to improve the specificity of the match between the RNA and the peptide so that the RNA would make exactly this peptide that was its helper, and so that further improvements could be discretely and efficiently made.

In the course of this selection process, another very important step was taken. We've been talking about "peptides." Peptides are chains of amino acids, any amino acids. "Proteins," however, are chains of twenty particular amino acids. These twenty came to be preferred, and chains made exclusively of them came to dominate in the RNA-peptide cycles, so from now on we have an RNA-protein connection.

The order of the links in the RNA chain determines the order of the amino acid sequence of the protein, so we call the RNA sequence the "gene" for the protein because it "generates" the protein, is the "beginning" for it. Notice that this now is a matter of *information*, although the RNA's nucleotide links and the amino acids relate to each other in terms of *energy*. Information is the order among material things but is not itself a material thing. Yet it will develop its own holistic structures and relations. Meanwhile, "gene" is the name for the relation between the order on the RNA and the order on the protein.

But how does the gene work? There is a code relation between the RNA sequence and the amino acids that will make protein. According to this code, three nucleotides specify one amino acid. It is a little complicated to explain just how this comes about, but the central reason is the same attraction between the bases A-U, G-C that we saw above (p. 99). Because of this, units in an RNA strand can bond to one another, following this matching rule. The strand bends back on itself in a hairpin shape, and at the loop end of that shape there are exactly three bases exposed: the coding triplet.

Why three? Because two are too few and four unnecessary. Look at it this way: There are twenty amino acids involved in biological proteins. But there are only four different bases in RNA. We have to make a different combination out of those four for each amino acid. If we take the bases two at a time (use twins instead of triplets for coding), we get only sixteen different combinations, not enough. But if we use all possible combinations of the four bases taken three at a time, then we get sixty-four different combinations, plenty. In fact, we have more than enough and most of these will have to code for an amino acid that other combinations are also coding for. Redundancy. That can be a good thing. And some combinations can be used to mean "Stop — end the chain here."

There's another reason as well for triplets rather than either twins or quadruplets. In the protein assembly procedure, two bases wouldn't make a strong enough bond to hold things steady while the amino acid was being fastened to the next member in the growing protein chain. And four would be so strong that the RNA and the protein couldn't separate when the chain was finished. I mention these details only so that you can see that there are natural reasons why things are the way they are. These arrangements are not arbitrary. They are this way because this is the way that works.

That is a highly simplified and abbreviated description of the basic autocatalytic cycle between nucleic acid and protein. Now we approach the formation of the cell. It will include a number of these cycles. Consider that just as the RNA and the protein promote each other's assembly, so one such autocatalytic cycle might promote the mutual assembly of another cycle. In fact, there might be several individual cycles, each performing some function relative to the others that is helpful. A kind of group symbiosis, or community, a cycle of cycles. It's called a "hypercycle."[9]

William F. Loomis, in *Four Billion Years: An Essay on the Evolution of Genes and Organisms,* says that there were probably an enormous number of these hypercycles all over the planet, all working out different methods of mutual assistance in replication. A good supply of the materials for making both RNA and the various proteins was needed, and they had to be close enough to each other that the reactions would take place. They needed to be confined and kept at hand. Having got the "code" established, life now needed the "cell." "Compartmentalization of successful hypercycles would have the dual consequences of concentrating the components and allowing independent competition among different systems."[10]

Two benefits must be secured by the cell. It must keep the raw materials within reach, and it must allow them to move around freely. What is inside modern cells as cell sap is still somewhat like what was (presumably) in the liquid medium in which these reactions may have been taking place three and a half billion years ago. Free circulation is protected in this way. But confinement becomes more important.

The confining is done by a membrane formed around a hypercycle group and a sufficient quantity of cell sap. All living cells have such a membrane, and it is everywhere made of a "lipid bilayer," a double layer of molecules called phospholipids. We have already discussed lipids (oils) as hydrocarbons and noticed their hydrophobic (water rejecting) property. We discussed soap, a substance that joins a hydrophobic molecule to a hydrophilic (water friendly) compound. And now, of course, speaking of enclosing membranes, we think of soap bubbles.

A cell membrane is a lot like a soap bubble. The phospholipids of which it is made have phosphate heads, which will be attracted to the water, and two long tails each, made of hydrocarbons, hydrophobic. These molecules line up with their hydrophilic heads all pointing one way and their hydrophobic tails the other way (⧔⧔⧔). That's one layer. Another layer just like it joins its tails to those of the first layer, hydrophilic heads on the outside of the two-ply fabric (⧨). Shaped into a hollow sphere, the heads of one layer are on the inside of the sphere and the heads of the other layer are on the outside of the sphere, with the tails of both in the middle of the bilayered membrane (see Fig. 8).[11]

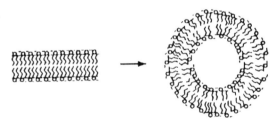

Figure 8

It is not hard to get phospholipids to organize themselves this way — a little agitation of the water medium in which they are floating will cause them to shape into such droplets or bubbles, thereby enclosing some portion of the "soup."

Would they be apt to form around RNA? Not directly. RNA by itself has negatively charged phosphate groups which are repelled by the charges on the surfaces of the bilayers. But (and isn't this convenient!) RNA molecules with protein joined to them are a complex that can act as a facilitating template for the formation of *bilayers!* So, naturally the bilayers enfold such RNA cum protein readily — a hundredfold more efficiently than if the RNA were bare. Therefore, the droplets, when they form, will preferentially form around our hypercycles, and we will have a cell.[12]

The membrane is a wonderful structure. It behaves rather like a liquid; its composing molecules, though densely packed, can easily slide along each other within the bilayer. This makes the bilayer flexible and moldable; it can adapt to nearly any shape of surface. The membrane is continuous and self-sealing, always a closed sac. Nevertheless, two bubbles can merge to form a single bigger bubble, or one bubble can split into two, each of them sealing itself off again. Both of these behaviors are important for reproduction.

But haven't we sealed off the cell rather too well? Doesn't it need to take in fresh supplies and to discard unwanted materials? Yes, it's a "driven, dissipative system," and successful cells are the ones that find ways of transporting materials through their membranes. Biologists think that cells found successively more sophisticated ways of fine-tuning such processes. The first way was just to leave tunnels open through the membrane; they were made of tunnel-shaped proteins called "porins" (because they make "pores"). Then there were "transport facilitators" for particular substances, letting them flow in either direction as long as it was from high concentration of the transported substance to low concentration of it.

More fussy were the "gated channels," governed by a gate that is unlocked by a chemical or electrical signal. This type allows traffic in only one direction. All these are passive mechanisms. The next improvement was "active transport," or "pumps," with additional energy put in to force substances to move against the usual flow, from low concentration of the transported substance to a high concentration of it. With pumps the cell can pick up desired molecules outside, even when they are scarce, and it can discharge wastes into an environment already polluted.[13]

This is a bit of detail, but it gives you some idea of the kind of thing that even very primitive cells were able to do and were rewarded for doing, for the genes that coded for these devices — that is, for the proteins that either were the devices themselves or the enzymes for assembling the devices — these genes were so benefitted by having the devices in their cell that they were able to replicate more readily and leave many copies of themselves with the instructions for continuing to make the devices. The cells so outfitted inevitably became more numerous than cells not so outfitted. That's how evolution works, by "natural selection."

The code and the cell thus work together. The genes code for the materials that make up the cell and function (according to their natural chemistry) in particular ways. These materials function in the cell community to facilitate the acquisition of raw materials, to catalyze the synthesis of more complex molecules, and to rid the cell of unwanted or noxious materials. All of these activities enhance the replication of the RNA, which in turn helps to make more of the materials that help to make more of it. The code makes the cell and the cell promotes the code.

We have one last behavior to tell about to bring us fully to what we recognize as a living cell, and that is cell division. Cell division is necessary. The cell's growth is limited, because the volume of material inside needing servicing increases faster than the surface area of the membrane through which the traffic lanes pass. Raw materials and wastes can't move in and out fast enough to keep up with the needs of the structures inside. However, if the cell were to make a bud, put out a further bubble or a branch, thus increasing the surface area (opening up new lanes for traffic), the pressure would be eased. If the tendency to do this was derived somehow from the genetic code, then the cells with that code would continue their lineage beyond their colleagues who perished of internal crowding, starvation, and pollution.

Growth of the bud or branch with all components of the hypercycle inside will eventually cause it to pinch off; both membranes will then seal up, and there will be two cells where there had been only one. Both could then grow in comfort and with speed until they were again so bloated that budding and pinching were needed to ease the strain. If other cells, with different sets of genes, were doing something similar, there would be a question as to which kind of cell multiplied more rapidly and used more of the food and other benefits of the environment. In a limited environment, one of them could crowd out the others.

Remember that there was always this kind of competition for building materials: when molecules were being assembled, when atoms were gathering electrons, when atomic nuclei were compounding. If things are beginning to sound a little more like human struggles, let us be aware that the heritage goes all the way back to the beginning and will continue in different forms and on different levels all along the path of cosmic development.

The competition will now be among cells — that is to say, among sets of genes (called "genomes") that code for making cells in certain ways. The way the cell is structured and behaves will determine how well that genome gets replicated and therefore how well the cell gets replicated. Any little variation that improves this situation relative to competitors will have a bigger share of the general population. It will out-replicate the others. This success in dealing with environments and situations makes the variation look as if it has been "designed" for just this purpose. But if you look closer, you see that the innovation was one of the things that was likely to happen because of the chemistry that was already in place. The new things build on the old things. And as the better working ones crowd out the poorer ones, the population as a whole comes to be characterized by the innovations. Those innovations then become part of the foundation on which the next round of innovations is built (like people making tools to make tools to make tools to . . .).

Even the way of encouraging innovations can vary. Instead of making only one innovation at a time, if it happens that a large number of experiments are under way at the same time, there will be a much higher probability of a really good way of doing something emerging and taking over the whole field.

But all this comes out of the dynamics, the processes, the functions of the spontaneously assembling natural bodies. Nothing is imposed from the outside. There is no guiding hand. Each stage of organization leads naturally to the next on the basis of the way things are already happening. We are modeling a universe that makes itself, from the inside out, as an act of ecstasy, not one that is made from the outside by imposition.

Chapter Seven

THE EVOLUTION
OF EVOLUTION

 REFLECTING ON WHAT WE HAVE SEEN of chemistry turning into biology, we can notice several things. The cell is made out of molecules, but as a cell it has a new wholeness and unity of its own. It will relate to other cells as its peers. From here on, we will have to be careful not to confuse levels of organization. We must not expect to account for biological phenomena in chemical terms alone. There will be biological properties that are not reducible to the components' levels of organization.[1]

Since to create a new level of organization is to unite components from previous levels, we become strongly aware that first things have to be different; then they can come together and share their diverse information, matter, and energy, thus composing the new-level being. In other words, "selfhoods" have to be "severed" in order for more complex systems to form and to operate. This separation is not something that "ought not" to be — not if creating is going on. Creating requires it. It is a "truly necessary 'sin' that merits (enables) a great redeemer," namely, further creation, greater complexity, and eventually consciousness. We need to remember this, because it is the root to which "evil" can be traced, a root which is not in itself evil.

In the created order we are always working with the characteristics of finitude. Much of what we will be watching in biology will have to do directly with limited supplies of desirables. Desirables can be matter, energy, location, access to variation (including mates), and later such intangibles as knowledge and social position. We will see that what succeeds, succeeds. Those organizations (even such simple things as crystals) that happen to make more of themselves — replicate their patterns, leave progeny — will become more prominent in their respective populations and crowd out alternatives in the competition for limited supplies of the relevant "desirables."

Self-organization characterizes the cosmos at every level and is the general theme running through the whole. Alfred North Whitehead saw these levels of organized reality as "organisms." He recognized that an essential feature of such "organisms" was the interactions that formed them and the interactions they then had with one another to give rise to "organisms of organisms."[2] We now speak of "systems." But it is this feeling for the organism — something like being alive — that we recognize in the "system." It means, among other things, that movement is fundamental and primary, not an afterthought. What is structured is movement itself. Reality is like a dance. Whitehead regarded "reality" as a "process."

Edward Fredkin, too, says that "there is an information process, and the bits [binary units of information, the basic to-be or not-to-be (represented as 1 or 0)], when they're in certain configurations, behave like the thing we call the electron, or the hydrogen atom, or whatever."[3] In other words, all reality is system, configuration, organization of reality-process that is meaning.

A system is a set of units interacting with one another; better, a system is a set of interactions; better yet, a system is a meta-interaction of interactions. The behavior of each player depends on communications from the behaviors of other players. There is no starting point, no first player, no responding in sequence. Everyone plays at once; everyone affects many, if not all, of the others in the system; everyone is affected by many, if not all, of the others. All of the interactions are necessary for the system to be itself. And it has — or is — an "itself," its own peculiar unity and character, emerging from "the simultaneous and cooperative interaction of all the elements."[4]

And this means that "whole" and "parts" are given together; parts do not precede the whole. When the wholes of one level of organization become parts of a larger whole, that whole is already present simultaneously with their becoming its parts. The interactions within the context of the meta-interaction is what differentiates the parts as parts. And it is their integration by the interaction of themselves as interactions that constitutes the whole. Distinction and union arise together. This is just how the Trinity was described in chapter 2. The organismic or systemic or configurational informational universe is an expressed (ecstatic) image of the Trinity.

But it is incarnated in the forms of finitude. We are now going to start watching these forms of finitude knit themselves up into such complexity of behavior and consciousness (see the next chapter) that the image of the Trinity as incarnate in them will become explicit (this is what I called the Theotokos, the God-bearer).

As the systems build up ever more inclusive wholes, they will go through phase transitions. (You remember that I said that phase transitions would come back.) There were phase transitions when the fundamental forces "froze out" and separated and the distinct particles of matter and radiation appeared. Being separated and distinct, they were able to enter into various interactions with one another and form new, emergent unities — nuclei, atoms, stars, galaxies, then molecules and planetary systems, and in our story to date, chemical reactions, autocatalytic cycles, hypercycles, enclosed in lipid bilayer spheres with two-way traffic to a supportive environment, living cells. The passage from chemical reaction to living cell is a phase transition. A new kind of wholeness, a new meta-interaction of interactions. A new unity, a new selfhood, with new kinds of differentiation, "part-ness," and gradually appearing specialization of function. It happens automatically when there is enough diversity and enough interaction.[5]

And what characteristics does this new selfhood display when adequate diversity and interaction enable it to emerge? There are three essential characteristics: (1) the ability to metabolize, meaning to transform matter/energy/information taken in from the environment into the forms of its own processing; (2) the ability to reproduce, i.e., to replicate itself (whether a gene, a cell, or an organism); (3) the ability to evolve, i.e., to suffer minor changes which, in interaction with the environment, affect the replication rate. This last means that if the change works with the environment in such a way that more copies are made of it than of its competitors (for what are desirables for all of them), then that change will tend to prevail.

In this chapter we will continue to look at ways of self-assembling, self-organizing, self-creating. This will now include and focus on evolving. In particular, I want to trace the successively better ways of evolving, which themselves have appeared as a result of evolution. We will cover the genetic code, bacteria and their gene-swapping, the eukaryotic cell and sex, adaptation and selection, symbiosis and coevolution. Along the way we will notice the importance of error, of failure, of death and extinction, of randomness and historical development, of deception and of pain. We will also see the appearance of adaptation, cooperation, and ecology. All of these features will illustrate what we outlined in chapter 3 as the nature of finitude.

The First Cells

A cell, as we have already seen, is a system that communicates with its environment; it is an *open system,* it has to take in material and energy from the outside, and it has to discharge its wastes. It is "driven" by this external energy, and it "dissipates" the matter and energy it can't use. Such a "driven dissipative system" recycles its environment and in the process preserves its characteristic form and augments its own existence.

It is amazing to consider that all living systems, which look to us like definite stable structures, are really "flow-throughs." The form does remain steady (comparatively) but the material of which the form is composed is in constant change and motion, incoming and outgoing. We are all systems of interactions — not so much *things* as *processes*.

This means that the *information* in the system is more important than the matter. And this is what evolution is concerned with: the form, the information. It is the informational system that evolves. What presses it to evolve is that the system is what is called "far from equilibrium." Or we could say that it is highly organized. Being in equilibrium means being in the most probable state, being average, random. Far from equilibrium is special, not average. In the crossword game Scrabble, the tiles are initially in random arrangement, but as words are spelled on the board, constraints tighten, fewer constructions are possible in each situation. Organization of the letters will be physically very improbable but linguistically more and more probable. This is increasing information.

Living systems organize their molecules and their physical and chemical processes in biologically significant ways. While this way has to be possible within the context of the environment, the organizational form of the system is not determined by the environment. The system itself sets its own mode of organization. This is part of what I am calling "self-creating." The environment supplies the system with needed inputs and carries away its outputs, and the system has to adapt to the environment (or adapt the environment to it) if it's going to stay in business. But the principles of its internal structure, processing, behavior, are immanent to it, not imposed from the outside. These principles, these forms, this information is what makes the living system to be what it is, able to conserve and renew itself. The system builds input materials into the *kind* of system it is (destroying the kind of system they were, if necessary). It is in charge of its kind, and it sorts and rearranges the materials accordingly. It is self-renewing and can maintain its character even though the materials keep changing. The matter flows through; the form remains.

In order to maintain, renew, and repeat this form, the living system has to be able to store the information, the instructions for arranging the molecules and the processes. You recall that the order of the nucleotides on the RNA polymer set the order for the amino acids on the peptide polymer. Most of the material in a living cell is made of proteins (peptides). So the information we are concerned about is the information on the RNA molecule.

A sequence of nucleotides that codes for a particular protein is a *gene*. The gene is the unit of hereditary material. Primitive genes could be only about seventy to a hundred nucleotides long; beyond this they would have too many copying errors. (Present-day genes, with more accurate replicating enzymes, may be a thousand or more nucleotides long.[6]) The total body of the genes for one organism is called the *genome,* or *genotype*. The genotype is distinguished from the *phenotype,* which is the thing made according to the instructions in the genes, e.g., a protein molecule. We also speak of a whole organism — one-celled, many-celled, modern plants and animals — as the phenotype. It is the *expression* of the information that the genome carries.

It is the phenotype that interacts with the environment. If this interaction is such as to keep the organism alive and enable the genome to copy itself and build another phenotype, then the genome is successful. It has made a phenotype that enables it to stay in business by copying itself. We tend to think that the genome is the phenotype's way of storing its information and making copies of itself, but actually it's the other way around. The chicken is an egg's idea of how to make another egg. The information in the sequence of nucleotides determines the phenotype, but the phenotype can't alter the sequence of nucleotides. The only way the phenotype and its interaction with its environment can affect the genome is by reducing or preventing its reproduction altogether. A genome that includes a gene that reduces the phenotype's probability of providing the conditions for reproduction will be represented in the population by a smaller number of copies. If the defect is serious, reproduction may fail completely and the genotype will be extinguished. This protection of the information in the genome means that every advantage that the organism gains in its relations with the environment will tend to be preserved and further gains can be built onto it, because the "burden of proof" is on the side of failure.

If the genome doesn't fail in a big way, it will continue. But how do advantages come about? Originally the nucleotide chains were assembled in no particular order. But those that happened to help assemble proteins that in turn helped assemble them increased by this very method and crowded out other random arrangements. Given a number of successful RNA arrangements of this sort, the winners might try combinations of themselves, whole RNA strings attaching to other RNA strings. Again, those combinations that coded for helpful proteins would take over the raw material supplies and leave competitors behind. This practice could be repeated until copying errors made it ineffectual.

Notice that the forward movement is dependent on the elimination of competitors at each stage of the compound assembling. There are other ways of obtaining new arrangements of the nucleotides, but the *selection* procedure will be essentially the same. Faster assembly, by that very fact, wins. But this means that slower assembly loses: it doesn't get raw materials or adequate location, or whatever it needs to reproduce (not just generally to stay alive but specifically to reproduce). This selective, or differential, dying out is what makes evolution work.

Interestingly, the main way of obtaining new advantages (at this primitive stage) also comes from what we would tend to consider failure — namely, copying errors. Of course, genomes need to be copied accurately if they are to be considered "replicating." Genomes that can't replicate correctly disappear. But a certain amount of error can be tolerated, the overall character of the genome being retained. If the error then gives an advantage to the phenotype in its interaction with the environment, those organisms that carry this error will make more copies of it and it will spread in the population.

Sometimes the advantage comes from the environment changing instead of the organism. If the organism has been harboring a gene that has been rather neutral in its value — no particular help but not a hindrance, either — and if the gene now provides just what is needed to cope with this shift in the environment, then the organism has a selective advantage over its neighbors who lack this asset. So it will be to the genome's advantage to engage in a certain amount of erroneous assembly, making new genes, because you never know when something you've put away in the closet (if it doesn't destroy the house in the meantime) might come in handy.

In general, then, advances in the methods of evolution will be advances in ways of obtaining variations, obtaining variations that have a high probability of conferring advantages, and obtaining them quickly. And here we should point out that as these evolutionary assemblies grope their way toward reproductive success, they are not operating each time from sheer randomness. They always build on what has been inherited, the information and the phenotypes that have survived from earlier interactions with the environment. This limits what can be done next rather considerably and points the sequence of changes in a more and more focused direction, which is irreversible.[7]

Bacteria Rule the World

The first cells were bacteria, and for two billion years (or more) they had the whole place to themselves. During this time they developed all the basic biochemistry by which the rest of us still live. And, for that matter, the bacteria are still the ones who run and regulate the planet. They manage aspects of our atmosphere that in turn moderate temperatures and radiation screens, and they make vital contributions to the soil and to the life cycles of plants and animals.[8]

Christian de Duve describes the ancestral bacterium as a single cell of unknown shape, probably surrounded by a solid wall (it would have been too fragile otherwise), with a plasma membrane inside that — a lipid bilayer with provisions for transport through it. It had to have a metabolic capacity to construct and break down all its constituent molecules and to support its energy requirements. Such a cell is called a "prokaryote" because it comes before cells that have nuclei to hold their genetic material.

At this time came another important step in the history of life, the advent of DNA (deoxyribonucleic acid, similar to RNA except that its sugar has lost an oxygen atom — hence "deoxy" — and thymine replaces uracil as a base). The problem was that RNA was doing two jobs, replicating itself and translating its code into protein assemblage. Hundreds of different bits of RNA were competing for complements so they could replicate, for materials needed for translation, etc. Confusion. This could be avoided by dividing the work into replication by one kind of molecule, translation by another. DNA now does the replication; RNA takes care of the translation.

With the appearance of DNA, three key reactions became possible, all in use to this day. The first was "reverse transcription," the assembly of DNA on an RNA "template." It works just like any other assembly of a complementary strand. However, the resulting DNA could not be used directly to line up amino acids for protein; that has to be done by RNA. But the *information* for doing so could be stored in the DNA and could be retrieved by making another RNA off the DNA. Retrieval is the second key reaction. And the third is the replication of DNA itself, which it could do just as RNA had done.

One further thing is important. DNA makes a complementary strand and then remains bonded with it in a double helix. This formation is extremely stable, an excellent way to store information. The double spiral can be opened by enzymes at any desired point and an RNA transcription made off that portion, and the helix closed up again. The result of all this is that the storage of the information for making the molecules that participate in the hypercycles is itself separated from the workaday activity of the cell. This information was therefore not easily altered. It became a world unto itself. What alterations took place in it came about from causes proper to its own world, not from the ups and downs of daily life on the RNA/protein circuit. This protected the genetic lineages (especially after eukaryotic cells appeared — see below) and enabled proper species to appear and to evolve as such.

There were other advantages to DNA. Since transcription to RNA could make whatever copies of the information were needed, not so many copies of the DNA itself needed to be made and stored. Transcription could be started or stopped by DNA sequences called "promoters" and later by regulatory genes. This became another source of variation and control, very important in adaptation and development. Since DNA was not itself directly involved in carrying messages about protein assembly, it could grow to great lengths and hold all an organism's genes together. This facilitated the replication of all the information for the whole organism at once. And the error rate in copying went down, too.[9]

Replication has been the name of the game of life from the beginning, with rapid replication being the winner. Bacteria are really good at rapid replication, as the home ec teacher will tell you when urging you to put the food in the refrigerator promptly. They make their proteins and copy their DNA, divide as soon as a copy of the DNA is ready, and keep on going. Every twenty to thirty minutes, twice as many cells. And, of course, it was natural selection that kept giving the prizes to the most rapid — that is to say, that the most rapid automatically got to more of the natural resources, and those reaching the resources quicker could replicate faster.

But what enabled natural selection to winnow out such tremendous replicators was the fact that the bacteria produced an enormous number of variants for the competition. And the more rapidly they replicated (or tried to), the more errors they made — more mutants for natural selection to select from, more chances to do it even better. In the twenty hours it takes a modern plant or animal cell to grow and divide, one bacterium can produce a trillion cells, including several billion mutations, which will cover just about every possible move from where the parent is now. So, although these mutations happen by chance and are random, among them all there is almost certain to be at least one new version that is better. And this will be true in every set of new mutations.

That's the basic way of getting new variations. But there are other ways. Bacteria are the ultimate in promiscuity. They engage in gene-swapping all the time. No one bacterium has enough information to handle all of its life processes, so it borrows from its neighbors constantly. And the neighbors are perfectly willing to lend. (Remember that the unit of replication is the gene. Gene-swapping that enables a gene to make more copies of itself will be selected for.)

There are several methods by which genes are transferred from one bacterium to another. Bits of self-replicating DNA called "small repli-cons" travel from cell to cell. Sometimes they are integrated into the main chain of DNA in the host cell; sometimes they float free in the cytoplasm. Occasionally they can do either. Another method occurs when a small replicon induces the whole bacterium to make many copies of the replicon until the cell is stuffed with them and breaks open, scattering the replicons. These small bodies are coated with protein and can survive and travel by river, sea current, or wind, and their formation is often triggered by adverse circumstances. Reaching another bacterium with similar metabolism, they perch on its membrane and inject their genetic material into it. There is also the method of "conjugation" by which a cell that grows a very thin hollow hair (a "pilus") from itself into another cell can send a bit of genetic material through the hair into the other cell.[10]

All the bacterial strains capable of fitting one another's genes into their programs thus form a kind of communicating society, or even a widespread organism, for sometimes the different strains seem to be helping each other resist antibiotics. (Of course, that's something that happens now, but similar cooperation may well have occurred in the past and helped to account for the bacteria's remarkable success.) This genetic sharing is an example of what I call "symbiosis," living to-gether. Perhaps such symbiotic cooperation helps the bacteria regulate the conditions of the planet crucial for life, that planetary symbiosis that James Lovelock calls "Gaia."[11] And perhaps a bit of living together paved the way for the next big jump in evolution, the emergence of the "eukaryotic" (well-nucleated) cell.

The Great Oxygen Poisoning and the Eukaryotic Cell

It came about this way. Three billion years ago the Earth was covered by blue-green and purple bacteria, on top of a layer of yellow, brown, and black bacteria. Those in the top layer, called "cyanobacteria," had evolved the chemical process of photosynthesis. They made sugar from carbon dioxide and water under ultraviolet radiation from the sun and with the help of chlorophyll as a catalyst. And they released into the atmosphere the waste product of their photosynthesis, free oxygen. For a long while — maybe a billion years — the oxygen bonded to other things, iron for instance, or was absorbed in the oceans, but eventually it began to accumulate in the atmosphere and became a serious pollutant. None of the other bacteria could live in the presence of free oxygen; it simply burned them up.

We think air pollution is bad now and that human beings have upset the balance of nature, endangering many species. But scientists tell us that this oxygen crisis in the bacterial age was the worst pollution threat that life has so far ever faced. As a matter of fact, 90 percent of living things did perish. But some of them could tolerate oxygen, and gradually there emerged some that positively required it. We are their descendents. The oxygen crisis, and the way life met it, was the great turning point in the history of the cell. When cells became able to use the poisonous oxygen, they had access to great energy.

What happened was that a new level of wholeness emerged, a new "selfhood." Just as atoms had interacted to make molecules and molecules had combined to make the first cells, so now the prokaryotes engaged in symbiosis, living together, to form the first eukaryotic cells. Certain nonphotosynthetic, but *respiring* (i.e., oxygen-using, or *aerobic*) bacteria established more and more stable relationships with larger *anaerobic* (non-oxygen-using) bacteria. Probably the aerobes originally invaded the anaerobes, but somehow neither destroyed them nor were destroyed by them. The anaerobes that acted as hosts to the oxygen users were those able to tolerate the oxygen on the outside. And they were safe from the oxygen inside because their own DNA was protected inside its own special membrane. That special membrane with the DNA inside is the *nucleus* of this new kind of cell.

The relationship proved of benefit to both parties: the large anaerobic host cell was able to use the energy-rich products of the aerobe's efficient metabolism, and the small aerobic partners got to live in the rich soup of their host's fermentation wastes and were protected by its cell membrane from the dangers of the outside world.

Lynn Margolis, a foremost spokesperson for this account of the origin of the eukaryotic cell, does not think that the nucleus itself resulted from symbiosis, but she does believe that the other *organelles* (bodies within the cell that function analogously to organs) in the eukaryote arose through symbiosis. These aerobic bacteria, for instance, became what we call *mitochondria,* which we all — all of us eukaryotic types — have. We can't live without them. It is the mitochondria in our cells that actually use the oxygen we breathe and make available the energy that runs the rest of the cell.[12]

The new wholeness preserves and even features the diversity of the symbionts. The mitochondria retain their own DNA, RNA, proteins, and protein-assembling machinery, inside their own membranes. Various other bacteria that took up residence inside larger cells contributed other skills, such as propelling the large cell or specializing as chloroplasts for plant cells. The functions became focused and the activities of the whole cell were differentiated but interactive. Differentiation plus interaction is the way new wholeness is made.[13] The same principle works as eukaryotic cells multiply as colonies, and colonies gradually develop specialized regions, functions, groups of cells, and at length become true multicellular organisms with distinct organs. And along the way they also develop some further improvements on ways of evolving.

The Origin of Sex

The self-creating universe is now fairly complex compared with stars and ready to become more complex yet in our immediate vicinity. The time is about nine hundred million years ago (called "BP" — before the present). Life started with bacteria, and bacteria had their genes strung on a single long, curly strand. That was an advantage, because the whole strand would be copied, and then, when the cell divided, each daughter cell would be equipped with a complete set of genes. As long as there was no mutation and no gene-swapping with other bacteria, that particular gene collection would continue making clones (exact copies) of itself.

But life is always on the move, so mutations do occur and gene-swapping goes on all the time. And that gives natural selection a pool of alternatives among which to select. One of the ways that the bacteria did their gene-swapping was by actually building a tube from one cell to another and floating the genetic material through. The later eukaryotic cells would do something similar. But they would combine only half their genes. Before this could happen, the cells had to invent a way of splitting up their genetic information.

This is called "meiosis" and is a very clever invention. In the eukaryotic cells, the genes are carried on chromosomes, strands of DNA wrapped around clumps of proteins called "histones."[14] The first cells had only one copy of each chromosome, but then some accident resulted in a cell having two nuclei. Maybe it failed to do cell division after having duplicated its nucleus. But it was an advantage, because now the cell had two copies of its vital information. Suppose there was a mutation in one set of its chromosomes and the mutation was harmful (as most mutations are). If there was only the one set of chromosomes, this was a disaster, but if there were two sets and only one was in trouble, the cell could survive.

Cells with two sets of chromosomes are called "diploid," double, as distinguished from those with only one set, called "haploid," single. The next thing that may have happened in those ancient times was that some of these diploid cells divided, giving one nucleus to each daughter cell. If there had been a mutation in one nucleus, these daughters now started separate lineages. And they might also fuse with other such mononucleated cells to make new diploids, thus mixing the combination of genes in the composite cell. This, or something like it, was probably the origin of sex.

An important refinement to this process occurred when a binucleated cell fused its two nuclei into a single diploid nucleus containing all the DNA from both the "parent" cells. But if the cell lineage is going to use this method of fusing haploids in each generation, it will need to reduce to the haploid state each time. Otherwise it would be doubling and doubling the number of chromosomes. This is where "meiosis," the reduction division, comes in. Meiosis is the process by which a single diploid cell becomes four haploid cells. It is a rather complicated process and consists of several steps.

The *first step* is the duplication of the diploid cell's chromosomes. Each chromosome now has an exact copy of itself, a "twin." The two are attached to each other. If each copy is visualized as shaped rather like a V, then when the two are joined at their points, they will make a shape rather like an X. We will be describing what happens to this X, but in the end it will come apart into the two Vs again.

Now we have to recall that the chromosomes in our diploid cell have come from two parents. In the case of a human being, twenty-three chromosomes have come from the mother and twenty-three from the father. Each chromosome from the mother can be matched with a chromosome from the father that is rather like it: that is, they both carry genes for the same characteristics in the same positions. These matching chromosomes are called "homologous." However, the genes themselves may not be the same: that is, they may both be for eye color, but one may code for blue and the other for brown. Such alternative genes are called "allels." This is one source of variation.

The *second step* in meiosis is that these homologous chromosomes, one from mother, one from father, find their partners and line up with each other. They line up in such a way that the corresponding genes actually touch one another, one X shape (two joined copies of the same chromosome, remember) lying on the other so closely as to look almost like a single body. At this point "crossing over," or "recombination" may occur. Corresponding sections of the mother and father chromosomes may be exchanged (see Fig. 9).

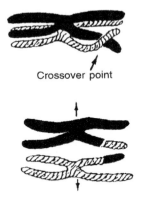

Figure 9

Suppose that the maternal chromosome consists in part of links ABCDEFGHIJ and that the paternal chromosome carries the corresponding abcdefghij. Then suppose that the break occurs between D and E, between d and e, and that the sections are interchanged. The recombined chromosomes will then read ABCDefghij and abcdEFGHIJ. But this switch will affect only one copy in the double chromosome — one of the Vs composing the X, but not the other. The Vs will no longer be exactly "twins."

Such breaks may occur at several places along the chromosomes, so that by the time the homologous chromosomes separate, they are no longer identifiable as "maternal" or "paternal," but are "mosaics" composed of more or less randomly selected pieces of both. Christian de Duve says that this phenomenon increases the variety of combinations almost to infinity and virtually guarantees that the offspring from the mating cells made in these meiotic divisions will have unique genetic compositions.[15]

When crossing-over has been completed, we come to the *third step:* the two members of each homologous pair separate. The twenty-three pairs come apart into forty-six double chromosomes (the X shape), and half of these forty-six go to one end of the cell and half to the other end. The twenty-three that go to either end are a random selection out of the whole forty-six. How many ways are there of doing this? Over eight million. So you can see that we are getting a lot of variation.

Step four: At each end of the cell we now have twenty-three (double) chromosomes, and the cell divides, encapsulating each bunch of twenty-three in a new membrane. This is where the number of chromosomes is reduced to one-half the number found in any other cell of the body. We are back to haploid, the number needed for cells that are going to mate with other haploids and thus make diploids.

Step five: Those two cells, each with twenty-three double chromosomes, will each divide again, but in the regular way. Ordinary cell division begins with duplication of each chromosome. But we already have "double" chromosomes — the X shape — because the chromosomes had made their copies at the very beginning of this meiotic process. So that duplication isn't needed. However, don't forget that these copies, or "twins," aren't twins anymore, because each of them has been subject to different crossing-over experiences and has become a unique mosaic.

In this second cell division, the X shape of the double chromosome comes apart into the two Vs, and each V (a single chromosome) goes to one end of the cell, and the cell divides. Recall that there are two cells undergoing this second division, so in the end we have *four* cells, each with a different mix of genes in it. These are the mating cells ("gametes") available for union with mating cells from another organism — which will mean still more variation in the resulting offspring. This long, complicated meiotic process is the secret of sex.[16]

Sexual Strategies

Robert Jay Russell, in *The Lemur's Legacy: The Evolution of Power, Sex, and Love,* points out that most organisms on Earth do not reproduce sexually. Bacterial reproduction, as we have seen, was rapid, and bacterial versions of gene-swapping offered opportunities for considerable variation. But, besides them, says Russell, "There are literally dozens of kinds of reproduction which are neither asexual nor fully sexual.... Some fish and reptiles are hermaphroditic (both genders alternate in the same individual); some reptiles and amphibians are capable of virgin birth (parthenogenesis)."[17]

Christian de Duve remarks that, for many organisms, as long as things are going well, the organism stays with its routine vegetative functions, simply copying a satisfactory genome. But if there is an environmental crisis, it abruptly resorts to sexual reproduction in a search for a genetic combination that will meet the adaptive challenge.[18]

And this, of course, is the advantage of sex. There is such enormous variation from one generation of mating practice in a population that a whole "space" of possibilities can be "searched" (almost every combination tried) and thereby *something* that can adapt be found.[19]

The earliest practice of sexual reproduction did not yet involve what is called "dimorphism," distinct males and females. There were just loose haploid cells looking for mates. But then a series of things happened. One of the first things needed was a way to prevent haploids from the same clone of cells from mating with each other and thus defeating the whole purpose of meiosis. Also, interspecies fusion was not a good idea because different species had usually had to adapt to different environmental situations and so did not have much to offer one another that would be relevant.

But in order for fusion to occur, there had to be surface molecules on the cell membranes that facilitated this operation. If these were of different types, capable of fitting together with an unlike type but not with a like type, then useless matings could be prevented. This was the beginning of "mating types." We are used to only two types, but paramecia (a species of one-celled microbe) have eight different sexes, and some fungi (e.g., Schizophylum commune, roadside mushroom), can have as many as seventy-eight thousand![20]

The next step was to recognize possible mating partners. A haploid cell released a bit of protein, and if another had a receptor for it (which means they fit together chemically), then the cells moved together and synchronized their cell cycles (the circle of events from duplication of DNA through the phases of cell division) so that when they fused the chromosomes would be in step with one another.

Finally, the mating types began to specialize along the lines of distinct reproductive strategies. One strategy was to emphasize the basic life process of a diploid cell: make a haploid that has other things that a new cell needs besides the information on the chromosome — store up some food for the new diploid — and be able to divide rapidly (by mitosis, regular cell division) as soon as fusion has taken place. This strategy characterizes maternal cells. Comparatively few of them are made because each is a large investment of energy. The other strategy is to make a very large number of haploid cells carrying nothing but DNA information and to make them motile so that they can mate with many other haploids. These are paternal cells. Paternal genes have more chances of scattering themselves broadly; maternal genes have a higher probability of surviving. If the two strategies are combined, the species has the best chance of adapting.[21]

Selection and Adaptation

Evolution walks on two feet: variation and selection. Variation gives living beings different ways of interacting with their environments. Selection picks out the better ways. Variation shows us the importance of error, randomness, and chance. Selection shows us the importance of death.

If there is to be a finite world that *grows,* one that develops and becomes more complex, more diversified, more interactive, and therefore more unified, and eventually more *conscious,* then it has to include chance, error, death, and pain. I think it is important that we see this and understand it. Otherwise, we may continue believing that these are "bad" things that "ought not" to be here, things that are "contrary to God's plan."

Of course, a universe that was merely *created,* built by someone else from the outside, the way one would make a machine, could be totally planned and then constructed according to the plan and wouldn't need means for correcting itself, for gaining information about its environment and finding new ways to interact. But it would not image its Creator by being creative.

A finite universe that is creative, that grows from the inside, following its own natural principles, has to start from a few comparatively simple natures (particles/fields) and build up its variety and complexity by intrinsic attraction and repulsion. In the beginning it doesn't have the capacity for "planning." Planning itself emerges, far down the line, from the interactions of previous interactions. We will look at this in the next chapter, on consciousness. Decision-making, free choice — let alone spontaneous creativity — are elaborations of more primitive acts of construction and selection.

But a *creative* universe has the capacity to become complex, living, sensing, and conscious by the compounding of its own natural tendencies, something far greater than the made-from-the-outside merely created world could ever be. A Creator who is really to be fulfilled as a creator who undertakes to make a self-image must make something that includes the note of creative capacity itself. This is the kind of universe we have.

And a universe like this has to grow by variation and selection. Variation without "outside" planning requires randomness (a pool of possibilities) and chance unions. If these unions are to become more complex (have more interactions of more different kinds and thereby produce interdependent unions), there must be some means of selecting among them. This means is the interaction of the variants with their environments, the different variations having different interactions which in turn affect the reproductive success of the variants. Selection, unlike variation — which takes place at the level of the genes (in the genotype) — takes place at the level of the whole expressed and developed organism (the phenotype) in its interaction with its environment. The environment is multifaceted; the interaction is ecological. We might speak of it as a "community" event or process. Reshuffling the genes, by mutation, error, crossover, and other devices, we might call "creative" work. And we might say that variation proposes and selection disposes. But both the creative aspect and the community aspect can be seen as images of trinitarian/incarnational Being.

Evolution is a history and a memory. The way the genes are organized and the way they respond to mutation-causing influences have themselves been shaped by evolutionary forces. When a certain type of evolutionary problem is solved, the genome, so to speak, "remembers" how to do it: that is, the genes that did it are preserved and inherited, and thus the same method is available next time.

Christopher Wills says that the genome accumulates "wisdom," which reduces the time required for the solution of similar problems when they arise again. A genome that becomes adroit at coping with challenging changes in its environment by responding promptly will survive in larger numbers than those that cannot. But a very special part of a genome's environment is its mutation-causing agents, which, according to Wills, co-evolve with the genes in such a way as to facilitate evolution itself. For, rather than being dependent on outside events providing suitable mutagenic agents, the very best way would be for the organism to make its own. Better mutations may be made by better mutagenic agents.

The most delicate and specific mutagenic agents are chemical molecules that can turn the genes on or off for transcription — the promoters and regulators we mentioned a bit earlier — and the enzymes that can cut out and rearrange particular portions of the DNA. We'll see some application of this in the "gene wars" and in modular units for rapid assembly. Genomes that can do these tricks will go places because the time required for the appearance of a useful gene will be considerably reduced.

Mutation won't be so much a matter of chance anymore. We will have a kind of symbiosis of the genome and the mutation-causing factors, and since this interaction is itself subject to selection pressures, the symbiosis itself will evolve in the direction of facilitating favorable mutations.[22] The self-making universe is getting a handle on how to make itself make itself better.

We need to notice that the very finitude of the material universe is the source of the selective pressure. In any local region there is only so much of the resources needed to make up the living organisms. They require space and protection, energy (light, heat), food, raw material for building their bodies and sometimes their homes. There isn't an endless supply of these things, and therefore at some point there isn't enough to go around. Those who succeed in getting what they need will survive. Those who don't, won't.

This is how the differential is worked. It isn't just a question of either living or not living, but a question of what proportion of the relevant population (those who are competing for the same resources) one's genetic line commands. Many factors enter into this competition for reproductive success. Merely living long is not sufficient. Organisms must be able to produce quickly large numbers of fertile offspring capable of adjusting to some range of possible changes in the environment, capable of obtaining protective habitat, food, and mates, and capable of defending against predators, including diseases. In general, the middle way favored by "stabilizing selection" succeeds best — don't go to extremes.

At least, this is so while the environment is relatively stable. When a change occurs, nonaverage individuals may be more successful and the new mean will lie in their midst in a few generations. This is called "directional selection." Or two different ways of coping may be equally successful but a compromise between them less successful. This is called "disruptive selection." It starts distinct lineages. Then each of them must seek to adapt to its particular environment.

Adaptation to the environment is a matter of finding a suitable "niche." That means a location and a mode of gaining a living and a strategy of reproduction that enable the lineage to continue. An environment rich in resources will have many niches. A population that is able to diversify a great deal will create new niches, even in an environment that is challenging. Organisms also have niches in the sense that they fulfill certain functions in an ecological community, such being food for others, or being predators and keeping down other populations, or (if bacteria) breaking down large molecules to help digestion or to return nutrients to the soil, or (if trees) providing shade and habitations, and so on. An organism is its interactive behavior, both within its own body and in its environment and community.

Niches are found by species rather than by individuals. A "species" is an interbreeding population. It may undergo directional selection and gradually turn into something rather different, or it may split into several distinct new species. The latter move is called "speciation" and is the source of creative diversity. Splitting into different species means that members of the distinct species cannot breed with one another; they are reproductively isolated. It doesn't necessarily take much to become isolated. Any mutation that interferes with any step in the reproductive path to a fertile hybrid between two lines can effectively isolate them from one another and constitute them distinct species.[23] Notice that it is not merely a question of having offspring but of having offspring who can in turn have offspring. Success in adaptation means having grandchildren.

Species can also become extinct. Sometimes this happens because the environment changes and the species can't change to fit into it. Climate changes, a new predator, loss of food resource, disease, can all contribute to extinction.[24] In addition, there are dramatic large-scale extinctions that wipe out many species at once. There have been five such global mass extinctions so far, at intervals of hundreds of millions of years, the most recent being the Cretaceous, 66 million years ago, and the worst being the Permian, 245 million years ago, when from 77 to 96 percent of all marine animal species disappeared. If marine animals are a reliable gauge for the whole planet, higher forms of life here very nearly lost it. What caused these events? Comets and meteorites have been suggested, as well as volcanic eruptions, all having the effect of blotting out sunlight by dust in the atmosphere. But these connections have not been proved. More likely are long-term climate changes, cooling, glaciation, itself caused perhaps by continental drift toward the poles.[25]

But what is especially interesting for us at this point in our discussion is the way life recovered after of each of these disasters. In each instance the living planet recovered to at least its previous level of diversity, but it took tens of millions of years. We should not conclude that Earth has some magical Providence looking after it on which we can unconditionally rely for protection. The near misses should rather make us alert to protect life ourselves. Many scientists believe that we are even now entering a period of mass extinction, brought on mainly by the expanding populations of human beings and our activities.[26] Nevertheless, the creative power of life and of evolution show in the fact that the planet has so far recovered each time with innovations and increased diversity. If we ourselves provide the innovations on this occasion, life, diversity, challenge, and innovation can all flourish.

Endless Innovation and the Gene Wars

A very early step that made innovation much easier in higher animals was "body duplication." You may remember that stringing copies of the same or similar things together is a fundamental strategy in nature. Carbon atoms, nucleotides, amino acids. Then there's duplicating chromosomes. Now we have copying a whole (simple) animal, so that we get what looks like a kind of segmented worm. Each segment is a complete organism, with alimentary, circulatory, reproductive, and other equipment. The segments are linked by joining their skins, alimentary canals, blood vessels, and nerve cords.

And with copying, there came the possibility of introducing a new level of variation. Each segment had its genes for making itself, of course. But now it also had a new set of genes which didn't code for making the body; they coded for making certain proteins which in turn could switch the body-genes on or off. These are the regulatory genes mentioned earlier. They could, for instance, put in an order for a duplication of the body segment, and the whole transcription would start over again and clone the segment. But then these regulatory genes underwent mutation — different mutations in different segments — and so the body segments came out somewhat different. A further layer of differentiation.

Christian de Duve says that "segmentation represents a major mechanism of evolutionary diversification, perhaps the most important one in the history of life. It initiated an extraordinary combinatorial game involving complete, originally viable modules that could be mutated, fused, reduplicated, deleted, and otherwise reshuffled, all by the magic stroke of single or sparse genetic modifications."[27] By enabling one small change (in a regulatory gene) to initiate a large change in body construction, significant branchings became readily possible. An ancestor could continue with its traditional body plan while its offspring, governed by the mutated regulatory gene, produced a variation that constituted a new species. In this way original single-celled organisms gave rise to worms, shellfish, insects, and eventually vertebrates.[28]

The regulatory genes themselves are marked by the interesting fact that they include a special sequence of about 180 base pairs that are highly conserved, that are the same in all of them, although the rest of their sequences can be quite different. The conserved sequence, called the "homeobox" because it is "homo" (the same) in all, codes for 60 amino acids carefully shaped to bind to DNA and thus control its untwining and being transcribed, that is, its being "expressed." Homeobox-containing genes have been found in worms, sea urchins, chickens, mice, and humans, in all of whom they seem to play a fundamental role in development. Development means the building of body parts according to the genetic information encoded in the DNA. The regulatory genes control sizes and shapes as well as positions of various features, such as limbs with their digits, or wings or antennae, or heads or tails, by turning the appropriate genes on and then off. Cell differentiation into so many different tissues, all from one single fertilized egg, is one of the marvels of life, but position seems to be the key to it, and regulatory genes the markers of position. As cells multiply, they develop different features by expressing different genes according to where they are located, that is, their position. If a cell has information as to its position in the developing organism and as to what genes to turn on in that position, it can carry on. And this information comes from the order of the homeobox genes, the order of the genes on the chromosome corresponding to the order of expression in the embryo, the same head-to-tail order in creatures as different as a fly and a mouse.[29]

Turning genes on and off, together with mutations, can have interesting applications. Consider the way selection acts on predators and their prey, favoring predators that are better at finding, catching, and eating their prey, but favoring prey who can avoid being found, caught, eaten. The two populations engage in "gene wars." Predators improve: their vision, hearing, sense of smell, speed of movement, accuracy of aim, means of catching (claws, teeth, tongues); their means of killing (stabbing, poisoning, suffocating, electrocuting) or paralyzing and preserving (injecting chemicals, wrapping in webs); their ability to swallow whole (dislocating the jaw), ability to chew, ability to digest (which may entail harboring other organisms as parasites in oneself!). Prey develop ways to hide, run away, reproduce in huge numbers, distract attackers, post sentinels, give alarms, prepare escape routes; ways to taste bad (or look as if they do) or to be hard to eat (full of spines) or poisonous. Both parties develop social behaviors favoring their cause, effectively cooperating and caring for their own. As each population achieves some advance, the other undergoes selection for a means to counter it. Thus they shape one another, or "co-evolve."[30]

Another way of making use of another species to one's own advantage is biological symbiosis. I've been using the word analogously; this is where it comes from, meaning "the intimate association of two or more species." There are three types. Parasitism exists when one species makes use of — usually eats — a host but doesn't kill it; the parasite benefits, the host is harmed. "Commensals" (who eat at the same table) live on the bodies or in the homes of other species but neither harm nor help them. And the third type of symbiosis is "mutualism," wherein both parties benefit by their association.

Mutualism is what most of us think of when we talk about symbiosis. It is the strongest bond across species lines, forming interdependent communities that behave as integrated organisms. An example is trees, termites, bacteria: dead trees are eaten — that is, bitten and chewed — by termites; but the termites can't digest the cellulose. Digestion is carried out by bacteria living in the guts of the termites. The bacteria benefit by having their food presented already chewed (they have no way to harvest it); the termites benefit by having their food digested (made water soluble so it can be carried into their cells). Even the broken up tree replenishes the soil, which grows more trees, and the methane released by the termite/bacteria combine has important effects in the atmosphere, keeping the whole planet fit for life.[31]

Another important example is the plant-fungus partnership whereby a plant shelters (allows to live in or on its roots) a fungus and feeds it with the carbohydrates the plant makes, in return for the fungus's supplying the plant with minerals concentrated from the soil. Almost all life on land depends on such a relationship; without it the colonization of the land from the sea probably could not have been accomplished. In the sea coral reefs are fundamental to larger communities of marine organisms, but they could not be built by the coral polyps without the energy supplied by the algae that the polyps harbor and feed.[32]

A favorite example of mutualistic co-evolution is the pollination of flowering plants by insects who are fed by their nectar. Successive selections may even shape them to match each other better and better until the species become absolutely dependent on one another, the insect's body shaped exactly to fit into the flower's bell.

Insects also relate to plants by resembling them, looking like twigs, leaves, thorns, bark. Sometimes the color of a butterfly will change from green to brown to match the changing leaves. There is a case of moths in England changing from a pale color to match lichen-covered trees to quite dark to match soot deposits as the industrial revolution progressed.

Color can also be used as a warning sign; poisonous or unpalatable animals may exhibit bright colors to discourage predators. And then an interesting thing happens: tasty, nonpoisonous animals evolve to mimic the truly uneatable ones. This is a disadvantage to the model because in time the predators will learn that the warning signal doesn't mean what it says and will start to eat both the mimics and the models. So the models have a tendency to evolve some change in warning sign to distance themselves from the mimics. But then the mimics catch up with them again. The gene wars are on once more.[33]

Notice that mimicry, like camouflage, is a matter of deception — lying, if you will — and nature rewards it. By employing it, the organism escapes destruction and lives to reproduce the genes that code for that particular trick. Predators also disguise themselves, wearing striped skins to blend in with the tall grass, or appearing as harmless rocks on the tidal sea floor. Other forms of deception, trickery, and cheating occur, such as the parent bird acting wounded to distract a predator away from a nest, or such as the cuckoo laying eggs in another species' nest, where its offspring will destroy the rightful residents and deceive the parents into rearing it. Genes for doing this sort of thing are selected for, they are successful, and they are passed on. When we trace the natural history of what we call "evil," we will need to recall this.

Since success in life depends on a three-way fit among the genotype, the phenotype, and the environment, another thing that helps is gaining some control over the environment, and living organisms have done this from the very beginning. In fact, alteration of the environment in such a way as to favor the alterer is almost a definition of life.

Richard Dawkins has developed a theory which he calls "the extended phenotype," in which he argues that "phenotypic expression" of genes can include characteristics outside the particular cell in which the gene sits and even outside the body in which the gene's cell resides.

An example of this is the way social animals — e.g., bees or termites — work together to benefit all. Each individual is stimulated by the others to perform a particular task which is integrated into the whole. But that means that each individual must have genes for producing whatever it is that stimulates the others and also have genes for reacting to stimulation from the others. Dawkins remarks that this is suggestive of the way differentiating cells stimulate one another during embryonic development. In development, the embryo is the phenotype produced by cooperative action of genes affecting activities outside their immediate cells. Among the termites, the termitary, the big earthen house (several feet high, with ingenious arrangements for ventilation and air conditioning) is the "extended phenotypic" product of the cooperative action of genes affecting activities outside their immediate bodies.

A beaver dam would be another example of a shared phenotype, or result of shared genetic programming. The programming has to include not only how to cut down trees and drag them to the stream and secure them with mud, and so on, but how to relate to the other workers and how to resolve differences in case some workers are programmed to build to one height and others to another. Both the behaviors and the dam itself are extended phenotypes of the individuals' genes, according to Dawkins. Beaver families who can work together to build good dams will be favored by natural selection over beaver families who can't.

But every living thing has to live in an ecological community and will succeed only to the extent that its genes do shape it to adapt to the structures and behaviors of the other entities in that ecosystem. Each of them will be shaping and reshaping to adjust to the others and to influence them to adjust to it. That is to say, the way one organism's genes make it will have an effect on the way other organisms' genes make *them*. Dawkins concludes that

> in theory, genetic action at a distance could include almost all inter-actions between individuals of the same or different species. Just as every gene is the centre of a radiating field of influence on the world, so every phenotypic character is the centre of converging influences from many genes, both within and outside the body of the individual organism. The living world can be seen as a network of interlocking fields of replicator power.[34]

The way of evolving has evolved again, we may say, because the con-trolling information has extended itself beyond controlling the structure and behavior of its own immediate body to the bodies and behaviors of others. And always the symbiosis, the networking, the interlocking, the community aspect increases. It becomes more extensive, more complex, more necessary, and more immanent. It comes more and more under the direction of the parties to the community.

Modular Assembly, Junk DNA, and Toolboxes

Sometimes we look at a complicated animal and think how incredi-ble it is that such a combination of small parts (all the way down to atoms) could come together by chance in such a functional way. The improbability is so astronomical that some outside cause must be in-voked to account for it. But by this point in our tracing of the history of the universe we are beginning to see that it isn't all a matter of chance and improbability. There is a random pool of possibilities, but what is drawn from that pool is always something that will fit in with what has already been assembled. As Christian de Duve says, "At each stage, *evo-lution can work only with the materials that have survived from earlier trials....* As evolution proceeds in a given direction, the range of avail-able choices narrows, and its commitment becomes increasingly focused and irreversible."[35]

This historical development, or building on the past, takes place by modular assembly. We saw this happening with molecules put together from previously assembled units, cycles organized from self-assembling large polymers such as RNA and protein, hypercycles of cycles, eukaryotes as symbioses of prokaryotes, multicellular organisms composed of unicellulars, whole body duplications followed by variation. The same sort of principle applies to the assembly of genes. Minigenes can be combined into large genes. But there is a finite number of ways in which such combinations can be made. In a large population every one of these possibilities can be tried, and the ones that work with the environment will survive and replicate. The better replicators will edge out the poorer ones. That is natural selection, and it means that the role of chance is still further reduced. In every generation every organism that is not prevented from reproducing will reproduce, or, put in terms of genes, unless a gene is so destructive that it prevents its carrier from reproducing, it will continue to be carried.

DNA sequences that are "expressed" (translated into proteins) are called "exons." But eukaryotic DNA includes sequences that do not express, may not be codes. These are called "introns" and have a usefulness of their own. Although at transcription the introns are excised and the exons spliced together, all this extra intron DNA, called "junk DNA," has been increasing in proportion to the coding sequences as we go up the evolutionary ladder. In humans less than 5 percent of the DNA codes. Maybe the "junk" just accumulates because it isn't worth the trouble to get rid of it. Or maybe it's available (like key blanks) for future coding.

One thing that introns do now is interpose themselves between exons, thus dividing genes into minigenes. The minigenes, or exons, become modular building blocks for assembling a variety of genes. Having introns that function this way has evidently been conferring some advantage, because it has continued and increased. The advantage would seem to be yet another way of gaining variation by reshuffling the components of genes within the genome itself. Even without sexual crossing-over, new mosaic genes can be constructed. An especially useful exon can be copied and inserted into many different genes, like a basic ingredient in a recipe with a number of variations.

If you look at proteins, you see that they in turn are constructed from modular units called "domains." The function of proteins is such that certain tasks, such as binding to a certain kind of molecule, have to be performed in each of many cases: something basic has to be done, and then some variable task is added. The basic function is performed by one domain and the variable one by another. So it would be convenient if the portion of the gene for the basic function could be kept separate and used over again. This is what intron spacing of distinct coding sequences accomplishes. A new protein can thus be assembled without having to start from scratch. Any parts that are to be used again can be coded for by their appropriate exons and only the really new part has to have a new exon to be inserted in the total gene. Also, different proteins can be assembled by simply making different combinations or different arrangements of existing exons for existing domains. Ready-made units are available and modular assembly can take place quickly, thanks to the introns, the regulatory genes, and the splicing apparatus.

Christopher Wills likens the basic repeated domain of a protein to the handle of a set of snap-on tools and sets of tools to the contents of a toolbox. Evolution selects in favor of good toolboxes. An example of how effective the toolbox and its snap-on tools can be is our own immune system. Humans can synthesize more than a million different antibodies, targeting distinct antigens. If we had to have a separate gene for each kind of antibody, we would use up a lot of our DNA on antibodies alone. But with the help of the toolbox we can make up antibodies by using only a few genes to code for products that pass through several combinatorial processes.

Because this is an especially impressive example of the self-creating capacity of the organized cosmos, it is interesting to look at it in a brief outline. (It is, like most biology, much more complex than this.) One of the things the immune system does is protect the body against disease — invading pathogens, which cause specific diseases, or more generally antigens, that is, any protein or carbohydrate that provokes the immune response, including allergic reactions and auto-immune illnesses.

The antigen is a molecule and it is met by another molecule called an antibody. The antibody has been secreted by cells called "plasma cells." They have been derived from B lymphocytes, found in lymph nodes and spleen, and ultimately descended from "stem cells" in the bone (hence B) marrow.

These B cells have a unique feature: their genomes can be rearranged in very specific ways so that they will synthesize particular antibodies — another example of "self-making." Each B cell genome starts out with a few hundred different DNA sequences for making parts of antibodies. Only one sequence can be used for each part. There are about a dozen parts. That's a lot of choice and a huge number of different combinations can be made. Each B cell makes one combination of choices. That commits it to synthesizing that particular antibody. But the B cells each make different choices and different combinations, so that among them all, the B cells can concoct an antibody for just about any strange molecule they are apt to meet.

Stimulating the committed B cell to begin secreting its antibody in volume is another operation. We don't want to invest in mass production of an antibody until we know that it is the right one for a particular invading antigen. This determination is made by a "consultation" among the B cell, a "macrophage" (large cell that eats unwanted matter), and a T cell (from the thymus gland). Each of these three cells has receptors on its surface for recognizing some part of the antigen. The three of them can link together by sharing antigens among them, the T cell and the B cell sharing by binding to different parts of the antigen, and the macrophage, able to hold both parts of the antigen, linking with the T cell through one part and with the B cell through the other part.

If the B cell is offering the right antibody for this antigen, the three cells will be able to make this link-up. And when they are so linked, they will begin to secrete various chemicals that stimulate one another to further operations. In particular, they all secrete factors that stimulate the B cell to differentiate into a "plasma cell" and devote itself to manufacturing and dispensing the specific antibodies for this antigen. And the T cell produces "inducing molecules" that incite the macrophage to synthesize the right digestive enzymes for consuming the antigen after the B cell's antibodies have bound and neutralized it. It's a cooperative operation, based on a kind of chemical "conversation" by which one cell can induce certain behaviors in other cells.

This process takes a little time and works by its own version of natural selection. Only those B cells that have the right antibody are able to make the link-ups and thus be stimulated to production. But more B cells are constantly being sent out into the world from the stem cells, and some of these will happen to make the right combination of gene modules for manufacturing the needed antibody. All those that do will be "selected" for engaging in production. Those that don't will be recycled. Gradually we will acquire a sufficient quantity of right antibody producers to cope with the invading antigens. Adapting to the antigen is like adapting to the environment. Eventually you get a good "fit."[36] The system is extremely flexible at minimum expense and can create a huge repertoire of response capabilities from a modest outlay of initial variants.

The success of the immune system is due in large part to the general practice of splicing exons. It seems that perhaps no more than about seven thousand exons may be enough to make up all the known eukaryotic genes. And this shows that obtaining order, good order, meaningful and creative order, from the random pool of possibilities — by interaction with the environment and interaction within the genome — is entirely possible by the very laws of probability, not improbable at all. At any stage of modular assembly, the entire space of possible combinations can be assembled and exposed to selection pressures.[37]

Edward O. Wilson, in summing up the power of evolution to be self-creative, points out the vast array of variations and the speed with which natural selection can act — a dominant gene with a little head start can crowd out its recessive alternative in twenty generations, or if the advantage of the winning gene is total, the contest can be settled in a single generation. He then focuses on the probability issue and the argument that putting together anything living is too improbable. He proposes this answer: Suppose a new trait emerges if two mutations on different chromosome sites occur simultaneously. If each has a probability of one in a million, the probability of both together is a trillion, impossible. But suppose that one of these mutations, by itself, confers an advantage. Even if slight, this advantage will cause its carriers to prevail in the population. Since it is now established, it is a question only of obtaining the other mutation. And its probability is one in a million. But populations are often of more than a million, so the appearance of the mutation is a virtual certainty.[38]

Any one mutation may cause profound effects, such as the shape of a skull or the length of lifespan. Murray Gell-Mann points out that sometimes a small change can set off a cascade of effects not only in its own species but in others that then have to cope with the new situation. A single change might open a gateway, say on the biochemical level, so that a whole new realm of possibilities appears. But in every case the changes can work only on "what is already present. Nothing is invented out of whole cloth."[39] Stuart Kauffman argues that selection can operate only on preexisting order, on what has self-assembled, and that it must be limited to a restricted space of possibilities if it is to succeed. The space within which selection is to work must itself be selected for. Building up complexity by the modular mode answers to these conditions. This is how "evolution" works, and "evolvability itself is a triumph."

But, given that this is how it works, then our own appearance in the universe is neither strange nor miraculous, says Kauffman. We have emerged in the usual way, not ad hoc, not by accident, not "merely tinkered together," but another instance of "the robust, self-organized, and emergent properties of the way the world works." So we are to be expected. We belong to this universe.[40] Christian de Duve says that "To [Jacques] Monod's famous sentence 'The universe was not pregnant with life, nor the biosphere with man,' I reply: 'You are wrong. They were.'... My reading of the same facts is different. It gives chance the same role, but acting within such a stringent set of constraints as to produce life and mind obligatorily, not once but many times."[41]

Gell-Mann supports this last contention:

Astronomers and planetary scientists are not aware of any reason why planetary systems should be especially rare in our galaxy or in other similar galaxies elsewhere in the universe. Nor have theorists of the origin of life come up with anything so remarkable about the conditions on our own planet some four billion years ago that the origin of life (or something like life) on a planet would be a particularly improbable event. It is likely that complex adaptive systems abound in the universe and that a great many of them have evolved or will evolve intelligence.[42]

Chapter Eight

THE SELF-CREATING UNIVERSE: PATHWAY TO CONSCIOUSNESS

 LET US PAUSE HERE before our "final assault on the summit" to survey what we have discussed so far, the theological and philosophical suggestions and the scientific descriptions and explanations that can be appended to them. The basic idea is that the universe is "God's ecstasy," that is, a making manifest of the unmanifest, a finite "exegesis" (John 1:18) of the infinite. The bond between the absolute, infinite, formless, unmanifest on the one hand and the relative, finite, formed, manifest on the other hand is not causal, not interventionary, and not explanatory. It is, rather, incarnational, self-presencing, and self-expressing.

The infinite cannot be a member of the causal order of the finite; it cannot act as one agency among others to intervene in the natural order; and it cannot serve as an explanation of why or how the natural order is the way it is. Anything that acts as a cause in the finite order must itself be a finite agent. Anything that can serve as an "explanation" for an item in the finite order must itself be described in finite terms. We probably don't realize that we would be finitizing the infinite to try to relate it to the finite as something the latter "needs" as a cause or an explanation. But once attention is called to that, it is fairly obvious.

It also becomes clear that such a "need" relation is poor, superficial, and naive compared with the depth and intimacy of the incarnation metaphor. If the Reality is truly, wholly, and thoroughly "God" and truly, wholly, and thoroughly "cosmos," as the incarnational formula says, then we have the possibility of a theology of the cosmos that is believable, congenial to our other ways of studying and relating to the world, and inspiring, revelatory, and meaningful.[1] "Incarnation" itself is not in service to any other goal. It is the Reality, the Whole Reality. It is because it is, in itself and for itself. That is the overall thesis.

The second point is that the infinite is in its own terms a community of interactive members, united by self-sharing. "Symbiosis" is a fundamental fact of Being. These same qualities therefore appear also in the finite reality: it is one, it is many, it is community, it is united by inter-action, it manifests symbiosis. In addition, the finite is characterized by process, by evolution. Evolution itself works by interaction, making new wholes of the union of previous wholes. This compounding creates new entities, new relations, new behaviors, and new abilities to create yet further compounds of interactivity. This is the "self-creating" aspect of the universe.

I said earlier that if we see the universe as derived from or intimately related to the infinite, and if we conceive that infinite as Creator, then the universe also must be creative, since things made must resemble their makers in some deep way.[2] But now, perhaps, we can say something a little better: just as the Whole Reality is both the infinite and the fi-nite — is the Incarnation — even so the Whole Reality is the Creator, self-creating in the finite by an act of ecstasy on the part of the infi-nite. Or, we can say that the finite is the ecstatic aspect of the infinite's interior enstatic aspect. Or, we can simply say that the Reality can be ex-perienced by us under these two aspects, which are in themselves united in the Incarnation.

The third point is seeing how the metaphysical characters — being one, being many, being interactive, self-sharing, making new wholes, compounding, being more, being in every possible way — are actually played out at successive levels of the cosmic reality and seeing how the universe does (according to our current scientific understanding) liter-ally "create itself." The outstanding instances of this that we walked through were the cosmological inflation in which matter and radiation appeared, the formation of the enclosed chemical hypercycle in which life appeared, together with life's own ways of creating further forms of living, even further methods of generating variation and ways of changing forms, behaviors, and information exchange.

Now we are going to look at the emergence of biologically based consciousness from the complex interactions of living cells and their chemical creations. Many of the same ways will be repeated: make many copies of the same thing; combine these in various ways; let those that can sustain themselves in their environment make more copies of them-selves; try all (or many) possibilities; use order, sequence, and variations in sequence. Let groups and sequences act as whole units. Compound these. Repeat.

The fourth point is to watch for some of those things that we humans tend to consider negatives, faulty, undesirable. See what their remote be-ginnings are, how they develop. Things such as competition, crowding out, death, pain, deception, domination. Ask whether they could have been avoided — how? Remember the nature of finitude and the nature of self-evolving, growing from the inside out, without prior planning and control from some outside position. Also, of course, watch for the beginnings and development of what we consider the good things: sharing, love, cooperation, pleasure, beauty, meaning, creativity.

The appeal of the incarnation metaphor may become stronger as we approach human consciousness and the puzzles of trying to account for our interior experience of ourselves as conscious in terms of movements of molecules and interactions of cells. But before getting into how the brain operates and the deeper mysteries of consciousness, let us consider first the biological usefulness of sensation.

The Value of Sensation

Consciousness has to do with the processing of information, and the information is obtained by communication. Probably the real starting point of the pathway to consciousness would be the fundamental forces themselves, the primordial channels of communication. Certainly communication is going on in the chemical world, which operates by the electromagnetic force. This is continued and greatly elaborated in the biological order. Even a single cell, if it is motile, will become capable of moving toward a favorable environment and away from an unfavorable one. Sometimes this will be a matter of salinity or acidity, sometimes a matter of light or temperature. The molecules on the surface of the cell will be able to react to the environment, and the cell will move in a favorable direction, following a "gradient," an increase of the favorable condition.[3]

The most primitive sensing mechanism works this way: A molecule stretches through the cell membrane, part of it inside, part outside. The outside part binds with some approaching molecule. This causes the inside part to react in some special way. Suppose the approaching molecule is something the cell normally takes in but can get too much of. If the sensing molecule closes the admitting pore when its outside part is bound, the intake will be moderated. The switch, or trigger, can initiate various operations this way: taking in food, shutting out danger, prompting cell division, stimulating other chemical reactions inside the cell. We saw these things going on in the immune system.

If the molecules that bind to the receptor on the outside are produced by another cell, that other cell has a way of influencing events in the receiving cell. This is communication. And if one of the responses the receiving cell can make is motion toward or away, then even more effective sensation has been achieved.

This is how sensation, the minimal form of consciousness, starts. Detect the resource you need to stay alive. Food "smells" good. Moving toward and moving away are the beginning of "good" and "evil" as categories of judgment. "Good" is that toward which we move, and "evil" is that from which we move away. Decisive action starts here, too. Creatures who make poor decisions leave fewer progeny.

Since leaving progeny is the name of the game, gaining information about possible mates — species, location, readiness — is important. This too is done by chemicals. Even comparatively simple and primitive organisms send out "pheromones" — scent molecules released by females (usually) to guide males to them. These are powerful molecules relative to their receptors on the males; extremely small quantities diffused in water or air will lead males to mates. This can work even if it is only the mating cells, the gametes, that are communicating and meeting. It may also happen, in a pleasing example of self-sharing and cooperation, that two mating types will synthesize the pheromone between them, passing the transforming molecules back and forth.

Chemical signals are also used for avoiding what is harmful. When a sea anemone is attacked by a slug, it draws in its tentacles, closes its mouth, and releases an alarm pheromone. This spreads through the anemone colony and other individuals close up as the signal reaches them. Repulsion, the first sign of pain and fear, is making its appearance. And deception is on the scene as well. The bolas spider makes a sticky ball of websilk suspended on a swing line. She then emits fake pheromone of a female moth. The deceived male comes flying, she swings the sticky ball at him, and there's dinner. Plants can play at this game as well. Certain orchids look and smell like female insects; males are tricked into attempting to copulate with the flower and in the process they pick up pollen, which they obligingly carry to the flower's mate.

Social domination and aggression are also made possible by sensation and communication. A queen bee can control a whole hive, suppressing maturation in workers and inhibiting the nurturing of any other queen by communicating her pheromones. Certain ants send out scouts to locate other ant nests; when they return with the information, the whole colony turns out, travels to the other nest, kills and eats many of the inhabitants, and takes the rest home as slaves. However, this talent for communication can be turned against the ant by a beetle who lurks in ambush beside the trail leading to the ants' aphid pasture. When the ants return full of sweet aphid juice, the beetle gives the code tap on the ant's head that prompts her to regurgitate a sweet drop. The beetle feeds this way until the ant realizes that she has been duped, whereupon she attacks the beetle. But he just hunkers down under his shell until she gives up in frustration.[4]

There are, of course, other kinds of stimuli for other kinds of senses: light for vision, sound for hearing, pressure for touch. Creatures can also respond to temperature and even electricity. There are various sorts of limitations on the ranges of these stimuli to which responses will be made, and variations among the different species, some being able to detect with amazing accuracy what others do not notice. Sensations are selected for if they provide the species with some advantage in fitting in with its environment. That means that receiving information is of no use unless it makes a difference in what the individual does, a difference that affects the reproductive success of the species. So a connection has to be made between incoming information about the environment and actions taken with respect to the environment. This is done by the nervous system.

The Neuron and Its Assemblies

The smallest unit of the nervous system — its "atom," for nervous system purposes — is the neuron, the nerve cell. It is composed of a cell body in the usual way, but has a great many fibers, or tendrils, branching out from it at either end. One end collects "messages"; the other end transmits them. Even a single neuron is a very complicated affair, operating by electrical polarization (collecting a charge) and depolarization along its membrane to pass a message from one end to the other, and by highly specialized chemistry to pass it on to the next cell at exchange points called "synapses" (see Fig. 10).

The neuron's input end is a forest of dendritic fibers, branching and subbranching and receiving chemical signals from other neurons through its thousands of synapses. As all this information is funneled toward the cell body, a number of factors act to process it. The cell membrane, which is allowing sodium and potassium ions to pass in and out through its pores, has a certain electrical voltage. This voltage changes according to the way the information processing is developing, and each "patch" of membrane in turn influences the patch next to it. Eventually the impulse reaches the long fiber at the other end, the axon, where the message is passed on to all the further cells with which the axon's branches communicate.[5]

Passing the message from cell to cell is done chemically. Each axon fiber ends in a tiny bulb, or button, which releases certain molecules called "neurotransmitters" into the narrow space of the "synaptic cleft"

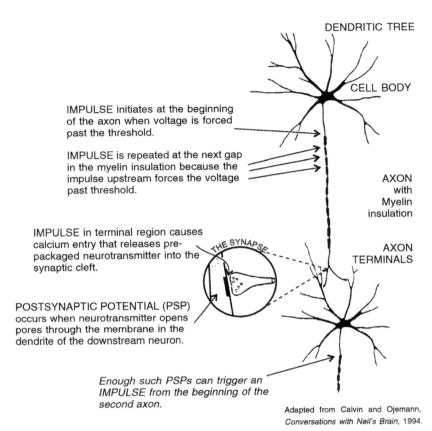

Figure 10
THE NEURON
The Functions of Its Parts

Within the figure:

DENDRITIC TREE

CELL BODY

IMPULSE initiates at the beginning of the axon when voltage is forced past the threshold.

IMPULSE is repeated at the next gap in the myelin insulation because the impulse upstream forces the voltage past threshold.

AXON with Myelin insulation

IMPULSE in terminal region causes calcium entry that releases pre-packaged neurotransmitter into the synaptic cleft.

THE SYNAPSE

AXON TERMINALS

POSTSYNAPTIC POTENTIAL (PSP) occurs when neurotransmitter opens pores through the membrane in the dendrite of the downstream neuron.

Enough such PSPs can trigger an IMPULSE from the beginning of the second axon.

Adapted from Calvin and Ojemann, *Conversations with Neil's Brain*, 1994.

between it and the receptors on the dendrite of the next cell. There are dozens of different kinds of neurotransmitters known so far, having different effects on the receptors. The "strength" of the synapse is determined by the amount of transmitter released. In general, synapses are stronger the more they are used, but there are many variations. The number of receptors on the receiving cell that can respond to a particular transmitter can vary. The speed with which the transmitting cell can reabsorb its transmitter molecules and be ready to "fire" again can vary. All this adjustability at the synapse, added to the several different kinds of processing and voltage regulation going on as the impulse passes through the cell on its way to the axon, is what enables the brain to learn, to remember, to create. Without it, the living circuitry would be as rigid as our electronic machinery's.

Recently, discoveries have been made indicating that brain neurotransmitters may reach other parts of the body and be received and have effects there. Not only that, but these other tissues — especially immune cells — may also be able to synthesize transmitter molecules and send them out. Meanwhile, hormones, which we had thought were produced only by glands, are found being produced and stored in the brain. Much of this exciting work has been done by Candace Pert and her colleagues at the National Institute of Mental Health. They have shown that there is a whole family of peptides (short strings of amino acids), maybe sixty or seventy of them, all of which interact among three major systems: the nervous system, the endocrine system, and the immune system.

These peptides include neurotransmitters, hormones, endorphins, growth factors, and other special molecules that attach to a multitude of specific receptors on the surfaces of all body cells and stimulate those cells to certain behaviors. Internal "extended phenotypes" again! Remembering the important contribution of the hormones to our emotional experiences, as well as the cognitive activity of the brain and the "identity" maintaining function of the immune system, we can say that we have here a genuine "psychosomatic" network of unifying interactivity for the entire body. It is so pervasive that Pert has declared, "I can no longer make a strong distinction between the brain and the body."[6] All this intercommunication and cooperation, sharing of energy and information, is how the living body keeps in touch with itself, spreads its news and assistance, and accounts itself one single unified being.

This is the sort of interwoven behavior that has been undergoing evolution since nervous systems and endocrine systems first appeared, adding senses, improving its intelligence and range of activity, especially among the mammals and particularly among the primates. But we are intensely interested in ourselves and how we work, so we will skip directly now to the human brain and say a little about how the neurons operate in clumps and assemblies and sequences, with a clear accent on how these operations are instances of "self-creating."

There are about two hundred billion neurons in the whole brain, thirty billion in the cerebral cortex. They each have tens of thousands of synapses with other neurons, say maybe a quadrillion synapses in the human cortex. That's a lot of intercommunication. When they stimulate one another, they behave somewhat like the small light bulbs on a message board in a stadium, says William Calvin.[7] The lights turning on together make a pattern. The pattern as a whole is intelligible. If some of the bulbs turn off and others on, the pattern can appear to move across the board. The pattern will still be the same, even if it is carried by different bulbs. Such a pattern, emerging from the connected firing of a group of neurons, is a cell assembly.

It usually takes some amount of assembling to produce anything intelligible from the raw data coming in over the sensory neurons. Each of them picks up only a very small piece of information, so quite a number have to be put together and compared in various ways in order to determine a useful response to the information. For instance, a single neuron feeling pressure on your wrist can't tell you much, but if you get enough of them reporting together, you will know it's your watchband. More complex comparing and checking out are involved if you step on a sharp tack. You might think the obvious thing to do would be to withdraw the foot from the painful contact, but you'd better make sure that your other foot is securely on the floor first! This will involve an assembly of assemblies.[8]

The concept of the cell assembly originated with Donald Hebb (*The Organization of Behavior,* 1949), who suggested that if a particular stimulus was repeated enough, firing through the same group of cells, it would lead to the development of a closed system (think of a hypercycle) capable of acting as a unit on some other such system. A sequence of such units, each activating the next, would be a "thought process." Sounds like modular structuring again, doesn't it? And like modular structuring, neural assembly units can mix and match: neurons can be members of more than one assembly, and assemblies can be members of more than one superassembly. If a significant number of members of one assembly are also members of another assembly (like interlocking directorates), cross-stimulation can occur.[9] But don't limit this operation to certain fixed cells. It's the pattern of turning one another on that's important, and the pattern can be passed to other neurons, just as the message on the light board can be passed to other light bulbs.

It may be worthwhile to say again here that emergents — these assemblies are emergents when they act as whole units in their own right, communicating with their peers, other assemblies — have their own novel properties and possibilities/customs/laws of behavior, which cannot be predicted from the properties of their components. But these new properties cannot be reductively "explained by" reference to the lower orders but are perfectly intelligible in well-ordered ways that lead to appropriate expectations on their own level of organization. As we come to more and more creative levels of organization and behavior, just what constitutes an "appropriate expectation" may have to be left more and more open, but we need not conclude that intelligibility has declined or failed. There is an intelligibility appropriate to each level; that is the point. We are not entitled to insist on the kind of intelligibility we were used to on a lower level being imposed on higher level emergents. Alwyn Scott, for instance, says, "There are at least as many hierarchical levels between the nerve fiber and the mind as between atomic physics and the nerve fiber."[10]

The emergents seem still to be coming about by evolutionary methods. The basic idea is that the brain "constructs, tests, and modifies hypotheses" about what it's perceiving, says David Layzer.[11] Some researchers think that it is the presence of this active *construction* of an assembly that indicates "consciousness." They stress that it is active, the brain taking some initiative, not merely responding passively. The brain, in its neuronal way, is "creating" a perception or an idea. And then it subjects this hypothesis about how the world is to real interaction with the world. This is the selection part of the evolutionary procedure. Modification and improvement naturally follow.

Gary Cziko, who believes we can give a good account of the world without invoking miracles, offers a refinement of the construction idea. Following the work of William T. Powers on "living control systems," he proposes that we modify and correct our behaviors as ways of controlling future perceptions. Not so much controlling the world or our interaction with it directly, but controlling our perception of it. Sensation brings news of the interaction, a perception is constructed, behavior is set in motion in accordance with that and the interaction with the environment is sensed again. The circle is so tight that both the behavior and the sensing are going on simultaneously. The control system compares the newly constructed perception with some model or ideal or desired perception and keeps amending its behavior until it gets a satisfactory match.

Where does the ideal perception come from? That's what is inherited and what is subject to evolution. Behavior itself is left free so that it can change to meet a constantly changing environment, but meet it in such a way as to obtain the desired perception. Balancing might be an example. We move in a way to keep our balance perception level, but exactly how we move depends on many things in the environment. The capacity to shape up such controlling ideals and to nest them so that they form systems within systems is what evolves and becomes more elaborate by adding what Alwyn Scott called "hierarchical levels," levels of compounded emergents.

The interesting thing, for Powers and Cziko, is that the whole system (let us say nervous-endocrine-immune) is evolving in terms of what it experiences; it is selecting methods of organizing what is perceived.

The nested control systems do not tell the subsystems what to do but what to perceive. Anything they can do to bring that about will be acceptable. Notice that this reference point originates within the organism. The cycle of interaction with the environment starts from it and returns to it. We might say, in our familiar language, that the reference point is what the organism is trying to achieve. Something like what we call "purpose" or "goal." Something to measure against.

The nested control systems can also select and winnow subsystems in terms of whether they conform to the reference point of the supersystem. Remember the thumbtack we did not withdraw from because our other foot wasn't on the floor. Particular perceptions have to be in service to more overall systems of sensing well-being.[12] At this point we might begin to put some human words on these systemic operations. If the reference ideal is "purpose," we may recognize matching it (or even progressing toward matching it?) as "pleasure," and failing to match it as "pain." Notice, of course, that the perception "pain" is highly useful in this scheme of bringing the organism into a favorable state.

The actively constructed nested assemblies/systems idea helps us to understand such everyday experiences as learning, remembering, and planning. Learning to read can be an example, says Scott. First we have to perceive the distinct natures of the letters, not confuse P with F; that takes a certain assembly. Then we learn how to see the letters together as words (new hierarchical level) by igniting an assembly of the assemblies of the letters. This new unit of operation in turn enters a larger assembly of words that form phases and sentences. Remembering works the same way. We recall an experience by reconstructing it, getting the assembly of assemblies of assemblies — whatever level is needed — or the interlocking of elements from various subassemblies, to light up all together. (Sometimes it doesn't come out exactly the same, precisely because we are not simply retrieving something from cold storage but actively recreating it.) Memories stored in terms of nested assemblies are not so easily lost or damaged as if they had been put in some particular structure and location. And since it is the *pattern* of group stimulation that is the memory, it is not dependent on any particular cells to recall it; quite different cells might be involved in shaping up the same pattern. Nested assembly memory is said to be "robust." It can survive physical damage, it minimizes losses, it can rebuild itself.

Notice that once we have learned certain words, we never have to go back to spelling them out letter by letter as when we are in the process of learning. We build up an inventory of learned words and then use them in the next level of learning. Similarly with whole phrases and later with ideas. This is the same method we saw at work with the exons composing genes, the antibodies put together from preexisting subunits — the toolbox of snap-ons, the modular assembly that saves so much time, trouble, energy, and error, and gives such flexibility and variety. Relatively few things, thanks to the mathematical laws of *combination*, give us an extraordinary assortment of a great many things. The behavior of interest shifts to the higher levels of assembly where the assortment of components lies ready to hand and new combinations can be created very quickly, without any need to go all the way back down to "scratch" and expect to put together what is needed by random accidents. Because we do it step by hierarchical step, we never face the high improbability of sorting out and pasting together the enormous number of items on the lowest level.[13] Reaching the higher levels of arrangement is probable, not improbable, and even accelerates, as we see in technological civilization as well as in individual learning.

With learning and memory in place, planning becomes possible. It is a kind of looking at a possible past: if we had this memory, would that be good? If not, how can we adjust it? Form a hypothesis and test it against memories of relevant past experiences. Do the whole thing inside, without involving the interaction with the environment yet. Saves time, energy, and especially costly errors. When there is a sufficient inventory of memories and enough levels in the nested assemblies of desired perceptions, quite useful planning can go on, and clearly the ability to do it — to do this unspecified thing! — will be selected for when subjected to Darwinian competition.

Do you notice how we have gradually moved from selecting definite structures and behaviors to selecting methods and abilities that do not limit the structures or behaviors? how more and more room is being left for the cosmos to be creative? self-creative? And for human beings this creativity will be most clearly mediated by language.

We Talk to Each Other

Despite sharing 99 percent of our genes with the chimpanzees, and despite our clear continuity with the whole evolutionary sequence, there is no doubt that an enormous jump took place when the fully modern human being — *Homo sapiens sapiens* — appeared. Here are people talking to each other, cooperating in tool-making, hunting, and other activities, painting pictures on cave walls, singing, dancing, laughing, and doing things that have no tie to gaining a genetic advantage. If ever there was a "phase transition," this was it.

What brought it about? Not just bigger brains, though they were necessary. Other animals, such as elephants and cetaceans, have even bigger brains than we do. And indeed, some earlier members of the *Homo* line had bigger brains than we now do. There was a period during which the brain increased in size and then leveled off. The explosion of human culture took place after that. What made the difference was not just size; it was a certain way that the big brain (and its cooperating systems) organized its activities. And that way was syntactical language.

Syntactical language is language made of a modest array of units, put together by our familiar modular assembly and nested assemblies of assemblies, and governed by rules which determine meaning. The modest array of units at the bottom of spoken language is composed of "phonemes," the smallest bits of sound. These are put together to make "morphemes," the smallest units of meaning — whole words, but also such things as prefixes and suffixes, tense and plural endings. Morphemes, if not already words, combine to form words, and these words represent objects, actions, relations, categories of the world. People who monitor such things tell us that there are several million words in the English language and that the number is increasing at the rate of two hundred thousand to three hundred thousand a year. All that from forty-four phonemes in American English.

But the real astonishment comes when the words are arranged to form sentences. Sentences don't represent objects or actions; they represent propositions, assertions about how it is with the world, and reactions to the world and feelings about the world, and so on. How many sentences are there? We laugh. We know that's an absurd question. An endless number. There's no limit on the sentences we can make out of our several million increasing by hundreds of thousands words made of forty-four phonemes. Finitude has been turned into infinitude.

But it's very mysterious how words and sentences are made. This is where "syntax" comes in, the rules for how phonemes can be combined into morphemes and morphemes into sentences. All human beings have language, all children learn to speak whatever they hear around them, we all seem to know when a sentence makes sense and when it doesn't. But asked to declare what rule is to be invoked as criterion of this sense-making, we usually can't say. But we can tell whether it's right or wrong.

Some linguists believe that there is a universal, very general, grammar on which all human languages are based. Even peoples, such as the Australians, who until a couple of centuries ago had been separated from everyone else for about fifty thousand years, have the same forms of organization in their languages. There are grounds for thinking, therefore, that language is not a cultural invention but a biologically based capacity.[14]

It seems to come out of the ability not only to form "representations" of the environing world, as in perceptions, but to perform further processing with the representations. The sensation circuit had shaped up a perception and reacted to it by some motion. Both input and output were interactions or interfaces with the environment. If part of that output had been a vocalization, a word, an advantage would have been gained. If gestures and facial expressions had been in use previously, vocalization could have freed hands and eyes to continue with other tasks while still talking/listening. In any case, another channel of communication is always a significant aid to cooperation.

But such limited language — one percept, one word — would not have progressed until some further level of organization had been applied. As with other assembly programs, the items — in this case the matching internal representations or perceptions and the vocalizations — would have to be diverse enough and numerous enough for assembling to work on. Then the units could be grouped according to kind; assemblies of assemblies would be formed, representing categories, each an entire class of perceptions/actions.

Finally, these category assemblies could be combined according to certain rules. The rules are the syntax and involve also creating some additional words for the relations between the primary words — additional words such as conjunctions, prepositions, words like "because" and "unless," like "if...then." The whole procedure reminds me of the way regulatory genes relate to the exons that code for parts of proteins: they don't make the protein themselves, but they control and organize the genes that do, turning them on and off in ways that translate into biological meaningfulness.

With a syntactical language, a language capable of making real sentences, sentences with modifying phrases and relative clauses embedded in them, thinking withdrawn from action becomes possible. Derek Bickerton calls this "off-line" thinking.[15] A secondary set of neuronal activities appears which is "about" the primary set. It is responsive to the assembly of assemblies of neurons that represents the primary interaction with the world. It is stimulated by an internal trigger and contents itself with internal processing alone. Now imagination becomes possible, testing out potential lines of action without doing them, inventing new ways of doing things, telling stories about things that have not happened and perhaps could not happen.

Bickerton argues that the secondary activities, which are "about" the primary ones, are representations of relations among the ideas of the primary level. They are interpretations, based on connections among primary ideas and among other relations on the secondary level. This secondary level has the same "quantity," or extent, that language itself has; that is, it is unlimited. Therefore, the outcome of a train of thought cannot be predicted from the beginning input. Especially if the original stimulus is purely internal, that is, randomly generated, the probability of any particular outcome of the thought train cannot, even in principle, be computed. This, says Bickerton, is "absolute indeterminacy," something that has "no place in a machine," but "what the mind, of its very nature, has built into it."[16]

One of the metaphors used by neuroscientists for this thinking-talking that goes on in the brain is "narrative," or "the narrator."[17] Bickerton feels that this term suggests too much a "solo performance." He proposes instead "dialogue," for "what the mind constructs is...a constant interaction between individual and environment — a story that not only edits itself but is edited by its surroundings in unpredictable ways as it unfolds."[18] A further development of this idea is that the most important part of our environment when we are thinking-talking is other people. William F. Allman urges that the development of language-consciousness and self-awareness comes from the social context of human life.[19] Being able to live with others, survive socially, cooperate, depends on forming internal models of what the other person is thinking. We are now considering not only thinking about things; we are thinking about thinking, even other people's thinking. We are talking to each other and that enables and obliges us to think about what the other is thinking. An extraordinary new level of cosmic interaction!

The Word presides over the beginning of the truly human world. That world is made by words. All things human come into being through words. Talking to each other is the life that is the light of consciousness for human beings. It is a new kind of light in the cosmos, shining out of the preconscious darkness, a darkness that can in no way overcome it (see John 1:1–5).

What Is Consciousness?

But does this wonderful human brain-body explain human consciousness? Does it explain our sense of ourselves as actively engaging the world, or reflecting on ourselves, or especially reflecting on the fact that we are conscious? With human consciousness we come to a situation we have not faced in any of the other levels of the cosmic organization. We experience our own consciousness *subjectively*, as subjects, from the inside. All the other levels of organization we had observed from the outside, objectively, seeing them as objects of our cognition. But in the case of our own consciousness, we do something more than and quite different from knowing it as an object for our cognition. We know it by being it.

It is also true that we can reflect on the facts of our consciousness and can observe that some subjective experiences can be correlated in a rough way with certain objective observables: various interactions with the environment match pleasure or pain, blows to the head can knock you unconscious, anesthetics can put you to sleep and keep you from remembering, intoxicants can loose you to strange perceptions and regrettable behavior, even psychosocial incidents can terrify you, make you angry, depress you or exalt you. We can trace perception through certain areas of the brain; we can identify language areas and motor areas; and we can relieve certain illnesses by brain surgery.

But can consciousness — not the behavior of our bodies, objectively observable, but our subjective experience of being aware, of being conscious of being conscious, of being ourselves — can this be exhaustively explained and accounted for in terms of the objective observables alone? Some neuroscientists claim yes, others insist no. A strong example of the first school is Francis Crick, who believes that he himself, his joys and sorrows, his sense of being "I," his personal identity and experience of free will, "are in fact no more than the behavior of a vast assembly of nerve cells and their associated molecules."[20] In other words, nature has evolved a combination of molecules so artfully working with one another as to produce a creature which experiences itself as transcendent of the molecules, but which also discovers that this is an illusion and its sense of being a "self" is not true. The creature knows that it isn't there.

Calvin, who models intelligent behavior in terms of a "Darwin Machine" acting on Hebbian assemblies, suggests that the best model so far for what we call "consciousness" is the "currently dominant pattern" in a competition among assembly patterns for making copies of themselves in the brain (very much as genes compete to make copies of themselves — hence "Darwin").[21] He presents this view in a conversation with an imaginary character, whose question is set in quotes:

> "You mean that the real me is just...*hegemony*? The current winner that can temporarily dominate over all the other warring factions?" — That's the best model we have, at least for creating a new idea, speaking a sentence that you've never spoken before. After all, the darwinian process — variations, followed by selective survival and reproduction, repeated many times — nicely explains how new animal species arise over a timescale of millennia. And how your immune system creates better and better antibodies...during the course of several weeks.[22]

154 / GOD'S ECSTASY

Other views, a while back, included Roger Sperry and John Eccles. Sperry was converted by the clinical evidence he had seen (up to 1977) to the opinion that consciousness was not to be "conceived as an epiphenomenon, inner aspect, or other passive correlate of brain processing but rather to be an active integral part of the cerebral process itself, exerting potent causal effects [from] a position of top command,...the subjective properties [exerting] control over the biophysical and chemical activities."[23]

Eccles (in 1977) laid out his "hypothesis" as

> the self-conscious mind [being] actively engaged in reading out from the multitude of active centres at the highest level of brain activity.... [It] selects from these centres according to attention, and from moment to moment integrates its selection to give unity. ...The self-conscious mind acts upon these neural centres modifying... the patterns of the neural events.... *The unity of conscious experience is provided by the self-conscious mind and not by the neural machinery.... The experienced unity comes, not from a neurophysiological synthesis, but from the proposed integrating character of the self-conscious mind."*[24]

Daniel Dennett rejects the idea of a ruling mind: just as we might have been tempted to account for the wonderfully integrated operation of the termite colony by assigning it a soul, but now understand it to be the organized "result of a million semi-independent little agents, each itself an automaton, doing its thing," so we must understand that the organization of the human self does not entitle us to attribute to it a soul, a single "Dictator ruling from Headquarters." He proposes to exchange the metaphors of "Theatre, Witness, Central Meaner, for Software, Virtual Machines, Multiple Drafts, a Pandemonium of Homunculi."[25]

Both Bickerton and Scott are clear that the reality of mind is both more complicated than these metaphors suggest and more unified.[26] Scott (and he is mainstream in this) places the hierarchy of emergent phenomena in the center of his discussion of consciousness. Each level of organized reality has its own regularities and its own rules. These do not reduce to those found on their component levels, cannot be predicted from those levels and are not determined by them. (In this sense we may say — Scott doesn't — that each successive emergent "transcends" its components but "includes" them because they are now operative members of it.) As one climbs to higher levels of the brain, it is by no means sure that we can continue with the type of description we had been used to on the lower levels — quantitative, with mathematical relations among clearly identified relevant variables.

Scott cites biologist Brian Goodwin, who believes that his field has centered too much on the gene and needs to operate more in terms of the organism: organisms are not "mere molecular machines"; they are "as real, as fundamental, and as irreducible as the molecules out of which they are made." Similarly with consciousness, but with a difference. Biological organizations pass matter, energy, and information back and forth. The neuronal hierarchy that leads up to consciousness and culture conducts its business in information alone. Matter and energy are a kind of background means-by-which, but are not the relations of interest.[27] The *patterns* of activity are what interact and thereby allow to emerge still more transcendent and inclusive higher level patterns.

One can appreciate these (more or less modified) materialist views. After all, are we not claiming a "self-creating" universe? Are we not seeing it otherwise knit itself up by its own intrinsic relations into one emergent level after another, each with its own character, properties, laws of behavior? Did we not outlaw "intervention" by supernatural forces and insist that it all could be done from the inside out? An utterly independent conscious "soul" hovering over its material brain does look very like an outside Creator modeling a world like a clay pot, or putting a machine together with a screwdriver. Is it not more wonderful to see the intangible energy clumps build solid materials, see the nonliving chemicals form cycles of catalysis that make their community alive, see the self-contained cells organize and cooperate to constitute individual plants and animals with unified behavior and identity? And now, someone might say, out of the exceedingly complex interactions of the patterns of cellular behavior, out of the material, has come the immaterial: just pattern, just form, just information. Information acting on information, within each brain, between brains. Is that not more marvelous than a "ghost" hidden somewhere in the "machine"?

And yet, and yet, there's our immediate sense of our personal subjectivity. Many of these researchers feel, toward the ends of their books, that it hasn't quite been accounted for. Perhaps the notion that "we" are just the Hebbian assembly that is currently successful in the patterning competitions is itself nothing but a temporarily dominant pattern. Can a temporarily dominant pattern know that it is just a temporarily dominant pattern? We experience ourselves as transcendently unitary with respect to all these means-by-which the brain works. We believe that it is we who understand the brain, even when we say that the brain is setting us up with this illusion of transcendent selfhood. Maybe consciousness is a special case. Maybe, besides affirming an emergent in the usual sense, as with all the earlier levels of organization, we find something more has to be said. Maybe the jump from objective to subjective is itself the really new thing at this level, and if so, then by the rules of emergence, subjectivity cannot be explained in terms of objectivity. It has to have its own terms of organization, its own kind of reality, its own way of being scientifically understood.

David Chalmers, searching for a fundamental theory of the conscious mind, has ventured out on the limb of admission that "consciousness is a *feature* of the world over and above the physical features of the world." Not that it is a separate "substance," but "we know ... that there are properties of individuals ... ['phenomenal' properties: having 'conscious experience,' feeling in some way] that are ontologically independent of physical properties." He says straightforwardly that "materialism is false," where "materialism" is "the doctrine that the physical facts about the world exhaust all the facts": "*No* physical facts suffice to explain consciousness."[28]

He seems to be willing to "take experience itself as a fundamental feature of the world, alongside space-time, spin, charge, and the like." And given new fundamental properties, there must also be new fundamental laws. But these are *psychophysical laws,* specifying how phenomenal ... properties depend on physical properties.... They will be *supervenience laws,* telling us how experience arises from physical processes."[29] These psychophysical laws are the foundation of Chalmers's "naturalistic dualism," which holds that "there are both physical and nonphysical features of the world.... Experience is fundamentally different in kind from any physical feature.... The property dualism that I advocate involves fundamentally new features of the world." However, while consciousness "is not *entailed*" by the physical basis of reality, it remains "plausible" that it "*arises* from" it, in terms of the supervenient psychophysical laws.[30]

I confess that while this seems a most promising move forward, it is not clear to me how conscious experience can be "dependent on" physical properties and also be a "fundamental" feature of the world, "alongside space-time," etc. But perhaps there is more than one kind of conscious experience, a kind that is lawfully correlated with the physical basis of the world, and (at least one) kind that is indeed a "fundamental feature," not dependent on any other "basis." We have concentrated so hard on freedom from simple materialism for conscious phenomena of any sort that we have not considered fully that there might be a whole new kind of world here with a variety of internal distinctions.

Explanations, Primitives, and Incarnation

David Layzer remarks that "in general, science isn't very good at answering questions of the form: Why does so-and-so exist?" being better at How questions. In particular, "neurobiology stops short of explaining subjectivity."[31] But if subjectivity is truly "fundamental," this is quite as it should be. What does it mean to "explain" something? Presumably it means to give an account of something less well known in terms of something better known. Explanations are either of the axiomatic type — tracing back to axioms and definitions and ultimately to undefined terms — or of the dictionary type — going round in a circle, every word of any explanation having to be explained elsewhere in the explanation-network. Karl Popper says:

> Explanation is never ultimate.... All explanation is ... intellectually unsatisfactory because all explanation has to start out from certain definite conjectures, and these conjectures themselves are used as unexplained assumptions for the purpose of explanation. ... [Our] wish to explain them in their turn ... leads to the same problem again.... We must come to terms with the fact that we live in a world in which almost everything which is very important is left essentially unexplained.[32]

In practice, we feel that we have an adequate explanation when we are no longer motivated to ask for one. But that satisfaction depends on the context of all our thoughts about what we think we understand and what constitutes "understanding." This context is shaped by collective and social consensus, often accompanied by explicit criteria, such as conformity to some authority (living or written), or measurability or repeatability or other standard of public shared judgment. The definition of what constitutes an acceptable explanation, therefore, may have built into it certain exclusions that prevent certain things from being explained, or else oblige them to be explained in certain approved ways.

Erwin Schrödinger complained that many scientists excluded subjective experience from the world-picture they were willing to take seriously and then claimed that they had discovered that there was no such thing there in the real world. But, argued Schrödinger, who framed that picture and determined its contents? Human subjective consciousness is itself the picture-maker and even the picture.

Eugene Wigner said something similar, that the starting point in physics is not actually the position of a particle but the knowledge of the observer concerning the position of the particle. Therefore it is "unreasonable to describe the basic concept — the content of the consciousness of the observer — in terms of the derived one...the concept of the positions of atoms."[33]

Nevertheless, at this stage in the development of science — that is, at this stage in the cosmic organizational process — only explanations in terms of the behavior patterns of matter are considered by the majority to be acceptable, to be orthodox. It is professionally risky to try anything else. Alwyn Scott has an important word to say about this:

> In the realm of science, one's attitude toward what Karl Popper called "the great tradition of materialism" is often used as an index of respectability. Those who turn away from this tradition to consider the nature of consciousness run the risk of being marked as flakes who might also believe in psychokinesis (spoon bending), mental telepathy, clairvoyance, precognition, and the like. The safest course — especially for the young scientist — is to shun such temptations and concentrate on the data from a particular level of the hierarchy. Although prudent, this approach to the gathering of knowledge ignores a pillar of the scientific tradition: face the facts.[34]

It has been interesting to me to see how sensitive the consciousness researchers are to this danger. They are very concerned about being thought "mystical" by their peers. Their works invariably contain a disclaimer to this effect somewhere, usually in the form "There is nothing mystical in this."[35] It is most unfortunate that the history of science in Europe, suppressed and persecuted by religious/political power structures, has left a legacy of rather more restriction than is necessary in order to learn how the world truly works.

Since we ourselves declare what shall constitute an acceptable explanation, I propose to revert to the rather simple definition of explanation as accounting for the less known in terms of the better known, and to ask, What is better known to us than our own subjective experience of our own consciousness? And why should we not face the fact that an explanation of subjective experience cannot be had by excluding the subjectivity and admitting only a postulated objective arrangement? Empirical science deals with experience, not with what the authorities say we are allowed to believe. Introspective subjective experience is a fact of nature. The need to explain it away in order to conform to a scientific orthodoxy or to twist it until it meets the norms of the prevailing belief system is the same sort of limitation on knowledge that the empirical sciences suffered from religious authority.

Why not try acknowledging subjective experience of consciousness as itself a primitive? a primary reality, a ground reality — like spacetime, or charge, or spin, or any of the fundamental forces — something that cannot be explained in terms of something else, because there is nothing else prior to it or simpler than it or better known than it in terms of which such explanation might be couched? We don't experience our consciousness as a composition or an effect. We experience it as that which experiences everything else, directly or indirectly. (We are the ones who find out that there are activities in our brains that never rise to the level of direct consciousness.) We experience it as the prior on which all else depends, as the knower of the known. It is what sets out to know, and it is what knows whatever is found out.

It is not true to say that we don't know what consciousness is. It is only true to say that we cannot find a fully satisfying way of saying what it is in terms of something else. This seems to me to be the mark of an independent dimension. Just as we all know what time is but find it difficult to define it in terms of something other than itself, so conscious subjectivity is perfectly well known to us, nothing better, but it is not to be expected that it should be "explained" in terms of something else. Our experiences of sensations or particular feelings or particular ideas or judgments are not the root experience of subjectivity. We experience it as the ultimate witness and the original agent in the sense of the reality prior to any of these particularities. We experience it as intense and full being, as unitary, and as the standard of reality. Everything else is "real" only by reference to it. We have inverted the relation between the experienced and the hypothesized when we declare the material to be the standard of reality and conscious selfhood to be a (highly debatable) hypothesis. From the point of view of subjective consciousness, it is itself the experienced and any theories about it or anything else are hypotheses.

Subjective experience experiences itself as that which cannot be regarded or objectified. *Self*-consciousness is not a reflexive specialization of general consciousness. *Self*-consciousness is original or fundamental consciousness. Awareness of the external world is what is "later," what is particular "applied" and specialized activity of consciousness. It is naturally possible to be intensely unitarily conscious without any awareness of the "external world." These are our experiences. These are not speculations or assertions but raw data observations. We may choose to interpret them in various ways, including calling them all illusions. All I am saying is that this is what we experience as subjective consciousness. If we cannot reduce it to the terms of objective views, we might try to make a science which recognizes these experiences as themselves primitive, just as we recognize energy as primitive and don't try to explain it in terms of bodies in motion.

There are some interesting derivatives from this view. If our subjectively experienced consciousness is a primary datum, then it is not exhaustively accounted for as an emergent from bodily interactivities, even though some of its modifications can be correlated with some of the latter's. It must always be included in its own right as an independent ingredient. To invoke matter/energy relations to give an exhaustive account of the experience of subjectivity is just as extrinsic, inappropriate, and impossible as invoking deific or other supernatural entities to account for cosmic events. But if this is the case, then there would not seem to be any justification for excluding some properly generalized "subjectively experienced consciousness" from any level of cosmic organization. It must run all the way back.

David Chalmers is willing to consider the possibilities of some variety of what is usually called "panpsychism" (though he doesn't care for the term). He argues that although a fundamental property, as he holds "experience" is, might be instantiated in this universe only occasionally, it seems more plausible, other things being equal, that it should appear in some form everywhere. He is able to say this in his context because he defines "experience" in terms of "information" and "information" in terms of "causal interaction." This permits him to see a thermostat, for instance, as having "experience" because of the way it interacts with its environment and processes information. The level of "psychism" here is minimal and does not include self-consciousness, intelligence, thinking, or mind. These latter are specifically "psychological" properties, and he is claiming only "phenomenal" properties in a most general way. The advantage of admitting anything along these lines is that it avoids the problem of having to draw a line where "consciousness" starts or stops.[36]

If "experience" is realized everywhere, then Chalmers can make an ontology based on his "double-aspect" theory of consciousness. The two aspects are the "phenomenal" and the "physical." What links them is the notion of an "information space," an array of possible states different from one another.[37] A switch that can be either on or off is said to realize a two-state information space. That's a physical example. On the phenomenal side, there are states that differ from one another in virtue of their intrinsic qualities, and our consciousness makes the selection among them that is the "information."

Chalmers's claim, in setting up the "double-aspect principle," is that "whenever we find an information *space* realized phenomenally, we find the same information *space* realized physically. And when an experience realizes an information *state,* the same information *state* is realized in the experience's physical substrate."[38] Or, putting it more unitarily and making information itself the basic reality, information has two aspects, physical and phenomenal, and whenever it is realized in the actual world, both of these aspects appear.

Chalmers says that the most straightforward way to look at things is to regard physical and phenomenal as separate features, with only a regular and reliable connection of appearing together and having a similar structure: ordinary "property dualism." But he is interested in an idea he picked up from Bertrand Russell (*The Analysis of Matter,* 1927), according to which the intrinsic properties of the *physical* (about which physics itself says nothing, restricting itself to relations among its objects' extrinsic properties) might be a variety of *phenomenal* property. Or one could say that "the basic properties of the world are neither the physical nor the phenomenal, but the physical and the phenomenal are constructed out of them. From their *intrinsic* natures in combination, the phenomenal is constructed; and from their *extrinsic* relations, the physical is constructed."[39]

Chalmers's feeling seems to be that intrinsic natures have priority over extrinsic. The world cannot be made of pure "information." If information is based on differences among alternative states, the differences have to be differences *in* something. Besides, we always come back to the basic fact: We know that we are conscious. We have access to the intrinsic qualities of the phenomenal. Taking all this into consideration, a "double-aspect ontology" is obtained: phenomenal reality, with its directly accessed intrinsic qualities, grounds information spaces which are expressed in extrinsic relations. The internal aspects are phenomenal; the extrinsic aspects are physical. "Experience is information from the inside; physics is information from the outside."[40]

This is, in another language game, structurally similar to what I am proposing under the title "the Incarnation." (Did I not say that in the creation the Reality was "turning itself inside out"?) The theological concept of the Incarnation, when generalized to cosmic proportions, handles a metaphysical problem the same way the Trinity does: when we are confronted with two realities and cannot reduce either one to the other, the thing to do is affirm them both, together. The One and the Many. And the phenomenal/physical, or intrinsic/extrinsic. Or, ultimately, the Infinite/Finite.

The really fundamental level of the Incarnation is, of course, the Infinite/Finite. It is the Trinitarian Community expressing its intrinsic, or enstatic, self as extrinsic cosmos, this being its ecstasy. Within that cosmos we find the same schema again as finite consciousness (intrinsic) and physical structure (extrinsic). But inasmuch as the Infinite does express itself as the Finite, is intimately bonded with it through the Incarnation, we may say that the Incarnation is really the Whole Reality.

We can also say, if we like, that the Word plays the role of information, linking pattern in the intrinsic to pattern in the extrinsic. And the intrinsic pattern itself is *agape,* the active sharing of whatever is shareable, the Many interacting to make One. This is the nature of Being. Being gives itself, it extends and expands Being. It tends to be in every possible way. It tends to elaborate — copy, vary, interact, select, combine, make next level wholes with emergent properties. All this is natural. Incarnation is not something that "happens" outside the regular order on the decree of a supernatural agency. It is simply the ultimate How It Is.

All this is natural, is the nature of Being. Shall I go on and say, "There is nothing mystical in this?" No, I'm going to say there is something mystical in this, and this is what it is: It is the immediacy and irreducibility of a subjective experience of knowing by *being* instead of by *representing.* The object of consciousness is in this case the subject itself. When the subject is aware of the subject, not by reflection — that is, not by making a representation of the subject or of the act of being conscious or of the concept of "being the knower" — but the subject is aware of the subject by being aware *as* subject, aware *as* subject of subject by *being* subject, in a fully luminous (not unaware or unconscious) way, that consciousness is "mystical."

It is, from one point of view, a singularity, a case in which the usual functional relations no longer hold. But, from another point of view, it is the space in which all the functions are deployed. This casts it in the role of the infinite with respect to particular functional relations as finite. It is the ground and they are the expressions. Together they are "incarnation."

And this consciousness view is the direct access to the intrinsic nature of Being. What is "known" in the "mystical experience" is the ontological structure of the Whole. Because we ourselves exist on every level of the Whole. We are the incarnational union. We are not on only "one side" of it, the finite objective material side. We are the union of intrinsic/extrinsic, subjective/objective, absolute/relative, infinite/finite. It is the nature of Being to be this way. Therefore we are this way. We know ourselves as being this way; thus we know Being is this way. The knowing and the being are one. That's mystical.

Chapter Nine

THEOTOKOS: THE ECSTASY OF THE COSMOS AS GOD

 I'VE MADE FREQUENT REFERENCE to the trinitarian image reappearing at every stage of the cosmogenesis, and I've urged that viewing the Whole Reality as Incarnation is both meaningful and realistic. But I haven't said much about the third icon I proposed to use, the Theotokos, the Godbearer. We couldn't see it until consciousness had emerged and the transcendence of consciousness with respect to its material vehicle could be pointed to in a recognizable way.

Now I want to say just a little more about how human beings share our thoughts and about the higher levels of human conscious activities — morality, science itself, art, and spirituality — and then explain how I see this high-level consciousness as a kind of birth of the divine from the cosmos itself. In developing this way humanity will also exemplify not only the symbiosis that has marked each level of the cosmogenesis but especially the self-creating aspect, which I have chosen to highlight. When human society practices *agape* (promotion of the well-being of one another), the cosmos will be performing, on this very complexly organized level of itself, a divine act. By its consciousness and its caring the cosmos will become ecstatic — transcend itself and its investment in individual or group "self-interest" — and its ecstasy will give birth to divine life.

Thus the circle of the Trinitarian Life Cycle will be closed: the Infinite, incarnating itself in the Finite, will evolve through a series of self-creating emergent levels to the point at which the Incarnating Infinite can awaken within the activities of the Finite and know itself.

Memes in the Darwin Machine

We people experience our lives from the inside in terms of ideas and feelings. This is the emergent level in the hierarchy that cosmic organization has now reached. Is self-creating going on here too? Of course. Self-creating intensifies as we go up the hierarchy. And a couple of the old methods that have been with us from the beginning are still operative here: modular assembly and natural selection.

The method is called, by William Calvin, a "Darwin Machine," and what are organized by this method are called, by Richard Dawkins, "memes." Let's take the memes first. In the last chapter of his 1976 book, *The Selfish Gene,* Dawkins likened human culture to the primeval "soup" from which life emerged and replicated itself through the genes. Human culture is made up of ideas, pieces of behavior, technologies, games, beliefs, fashions, methods, ways of organizing society, art styles, courtesies and other customs, philosophical systems, all sorts of things. These units of culture, which can replicate — be copied, reproduce — he called "memes," from mimetic, imitative. "Just as genes propagate themselves in the gene pool by leaping from body to body via sperms and eggs, so memes propagate themselves in the meme pool by leaping from brain to brain via a process, which, in the broad sense, can be called imitation."[1]

Memes are passed mostly by language but also by pictures and by action and observation. They can spread very quickly, especially in our era of mass communication of visuals and language together. Entertainment, advertising, instruction, proselytizing for politics or religion or social attitudes/practices are all ways of transmitting memes. It reminds me of the variety of means the bacteria use for their active gene-swapping. Memes that confer an "advantage" in the human social cultural environment will be copied and spread. Some will speciate, split into subdivisions, easily, while others will be amazingly stable and conservative. Still others will undergo modification and gradual evolution.

Sometimes a crucial breakthrough meme appears and produces all sorts of "spin-offs" in what amounts to a whole new world. The idea of human equality and individual worth and dignity is such a meme. So is something like metalworking, the alphabet, the telescope/microscope, printing, the internal combustion engine, or, in our day, computers. Ideas, techniques, and social practices all influence one another. Memes mix and match just as modular genes to make up larger units of pattern transmission. And then they produce emergents.

And they seem to spread and survive (or not) on very much the same principles as genes do. That is, they constitute a "Darwin Machine," although at least some of them (fashions and fads especially) tend to come and go much more readily than genes. Nevertheless, they conform fairly well to Calvin's outline of the evolutionary *method:* (1) take a complex cultural pattern; (2) copy it (let other people believe, say, do imitations of it); (3) variations appear; (4) the variants compete for copying (fashion designs, VCR types, or political philosophies); (5) a number of different aspects in the appropriate environment give advantages to one or another variant (how well does it work/wear? how much does it cost? how available is it? how compatible with other items in its line? what social effects? what ecological effects? is it acceptable to my family, friends, religion? etc.); (6) winning variants tend to cluster around an already successful meme-system and to replicate even more than it has done. They are not random jumps but small sidesteps from an already preferred position. Succeeding generations are descendents of these winners. (Whitehead called all Western philosophy a series of "footnotes to Plato." Isaac Newton said, "If I have seen farther than other men, it is because I have stood on the shoulders of giants," i.e., Galileo, Copernicus, et al.)

Such a Darwin Machine, says Calvin,

> capable of operating on various time scales and in various media able to reproduce with inherited variation, [can be recognized] as one of the key organizing principles of the universe. In the brain, such a process need not run out of challenges, as memes from a rich cultural life always provide another set of complex patterns to analyze for possible hidden structure, repeating the process that we used as two-year-olds to figure out the syntax of the utterances we heard [and thus learn to speak a true language].[2]

Aaron Lynch, examining the new science of memes in *Thought Contagion: How Belief Spreads through Society*, identifies seven modes of contagion: "quantity parental" (meme encourages large families, whose children will probably adopt the meme), "efficiency parental" (meme makes it more likely that children will adopt it, e.g., by separating them from unbelievers), "proselytic" (meme includes the injunction to pass it on), "preservational" (meme includes fear-inducing threats against abandoning the meme), "adversative" (meme includes injunction to diminish competitors), "cognitive" (meme makes sense with rest of believer's cognitive property), and "motivational" (believer adopts/transmits meme because it benefits believer to do so). Several of these modes may operate in conjunction.

Thought contagion reshuffles ideas much as modular assembly makes up new combinations of genes or antibodies. The new combination may copy and spread faster than its components singly. For instance, in the first century of the Common Era there were many Gentiles in the Roman Empire who believed in the Jewish God (these people were called "God-fearers"), but they did not convert to Judaism because they wanted to remain citizens of their own countries and they were reluctant to adopt circumcision and kosher kitchens. When the Christians allowed them to join the church that believed in the Jewish God but did not oblige them to adopt new citizenship, circumcision, or kosher diet, they came in readily. The two memes together were a winning combination.

Completely new ideas can arise out of relations among old ones. The inflation scenario with which we began is an example. All the pieces of it were lying ready to hand, but no one had thought to put them together until Guth had his brilliant idea. The insight into natural selection itself is similar. Stock-breeding had been practiced for millennia, which was artificial selection. It was only required to put the observation that certain breeding lines in nature gained while others failed together with the idea that nature itself might do the same kind of selecting by encouraging or limiting reproduction to have a powerful new theory that swept through the whole of science.

Meme evolution is necessarily a combination of natural selection and artificial (deliberate) selection, because people are now quite freely and consciously trying to influence the beliefs of other people, to promote their own memes while retarding their competitors'. But out of this fray, which can get quite fierce and include both deception and other insidious devices and outright warfare, frequently come fruitful new ideas. It seems that we are living in a wide-open arena in which every idea takes its chances. Notice that cognitive cogency is only one among seven modes of transmission mentioned by Lynch.[3]

The Evolution of Evil

Even human behavior and its subjective counterpart, the most complex cosmic organization we know, have roots that reach far back into the past. We are troubled in our consciousness about what we regard as evil, why it exists, what we can do about it, and especially how to reconcile its existence — indeed, its prevalence — with a Ground of Being that is presumably good. This is a very difficult and convoluted problem, and it is usually rash to attempt any resolution of it. But one has an obligation in such a context as put forward here to take some account of it.

I will point out what I call the evolution of evil in terms of animal behavior and trace it back to the nature of finitude. Then I will work forward in terms of recognition of "rights." In both cases there will be a basic self-interest perspective. A third line will seek out the development of altruism, friendship, and empathy, for these have their roots, too. The three lines are intertwined, of course, and more or less subject to the Darwin Machine and some interesting models of game theory. A fourth line of exploration will treat of human psychology and what basic motives in it can eventuate in evil acts. Finally, I will try to relate all this to the theological structure of Trinity-Incarnation-Theotokos that I am proposing.

As I noted in chapter 7 (the section on "gene wars"), what we call evil has a natural history. Lyall Watson has written a book about it, *Dark Nature,* in which he gives many examples of behavior among animals that may be regarded as precursors to human murder, theft, rape, lying, cheating, enslaving, warfare, cruelty, deception, etc. Marsh hens peck blackbird eggs to kill the chicks; newborn hyena twins fight until one is killed; elephant seal females gang murder another mother's pups. Indeed, infanticide is common as a means of reducing the burden on parents or as a way of eliminating another's offspring. Ten percent of all species are parasites on others, and there is cannibalism in every animal species not vegetarian. Warfare is there already among insects and among primates. And at the human level, it is no use our imagining that people who live close to nature rather than in industrialized cultures have less crime, for African Bushmen have a homicide rate higher than the worst American cities.[4]

All this is in service of the genes' replication. It's as though the motto of the genes is "Happiness is making others unhappy." And the irony of it is that intelligence and awareness of the other and the other's probable behavior evolve in this context. Deception especially, or any form of cheating, takes intelligence, and, as Watson says, one of the rules of this game is "Cheat whenever possible."[5] But consider what cheating and deceiving imply. There has to be a mechanism for acting *contrary to the facts.* The organism has to "know" what is true and then invent behavior that is not true. And it does this in a world in which particular other parties will interpret this behavior as if it were true and that will have an effect favorable to the deceiver.

I'm not saying that this is explicitly conscious, of course, but it is objectively implicit: nature itself is making facsimiles of alternative realities, of conditions that are not actually so. This seems a strange thing to do, or at least a very complicated thing to do, even if we want to hold that it comes about accidentally. It happens all over the natural world by all sorts of different imaginative devices. Even if unconscious, this must be the forerunner of imagination and intelligence. This is a fundamental example of how something we value and something we (say we) disvalue are intimately tied together. It's not just that intelligence is neutral and can be used for either good or ill. It's that intelligence as such, in its neutrality, probably was selected for (at least in part) because of its advantage in the deception game.[6] And even more interesting is that it is precisely the untruthfulness, the unreality, of deceptive behavior that lies behind a most prized faculty, imagination. Lying is a form of creativity. Creativity is making something that is not immediately derived from a preexisting reality.

Closely related to the evolution of intelligence is the evolution of pain. This is the passive aspect of evil, evil not as we do it but as we receive and experience it. One of our frequent complaints against how the world is, is that there is so much suffering in it. But could consciousness have developed without it? What is pain, distress, discomfort, except the subjective aspect of interaction with that which is harmful to us? Just as advancing intelligence became more clever at deceiving others to its own advantage, so advancing consciousness became more sensitive to detecting interactions disadvantageous to it. "Pains" differentiated, became of various types, degrees, locations. Internally caused distress could be distinguished from externally caused. Social disturbances — unhappiness, shame, guilt, loneliness, disappointment — were advances over plain fear, anger, desire. These are names we give to internal urgencies to do something to alleviate the disadvantage. Even at the level of human consciousness, we are still strongly moved by discomforts of various sorts. The higher the level of organization and consciousness, the more sensitive and responsive the being is, the more capable of more sorts of suffering.

Putting it in teleological language just to show the strength of the link, if you're going to try to get consciousness to "emerge" from interactions of material particles, all of these "evils" are probably more or less inevitable. Complex unity is dependent on variety and interaction. Variety means there have to be different constructions of the cosmic stuff. The constructions have to maintain themselves to some extent in order to enter into significant interactions. This means that they have to defend themselves, probably augment themselves, certainly copy themselves. This entails gaining the supplies to do this from a resource location that is limited. Those structures that do gain the supplies make the copies. Those that are able to eliminate competitors will gain, and those that are able to detect and analyze hindrances will gain. And all of this comes ultimately from the fact of finitude: to have variety and differences, we have form, particularity — finite being; and then we have the necessity to maintain these beings in an environment of finite resources. In the end, all the activities that at the human level are labeled evil can be traced back through their predecessors to the fact of finitude itself.

But now let us turn to the human level and the evolution of the label "evil." Here the concept of inclusive fitness comes in; we protect (unless sorely tried) our own genes present in other bodies, that is to say, our kinfolk. We do not as a rule hurt them or steal from them (though these things also occur). There is a sense in which this is recognized as harmful to the group, thus evil. On the other hand, stealing from outsiders or killing them as competitors or dangers may well be considered good—until we need to make an alliance against a greater threat. Then it becomes evil to injure the allies. The men of our tribe will no longer take their women or their cattle. The men agree to recognize each other as brothers. But those outside this alliance are still fair game, and it is heroic rather than evil to harm them.

My suggestion is that very slowly the scope of evil has increased. Behaviors that had been good or had been merely natural without attracting any attention became recognized as evil. The notion of "right" appeared. Some people had a "right" to be left unharmed. To transgress a "right" was evil. As more people were acknowledged to have more rights, there came to be more "evil" in the world. One tribe, allied tribes, a nation, here and there the women, to some extent the children—these gradually acquired "rights." Up to our own day more and more classes of people have been claiming their right to self-possession and self-determination, and to the extent that their claim has been acknowledged by others, more possibilities of doing evil have been added to our list.

The Moral Era

With the notion of right came a new era — was it an emergent? — the moral era. This is different from the practicality of inclusive fitness. It declares that there is value in the other person due entirely to that other's own being without regard for how I benefit from the other. Because of that value in the other I am under absolute obligation to respect it, whether it is to my advantage to do so or not. That is the idea. How did we come by such an idea? No doubt its background was larger and larger communities of shared fitness and the experienced advantages of certain amounts of cooperation. This is still what I called point-of-view good and evil. That is good which benefits me; that is evil which harms me. When I contract to refrain from harming certain others, I am doing so in order to benefit myself.

But the moral concept is quite different. The goodness of the other is vested entirely in the other, transcending any relation to me. Therefore the harming of the other is objective evil, evil in itself. This escapes the genes. It may even escape the memes. Let us see. Let us look now at the natural history of altruism, friendship, empathy, and sympathy.

Already in *The Selfish Gene* Dawkins was explaining the mathematics of kin-altruism, the protection of copies of the same gene in different bodies. A parent shares one-half of her or his genes with each offspring. Siblings share half their genes. First cousins, one-eighth. Willingness to sacrifice oneself for a relative is strictly correlated with the degree of kinship: one must save more than two siblings or more than eight cousins![7]

Also in our background is the evolution of cooperation, and there is a well-known book about this, too, by Robert Axelrod. Starting from the game of Prisoner's Dilemma, he shows that "when the players will never meet again, the strategy of defection is the only stable strategy." This supports Watson's "Cheat whenever possible." However, says Axelrod, most actual exchanges in life occur between parties who probably will meet again, and this means that a totally different strategy wins. It's called "Tit for Tat," and works like this: on your first move, cooperate; if the other cooperates, cooperate again; if the other defects, then defect on your responsive move. Played as a computer program against other programs, it wins tournaments, and played in real life it can lead to cessation of hostilities in trench warfare, as actually happened in World War I. The secret is: don't be the first to defect; cooperate as long as the other does; retaliate for other's defection; forgive an isolated defection by returning to cooperation after retaliation. And be clear so that the other party can grasp the pattern in your behavior and know what to expect, leading to knowing what to do. This is how the cooperation can "evolve" through a series of moves.[8]

Lyall Watson calls Tit for Tat "altruism with teeth," and says, "It is self-realizing. An automatic process that leads inexorably to a distinct goal, creating good out of evil. . . . Systems that start in this way tend to grow: they contain a 'ratchet' which ensures that levels of cooperation remain the same or increase, but never go down."[9] Do they produce emergents? Might friendship be one? It seems to begin with "reciprocal altruism." This does not involve kinship. One animal troubles itself to a minor extent to do a good deed for another that is a large gain for the recipient — e.g., removes a parasite from the other's head. If later, after some time has passed, this donor has a similar need and the former beneficiary returns the favor, that is reciprocal altruism. It requires memory, continued relationship, trust, expectation, and works best as Tit for Tat, with retaliation for defection. Friendships form where reciprocity can be relied on. Notice that the time lag and the expectation of reciprocity and the possibility of disappointment give rise to a sense of "unfairness." Here is the beginning of the sense of justice and the notion that something is "due." The retaliation that helps Tit for Tat work generates the feelings connected with rightfully due rewards and punishments.

Friendship develops best between animals with a good bit of similarity in age and social status who share life stage experiences (parenthood, for instance). They begin to know what the other is experiencing through this similarity. Other friendships can form without that similarity, as between male and female. They can offer one another different sorts of desirables (such as protection in exchange for breeding), and they tend to share food exchanges, grooming, and other activities. Animals that live in community feel anxious if a close companion is absent or if there has been a quarrel; emotional distance produces the same distress as physical distance. Reunion is cause for rejoicing: elephants entwine their trunks, click tusks, dance around, trumpeting and flapping their ears; chimpanzees can remember one another for years and embrace and kiss when reunited; making up after a quarrel is done the same way.

A step beyond the empathy of sensing or understanding what another is experiencing is sympathy, which adds concern and an intention to do something to alleviate distress. The ethologists call it "succorant behavior." Frans de Waal has collected numerous instances of such caring for those who are hungry, sick, injured, in danger, handicapped, or dying. Animals grieve for their dead and, in some cases, bury them, both in rather ritualistic ways. Even without language there is evidence that the animals' behavior is shaped by "gratitude, obligation, retribution, and indignation."[10]

I think we can see from these observations that there is gradually arising out of the selfishness of gene-directed behavior, and perhaps partly as an accidental side effect of intelligence and the imagination that made deception possible, a capacity to feel for the other, to imagine what it is to be the other, to look from the other's point of view. When this transcends the interests of its forebears and its infrastructure in reciprocal altruism and becomes care for the other irrespective of any benefit to the one caring, then I think we may point to a true "emergent," a new level of being and interaction. And this ushers in a new age of the universe, the moral era.

In the earlier argument, in connection with the development of the sense of "right," we came on the insight that injuring the other is evil because the value of the other is ultimately in the other, not in the other's relation to me. Now we approach the same insight from the side of caring for the other. Sympathy, the will to the well-being of the other irrespective of benefit to myself, is also rooted — for the human being, but with the noted antecedents among the animals — in the recognition of the value of the other in the other's own selfhood.

The full realization of this seems to be coming on gradually, and the motives of the genes are still very active among us. Meanwhile, there are also memes for how moral values, as they come to consciousness, should be implemented and practiced. These memes are ideas, arguments, customs, and their accompanying feelings of what is acceptable. They tend to be ethnic or class bound or associated with religious or political systems. Here there is vigorous competition and dispute. But such supermemes as "co-existence," "tolerance," and "pluralism" also appear. A danger in this is a meme currently bidding for favor, "no-norms" at all.[11] But I want to push on to a level at which even the memes are transcended. And I am happy to quote Richard Dawkins himself at this point. This is from the end of *The Selfish Gene:*

> We have the power to defy the selfish genes of our birth and, if necessary, the selfish memes of our indoctrination. We can even discuss ways of deliberately cultivating and nurturing pure, disinterested altruism — something that has no place in nature, something that has never existed before in the whole history of the world. We are built as gene machines and cultured as meme machines, but we have the power to turn against our creators. We, alone on earth, can rebel against the tyranny of the selfish replicators.[12]

I said earlier that we become capable of the insight that there is value in the other that is vested entirely in the other's own being. This is seeing all the way through to the Ground of Being, to the Infinite, which is manifesting itself in whatever finite form is before us. It is because of this, because the Ground of Being is showing and it is the Infinite, that we are under absolute obligation to respect it. It is not a matter of a relative obligation (although we seem to have worked our way up to this realization by way of contracting for relative obligations) but an absolute obligation. There are no conditions attached, no if...then approaches. This is the Unconditional. This is the Ground of Being as unconditional *agape,* where *agape* is both the acknowledgement of the absolute value of Being in the other and an unconditional will to the well-being of that other.

This insight into the Ground of Being in its absolute, infinite, and unconditional nature is not just another meme. My way of saying it may well be only a finger pointing to the moon, but the moon itself transcends all memes, and whenever anyone sees it, that act also transcends all memes. It has no alleles, no alternatives.

It is this insight into the Absolute that lies at the root of our sense of, concept of, "sin." That sense includes the conviction that something absolute has been violated; it goes beyond failing to respect a relative claim that a finite being has on us. All the particular "sins," acts of disrespecting or injuring others, are based on this fundamental failure to recognize the Ground in the other, and this in turn comes from a failure to recognize it in ourselves.

When there is not profound realization of the ultimate security of being rooted in the Absolute Ground, then there are anxious efforts to secure being through finite actions. Many evils are products of love-deficiency diseases. But consciousness is always active (not merely passive) and therefore the individual's own responses in shaping attitudes and actions are also ingredients in the result. This is why we hold people "responsible" for their behavior, even when there is a severely predisposing background.

Love is security, and when love is lacking, other forms of security may be sought as substitutes. Food, promiscuous or forced sex, consciousness-altering drugs, wealth, fame, power are attempts to increase a sense of being, strong being, therefore secure being. Controlling others is power, and causing others pain is power. All too often the genes' motto, "Happiness is making others unhappy," becomes allied with human intelligent empathetic knowledge of just how to go about making the other unhappy. This is cruelty, what we call "evil" in the strongest sense, for it seems to delight in doing evil for its own sake.[13] Because we sense it as an affront to Being itself, we feel it as an absolute in itself. This is right as a moral feeling, for here we meet the foundational values.

But the real basis for sin, what makes it possible, is the failure to find the Absolute in oneself. Consciousness is at such a level in us now that we can desire the Absolute (in hidden, disguised, more or less unconscious or implicit ways) and yet not see that we are quite securely rooted in the Absolute. It is this incongruity that moves us as existential fear, insecurity, and frustration and is expressed as efforts to gain security, pleasure, and power. Notice that power is pleasurable for two reasons: it simulates security, which is a fundamental need of finite incarnation, and it is a finite expression of the quest for *transcendence, freedom, creativity.* This is why theologians have called sin an attempt to be God, to seize the power of God the Creator. Look how close together are our highest good and our greatest evil. They are both associated with *transcendence.*

The icon of the Theotokos represents the drive to bring divinity to birth in a cosmos that is being self-created from lower to higher levels, from the inside out. The Theotokos icon says to us: Divinity is within you; it is growing toward emergence. But the pregnancy may go undetected. We may not interpret our life in such terms. And so we may not realize our being as securely vested in the Infinite, in the Absolute, and yet, driven by the dynamic of the cosmos to bring its inside out, we may do all these harmful and wrong deeds. In this sense the whole program of sin is founded on falsehood and ignorance.[14]

This is why the Christian teaching on sin has these two notes: the Crucifixion showing the horrifying attack on the Ground of Being (in any of its incarnate forms), the absoluteness of sin; and the response, "Father, forgive them, for they know not what they do," the clear pointing to the ignorance behind the horror. The labor of the Theotokos is the struggle of the enwombed divinity to emerge from this ignorance.

The Ecstasy of the Theotokos

The whole creation has been groaning in labor pains...until now.
...For the creation waits with eager longing for the emergence of the children of God. (Rom. 8:22, 19)

Birth is bringing what is inside out. Ecstasy is bringing what is inside out. I am saying that the whole natural order, the cosmogenesis, is a cosmogestation. It is growing as an embryo grows, organizing itself, and progressing from stage to stage, "fulfilling itself," so to speak, becoming what it is. When the primeval energy has become matter and the matter stars, and the stardust living cells and the cells animals and the animals conscious and the conscious human being able to look back and see that this is what has happened, the cosmos has made another auto-catalytic loop, another recursion, another self-making emergent. And what the human consciousness does is reach all the way back and see the Ground of Being itself, see it being one and many, communicating being, being more, being in every possible way, thus being finite as well as infinite, being incarnate as cosmos and there repeating its one/many, being-communicating symbiosis in the forms proper to finitude. This seeing as such transcends the forms that make it possible and so is an ecstasy. The cosmos stands outside itself and sees the whole.

Toward the end of *Dark Nature*, Lyall Watson quotes Annie Dillard as agonizing: "I came from the world, I crawled out of a sea of amino acids, and now I must whirl around and shake my fist at that sea and cry shame!" at seeing all the dreadful things that happen in the natural world, including human behaviors. Watson agrees:

I'm afraid so, because in a limited, but very real, sense we are moral creatures in an immoral world. There was no other way it could have been. Natural selection was necessary, and is necessarily blind.... We are unplanned children of a world that made a pact with the devil, simply because it had to. There were no better offers on the table. So here we are now, free and seeing, faced with a blind parent and forced, not just to shake our fists, but to outwit him at every turn if we want to survive.[15]

I don't see it *quite* that way. My idea is more in line with the Easter *Exsultet:* "O truly necessary sin of Adam...that merited so great a redeemer!"[16] The Infinite Creator is incarnate as finite creativity, which has to go through the experiences of variation and natural selection in order to grow in an inside-out, self-creating way, and suffer whatever that may entail, to "fulfill itself" as *agape* ecstasy, as both thorough self-giving or self-expression in the finite and as transcendence of the finite. That is, the finite transcends itself in realizing that it is the incarnation of the Infinite. The ecstasy of the Incarnation is matched by the ecstasy of the Theotokos.

I am inclined to interpret the commandment "Honor your father and mother" in this context. Do not despise your ancestors and antecedents; remember your predecessors in the universe-process, the way by which you have come to this point. Nevertheless, you are now going to transcend that self-centered path, and the way by which you have come is no longer the way by which you will go. This is a phase transition. There will be new rules in a new world. Although stealing, deceiving, killing, and raping worked well in the natural selection world, it is no longer necessary for you to do these things. You are released (redeemed) from them. As the Talmud says, "Under the sun there is nothing new, but over the sun there is something new."[17]

The Theophany (revelation of God) at Sinai is the turning point. On that occasion the inner essence of everything was revealed. Gershom Scholem, expounding Kabbalah, says, "There is nothing in [all the worlds] that is not God's manifest glory and essence."[18] According to Moshe Braun, every created thing has God's Voice within, giving it vitality, expressing it in being. The original Light of creation is "found in the inner part of every created thing. Thus, although on the outside, things appear to be separated, in their inner spiritual nature, they are united. And when God reveals Himself, as He did on Mount Sinai, the physical differences disappear, and all that is left is the inner light, which is Divine and unified as one." God's Kingdom is hidden in the natural world, "in every particle of nature, and if people would see it they could not possibly sin."[19]

That is closer to my view. The birthing struggle of the Theotokos is the effort to "live up to" Sinai, to *see* this. But consider that someone has said these things, has had enough vision to paint this picture of Reality, to tell this story. Complexly organized stardust has done this, elevated itself to this aspiration, to this grand insight into Universal Unity. This is the ecstasy of the Earth, reaching out of itself, well beyond itself. There is another saying from the Talmud that I like: "Who has Wisdom? The one who sees the unborn."[20] Our effort is to "see the unborn" in the Theotokos and help bring it to birth. I see the ecstatic movement of the Theotokos as the "awakening from below" that is responsive to the descending "Blessing"[21] by which the Infinite turns "itself inside out and back again," as Rabbi Lawrence Kushner says.[22] This is what I call the Trinitarian Life Cycle: Transcendent, Incarnate, and Realized.

The ecstasy of the Theotokos is transcendent of nature, but it is also continuous with nature, is itself perfectly natural. I would prefer to enlarge the concept of "nature" until it securely includes all these transcendent acts of human consciousness, but without denying their transcendence or attempting to reduce them to the motions of matter. Transcendence, emergence, and integration of the components are the very pattern of the cosmic movement. These last movements of the *moral* insight into the absolute value of the other in its own right, the *metaphysical* insight into the rootedness of each finite being in the Infinite, and the *mystical* realization of the union of the Finite and the Infinite are all perfectly natural. Even the mystical is not "mystical"! For there is nothing outside the Total Real, which includes both the Infinite and the Finite, and the Finite includes the subjective conscious experience of this fact. All of this is inside the one natural order, the order of What Simply Is.

Cosmic Incarnational Mysticism

It is my contention that this theology of the cosmos, which we may call "cosmic incarnational mysticism," relieves us of certain problems of more familiar and popular theologies, gives us a more realistic and credible idea of God, and offers us both a more intimate relation with God and a more active, responsible, and exciting role in the creation.

The incarnational model relieves us of the classical "problem of evil" by not using its assumptions. Those assumptions are that God is both outside the creation and yet capable of acting as an independent agent inside the creation, changing some aspects of the creation without changing others. The incarnation model says that God is incarnate as the creation, thus acts as the whole of the creation in terms of the lawful operations of that creation, and thus cannot (any more than any other agency) change some aspects without upsetting others.

This also relieves us of the problem of why prayers are "not answered." Interventions from the outside to make certain events happen (or not) are not possible. Such interventions are always desired from a certain point of view without considering that the cosmos is an intricately interwoven net of lawful relations. The God incarnate in the universe as a whole and therefore as those lawful relations does not magically suspend this one or that to accommodate some particular party. The belief that such things can happen is what I call unrealistic, and makes a theology not credible. It is unfortunate that so many people make themselves unhappy by imagining that God could have made things turn out differently but refused to do so. Incarnational mysticism enables us to realize that God is thoroughly present as world, as everything that happens in the world, and that we ourselves are members of that God. It isn't the case, says the incarnational model, that Someone Else is doing this to us or is refusing to help us. Incarnation says it isn't Someone Else; it and we are joined in a most intimate union. If the religious value at stake is having a God who is close to you, as distinct from one who does favors for you, then you may want to rearrange the way you think about some of these things. I believe the incarnational model offers a way that is more realistic (facing the facts) and thus more credible.

The incarnational model accepts the mystical experience of people all over the world, of all historical periods, all traditions. These are among the "facts." How does it come about that the mystics all come to (very much) the same experience of some ultimate nondifference between themselves and the Ground of Being? Very simple, the model says, that's how it really is. The Ground is incarnate as the cosmos, and when part of the cosmos becomes conscious enough to find that out, that's the Theotokos rejoining the Ground as the subjective experience of being Ground incarnate as cosmos. The mystical experience is not an illusion to be explained away because it's outside the natural order or totally irrational. It's a perfectly natural coming to consciousness of what the subjective reality is, a kind of larger version of ordinary human self-consciousness.

The incarnational model also accepts all that contemporary science is proposing in the way of a self-creating world. The incarnate God creates the world from the inside in lawfully interconnected ways. Because of the nature of "incarnation," that's the same thing as "the universe creates itself." Incarnation says that both the Infinite and the Finite are thoroughly present, each aspect in its own proper way, and the Whole is One. I will repeat here what I've often said, that my favorite image for this is the dancer: the dancer obviously transcends any particular gesture and any whole dance; nevertheless, the dancing is nothing but the dancer in action.

In the case of the cosmos, we can say that God as Creator is incarnate as self-creating universe, including self-creating creatures within that universe, such as, for instance, ourselves as human beings. Creativity itself is what is evolving in the cosmos, and we are at the growing edge as the Trinitarian Life Cycle moves from Transcendent to Incarnate to Realized. We are in a position to realize ourselves as incarnate divine creativity. This has two effects. It makes the whole thing intensely meaningful. The universe is not some blind and uncaring organization of atoms; to see it so is to impose an interpretation on it. It can easily be seen as a gigantic artwork, full of whatever it is that comes out as "feeling" when it becomes incarnate. We are part of this, creative contributors to this. And this is the other effect: we bear some responsibility. We have to take our part in the work. We, for instance, are now in a position to do something about all the suffering that we were complaining of a moment ago. We are agents within the system and can have causal effects on other parts of the system. We have intelligence, we have empathy and capacity to feel for others and to care about them, we even have insight into the Ground present in every being and calling for an appropriate form of absolute respect.

What will we do? What are we "supposed to" do? What does "God want us to" do? Not a good way of putting the question, because it distances God from the world, but the answer I propose is Be! Be creative, be interactive, be agape, give being, unite, be whole, be in every possible way, be new. The self-creating world is unpredictable. It's like a musician's improvisation. There is no "predestination" and no "eschatology," either. No one sings a song only to come to the end of it. But the artwork will always resemble the artist. So the cosmos will somehow be like the Trinity, the vast Person-Community that is Agape, inter-being.

If the world is the Body of God, then it must be both honored as God and also dealt with in worldly terms. If we are members of the incarnate Deity whose essential nature is to be sharing community, then we must express this reality in appropriate community-sharing arrangements. It's not just a question of cultivating one's own interior. If what we discover by such culture is our membership in the Incarnate Transcendent Community, then we must live this out in terms of deep appreciation of ourselves, of our social communities, of our material, technical, informational, esthetic, and meaningful world.

The Incarnation has many dimensions. We need to be aware of them all and to honor and develop them all. This book has done no more than provide a little background on the wonders of the material world — and the greater wonder that we have been able, through our sciences, to understand some of it — together with the suggestion that it could be meaningful to regard this world and our scientific understanding of it in terms of an "incarnation" of the Deity-Community. It needs to be balanced by comparable books on society, ethics, and esthetics.

And, of course, if we are speaking of an *incarnational* mysticism, then such mysticism will manifest itself, not in withdrawal from the world and understanding of the world, but in realization of the Transcendent Reality precisely in the movements of the world — physical, chemical, biological, social, scientific, political, artistic, religious — and in active, intelligent, compassionate, responsible, beautiful, happy *working with* these dimensions. We are in the process of trying to do this.

And the contemplative? Does the contemplative have some special role? I say to the contemplative: Feel at home in the universe, study it, try to understand at least some of its innumerable marvels, including ourselves who are more and more capable of this understanding — marvel at that! Rejoice in the cosmos. In spite of all its hurtful ways, look at what it has done, is doing, is capable of doing. If you can see the God you love as present in, even as, this world, then feel that union and rejoice in that. And be active in it, contribute to it, participate in the building, in the artwork, in the healing, in the understanding. This is where Reality is. You yourself are both a member of the Finite and a member of the Infinite. You are a participant in the Trinitarian Life Cycle, for you are doing the incarnating and the creating and the realizing and the rejoicing. God's ecstasy creates the world, and the world's ecstasy realizes God. And you are right in the midst of it all.

NOTES

Chapter One: The Contemplative and the Cosmos

1. Pierre Teilhard de Chardin, *Letters from a Traveller* (New York: Harper & Row, 1962), 133, 305.

2. Keiji Nishitani, *Religion and Nothingness,* trans. Jan Van Bragt (Berkeley: University of California Press, 1982), 11–12.

3. Eric J. Lerner, *The Big Bang Never Happened* (New York: Times Books, 1991), 400.

4. Pierre Teilhard de Chardin, *The Phenomenon of Man* (New York: Harper Torchbook, 1961), 170; *The Appearance of Man* (New York: Harper & Row, 1965), 49.

5. I am borrowing the term "poise" from Aurobindo Ghose, who described the Absolute as having three poises: the transcendent, the cosmic, and the individual, but disclaimed credit for the idea, saying that he got it from esoteric Christianity! See B. Bruteau, ed., *Worthy Is the World: The Hindu Philosophy of Sri Aurobindo* (Cranbury, N.J.: Associated University Presses, 1971), 258–59.

Chapter Two: God as Person-Community

1. Jack Miles, *God: A Biography* (New York: Vintage, 1996), 98–99.

2. Einstein as cited by John L. Casti, *Five Golden Rules: Great Theories of 20th-Century Mathematics — and Why They Matter* (New York: Wiley, 1996), xiii.

3. Paul Quenon, "In the Womb of Angels," *Living Prayer* 19, no. 4 (1986).

4. Daniel Walsh, "Person and Community," Gethsemani Archives Document 5, Abbey of Gethsemani, Trappist, Ky., November 6, 1971, 4.

Chapter Three: The Incarnation and the Nature of Finitude

1. Fredkin as cited by Robert Wright, *Three Scientists and Their Gods* (New York: Times Books, 1988), 3–80, esp. 64–65.

2. Bruno Barnhart, *The Good Wine: Reading John from the Center* (New York: Paulist, 1993), 433.

3. Paul Davies, *Are We Alone?* (New York: Basic Books, 1995), 22.

4. Keiji Nishitani, in *Religion and Nothingness,* trans. Jan Van Bragt (Berkeley: University of California Press, 1982), has an interesting discussion of what he calls "circuminsessional interpenetration" in the context of the Kyoto School's understanding of *Shunyata* (Emptiness) and Heidegger's concept of *Dasein* (lit. there-being, in the sense of the facticity of existence): "all things are

master and servant to one another.... To say that a certain thing is ... servant to every other thing means that ... it is a constitutive element in the being of every other thing, making it to be what it is and thus to be situated in a position of autonomy as master of itself" (149); "... self-centeredness only comes about at one with other-centeredness, and other-centeredness at one with self-centeredness. And this is quite natural and as it should be" (264). I believe this is congenial with my sense of the enstatic/ecstatic relation.

5. See, e.g., John H. Holland, *Hidden Order: How Adaptation Builds Complexity* (Menlo Park, Calif.: Helix, 1995), 3, for examples of the importance of interaction in the immune system and the central nervous system.

6. See Stuart Kauffman, *At Home in the Universe: The Search for the Laws of Self-Organization and Complexity* (New York: Oxford, 1995), 24, on the emergence of new levels of reality as wholes.

7. G. Spencer-Brown, *Laws of Form* (New York: Dutton, 1979; first published 1969), xxix.

Chapter Four: The Self-Creating Universe: Pathway to the Stars

1. See John D. Barrow, *The Origin of the Universe* (New York: Basic Books, 1994), 4. An excellent, easy, readable book which nevertheless goes into the arguments thoroughly and has diagrams to help.

2. Paul Davies, *The Mind of God* (New York: Simon & Schuster, 1992), 63-68. In this book Davies, who is a physicist by trade, engages philosophical and theological questions as well as cosmological ones in a dialogue that shows where the questions lie and why. The expression "the mind of God" refers to the laws of nature.

3. John D. Barrow and Frank J. Tipler, *The Anthropic Cosmological Principle* (New York: Oxford, 1988), 15. Difficult technical resource. Argues in the end that we are so improbable as to be probably alone in the universe.

4. P. C. W. Davies (the same as Paul Davies in note 2), *The Accidental Universe* (Cambridge: Cambridge University Press, 1982), 39, gives a list of fundamental constants and derived quantities. The book details what would happen if various constants (including ratios of the constants to one another) were different. The extraordinary thing is that so many independent quantities are simultaneously constrained to quite narrow ranges in order for a universe such as our own to develop.

5. Joseph Silk, *Cosmic Enigmas* (Woodbury, N.J.: American Institute of Physics, 1994), 181. Scientific papers, accessible to the educated reader, mostly about galaxy formation.

6. P. J. E. Peebles, *Principles of Physical Cosmology* (Princeton: Princeton University Press, 1993). A comprehensive overview for students and scientists in other fields. Advanced mathematics, detailed explanations, criticism, and reflection. More helpful than popularized versions if you want to know what the theories and conjectures really are, what questions they undertake to answer, and how successful they have been.

7. Velocity is distance per unit of time (e.g., miles per hour): d/t. When it is divided by a distance d, that is the same as being multiplied by 1/d. Hence,

H = d/t x 1/d = 1/t. For the Hubble parameter, see Trinh Xuan Thuan, *The Secret Melody: And Man Created the Universe,* trans. (from French) Storm Dunlop (New York: Oxford, 1995), 186–87, 289–90. The latter pages give simple mathematical details of the cosmological parameters: expansion, deceleration, density. Popularized reflections of an astrophysicist (known as the Carl Sagan of France); readable, provocative. Technical topics in appendices, glossary.

8. Barrow, *Origin,* 3–11; a simple explanation and good diagrams.

9. Ibid., 13. See also Silk, *Cosmic Enigmas,* x; for details, see 190–96.

10. Thuan, *The Secret Melody,* 122.

11. Alan H. Guth, "Starting the Universe: The Big Bang and Cosmic Inflation," in *Bubbles, Voids and Bumps in Time: The New Cosmology,* ed. James Cornell (Cambridge: Cambridge University Press, 1989), 138. See also Barrow, *Origin,* 60–62.

12. Michael Rowan-Robinson, *Ripples in the Cosmos: A View behind the Scenes of the New Cosmology* (Oxford: Freeman, 1993), 127–31, 142. Author participated in the IRAS studies. On the relationship of density to geometry: General relativity predicted (and this has been observed to be the case) that light in the vicinity of a massive body, such as a star, will behave as if it is pulled a little toward the star by the latter's gravitational field. But, says general relativity, you could just as well describe what is happening by saying that the space is curved in the vicinity of a massive body — or, of a strong gravitational field — and therefore light, traveling in a straight line, as is its custom, will follow the geodesic (shortest distance) of the curved space and thus move around the source of the field.

If there are many massive bodies close to each other (high density), there will be a very strong gravitational field, and the space will be tightly curved all around them, approaching enclosing them in a sphere. Such a space is called "closed." On the other hand, if there are few bodies, distant from each other (low density, weak field), the (expanding) space will bend away from itself in every direction and will be called "open." The idea is that the gravity and the expansion are opposing forces. But if the gravity just balances the expansion, the space won't bend either way but be "flat." This is the way we actually perceive space to be, except in the vicinity of massive bodies. The universe, over all, is flat.

13. Michael Riordan and David N. Schramm, *The Shadows of Creation: Dark Matter and the Structure of the Universe* (New York: Freeman, 1991), 110. Easily understood text, with helpful pictures. See also Alan Lightman and Roberta Brawer, *Origins: The Lives and Worlds of Modern Cosmologists* (Cambridge, Mass.: Harvard University Press, 1990), 24, 40. Interviews with twenty-seven cosmologists, including people whose names have been mentioned here. Very interesting inside view, instructive. Lengthy introduction on the science itself (pages cited above), recommended reading list, glossary.

14. Jeremy Bernstein, *An Introduction to Cosmology* (Englewood Cliffs, N.J.: Prentice-Hall, 1995), 166–67. This is a textbook, not for popular or easy reading unless you already know a good bit of math and physics but very helpful if you do.

15. Peebles, *Principles of Physical Cosmology,* 396.

16. Riordan and Schramm, *The Shadows of Creation,* 167.

17. Peebles, *Principles of Physical Cosmology*, 405, 408.

18. Bernstein, *An Introduction to Cosmology*, 170.

19. See Riordan and Schramm, *The Shadows of Creation*, 97–99, 101, 108–110. There is a good deal more to this part of the story, which features Andrei Sakharov, who proposed an interaction that (1) did not require the number of baryons (particles that react to the strong force) to be constant, (2) did require violation of the principle that says that the laws of physics remain the same if particles are replaced by antiparticles and any process is replaced by its mirror image, and (3) went out of equilibrium (reverse reactions did not proceed at the same rate as forward reactions). The situation at the end of the inflation epoch fulfills these conditions. For details, see Bernstein, *An Introduction to Cosmology*, 181.

20. Bernstein, *An Introduction to Cosmology*, 174.

21. Leon Lederman with Dick Teresi, *The God Particle: If the Universe Is the Answer, What Is the Question?* (Boston: Houghton Mifflin, 1993), 398.

22. Guth, "Starting the Universe," 136.

23. Bernstein, *An Introduction to Cosmology*, 175, 150. Also see Riordan and Schramm, *The Shadows of Creation*, 168–69.

24. Guth, "Starting the Universe," 139. Barrow, *Origin*, 83, adds that with inflation we can draw no conclusion about a beginning to the universe. The inflation destroys all evidence about whatever preceded it.

25. Barrow, *Origin*, 76–81. The degree of clustering varies with how big a piece of sky you're looking at: less clustering on larger scales. Rowan-Robinson's *Ripples* (n. 12) is an engaging account of the history of these discoveries and the people involved from the perspective of a working astrophysicist in the midst of it all. For a technical account and a helpful diagram, see Bernstein, *An Introduction to Cosmology*, 195.

26. Rowan-Robinson, *Ripples*, 188, 195, 207.

27. Barrow, *Origin*, 83–85.

28. Murray Gell-Mann, *The Quark and the Jaguar: Adventures in the Simple and the Complex* (New York: Freeman, 1994), 181. It was Murray Gell-Mann who named the quarks and initiated their theory. This is a popular, readable, yet deep and far-ranging book that covers not only particle physics but complex adaptive systems as they move through the Darwinian process.

29. Thuan, *The Secret Melody*, 145, has a diagram of these two processes, and pp. 135–62 expand the discussion and present helpful and interesting drawings and photos.

30. Silk, *Cosmic Enigmas*, 49. Most of this book, as previously noted, is about galaxy formation, so many details are available.

31. Riordan and Schramm, *The Shadows of Creation*, 121. There is a lot of good material on this stage of the evolution on pp. 115–53, with drawings, photos, and computer simulations.

32. Barrow (*Origins*, 124–25) remarks that "the presence of carbon in the universe depends not merely upon the age and size of the universe but also upon two amazing apparent coincidences between those constants of nature that determine the energy levels of nuclei.... Fred Hoyle... in 1952... predicted that the carbon nucleus could reside in an energy level just greater than the sum of the energies

of the helium and beryllium nuclei...a 'resonant' state: one that has a natural level of energy waiting for it." So instead of it being difficult to make carbon from helium, it is clear now why it is easy and why plenty of carbon is made.

"And here is the second coincidence: Once the carbon is made, it could all be turned into oxygen by the nuclear reactions between carbon and further helium nuclei. But this reaction just fails to be resonant — by an even finer margin — and therefore the carbon survives." In the event, carbon and oxygen are made in about equal quantities; these two elements are the most abundant in the universe after hydrogen and helium (P. W. Atkins, *The Periodic Kingdom: A Journey into the Land of the Chemical Elements* [New York: Basic Books, 1995], 72.)

33. Atkins, *The Periodic Kingdom*, 72–75. If you want to see what an exploding star looks like, find a photo of the Crab Nebula (there's a black and white on p. 172 of Thuan's *Secret Melody*, but color versions are widely available, even on calendars, and on the World Wide Web see www.nasa.gov. It was first seen from Earth on July 4, 1054, in China. The debris is strung out across hundreds of billions of kilometers of space.

34. Thuan, *The Secret Melody*, 178.

Chapter Five: The Cosmos as God's Ecstasy

1. Michlo Kaku, "What Happened before the Big Bang?" *Astronomy* (May 1996): 38. "Physicists find it difficult to construct things in which protons have lifetimes [before decaying into other particles] long enough to create the chemicals for life." (The symmetry of a Grand Unified Theory, absorbing the strong, weak, and electromagnetic forces, requires the proton, like any other particle, to be capable of decay.) A minimum of ten billion years is necessary to create stable organic molecules. Such a special condition may have a low probability.

2. Ibid.

3. Paul Davies, *God and the New Physics* (New York: Simon & Schuster, 1983), 215.

4. P. C. W. Davies and Julian Brown, eds., *Superstrings: A Theory of Everything?* (Cambridge: Cambridge University Press, 1981), 124–25.

5. Ibid., 221–22.

6. Gershom Scholem, *Kabbalah* (New York: Meridian, 1978; reprint from Jerusalem: Keter, 1974), 95. See also pp. 109–11, which are of some interest in relation to my discussion of the Trinity and the "I–I" relation: the first emanation from the Infinite is "the force hidden within the third person singular of the verb *bara* [created] — [which] produced...the third [emanation]...called *Elohim*. *Elohim* ('God') is thus not the subject but the object of the sentence...*bereshit bara Elohim* [ordinarily 'In the beginning God created...' but now 'The Beginning created God']. But as His manifestation continues, God becomes 'Thou,' whom man is now able to address directly. However, God reaches His complete individuation through His manifestation in *Malkut* [the tenth emanation, called 'the Kingdom'], where He is called 'I.' This conception is summed up in... 'Nothingness changes into I.' " Cf. D. Walsh's claim that the first effusion of Love (which is God) is the Trinity (p. 34 above) and the second effusion is the company of persons who will be expressed as angels and human beings (see chap. 2,

n. 4, p. 181 above) and my use of the Theotokos, the evolutionary process by which divine consciousness comes to itself in manifestation. For more on Walsh, see B. Bruteau, feature book review of Robert Imperato, *Merton and Walsh on the Person,* in *International Philosophical Quarterly* 31 (1991): 353–63.

7. Ibid., 93. "It is called *Ein-Sof* [without end] internally and *Elyon* [divine will] externally" (p. 92, citing *Tikkunei Zohar,* end of Tikkun 22).

8. Ibid., 147.

Chapter Six: The Self-Creating Universe: Pathway to Life

1. See any elementary chemistry text, e.g., Theodore L. Brown, H. Eugene LeMay, Jr., Bruce E. Bursten, *Chemistry: The Central Science,* 6th ed. (Englewood Cliffs, N.J.: Prentice-Hall, 1994), 250ff.

2. Ibid., 259. Richard Bader, *Atoms in Molecules: A Quantum Theory* (Oxford: Clarendon, 1994), 290–95, gives a classification of atomic interactions. There are two main types: "shared interactions" and "closed-shell interactions." The former are characterized by delocalization; the latter include the ionic bonds, hydrogen bonds, and some other types. *Atoms in Molecules* is a technical resource book. An attractive and easy book is Lionel Salem's *Marvels of the Molecule* (New York: VCH Publishers, 1987): quantum chemistry taught almost entirely in pictures with brief texts for each two-page lesson.

3. See Ronald F. Fox, *Energy and the Evolution of Life* (New York: Freeman, 1988), 60–61. This is a fairly difficult book, but gives a lot of valuable detail. The author enlarges on the dry-heating phenomenon, which "automatically results in amino acid chains called...proteinoids. Biochemists have discovered that when proteinoids dissolve in water, they spontaneously assemble (*self-assemble*) into spheres about one micrometer...in diameter, called *microspheres* [he supplies a photomicrograph showing them]. The microspheres enclose chains of amino acids...approximately 10^{10} molecules of proteinoid...and other solutes in the water in which they form. Although the proteinoids contain no lipids, the presence of hydrophobic amino acid residues causes the boundaries of the microspheres to act as membranes (some are even double layered)." For another interesting example of prebiotic self-assembly, see "Self-Replicating Molecules That Are Not Alive," in Bryan Bunch, *The Henry Holt Handbook of Current Science and Technology* (New York: Holt, 1992), 166–67: Amino adenosine triad ester, AATE (also known as the J-molecule, from its shape), placed in a chloroform solution of its two components, an amine and an ester, will attach an ester to its amine end and an amine to its ester end. The newcomers are so positioned (consider the J shape) that they can bond to one another by the same kind of bond that amino acids use in making peptide chains. The newly formed J then breaks away from the original and picks up an amine and an ester, which it unites just as it itself was made. AATE can duplicate itself a million times a second if it has the raw materials. Other self-assembly experiments have made large molecules from as many as eleven pieces.

4. For further detail, see Christian de Duve, *Vital Dust: Life as a Cosmic Imperative* (New York: Basic Books, 1995), 46–64. This is a much longer book than the Fox, covering cells, multicellular organisms, and the emergence

of mind. It explains everything thoroughly, so gets a little technical, but is as readable as it is possible to be when dealing this faithfully with material that is itself so complicated. Also contains discussions of special interest for contemplatives, concluding that while chance has an important role In the development of life and intelligence, we ought not to conclude that the universe is meaningless.

5. Michael Crawford and David Marsh, *The Driving Force: Food, Evolution and the Future* (London: Heinemann, 1989), 62. This is a highly readable book which nevertheless tells a great deal about the evolution of life. Its focus is food, "nutrition as a major evolutionary pressure" limiting the directions selection could take, including the appearance of the human brain.

6. De Duve, *Vital Dust*, 61.

7. Stuart Kauffman, *At Home in the Universe: The Search for Laws of Self-Organization and Complexity* (Oxford: Oxford University Press, 1995), 47–48. This is an exciting book, full of new ideas carefully explained by the man who thought up many of them, intended for the general reader.

8. Fox, *Energy and the Evolution of Life*, 94, 155.

9. William F. Loomis, *Four Billion Years: An Essay on the Evolution of Genes and Organisms* (Sunderland, Mass.: Sinauer, 1988), 25–26. M. Eigen and P. Schuster, "The Hypercycle: A Principle of Natural Self-Organization," *Naturwissenschaften* 64 (1977): 541–65. Manfred Eigen is the name most associated with the idea of hypercycles.

10. Loomis, *Four Billion Years*, 27. This book is not very hard to read and it gives you deep detail on what is going on in living structures.

11. Figure from ibid., 29.

12. Ibid., 30.

13. De Duve, *Vital Dust*, 96.

Chapter Seven: The Evolution of Evolution

1. The importance of recognizing "levels of explanation" is stressed by William H. Calvin, *How Brains Think* (New York: Basic Books, 1996), 35–38. Lower-level entities and their relations may be necessary factors in an explanation, but are not sufficient. Spark plugs are needed to explain automobiles but are not of much help in explaining traffic jams. Alwyn Scott, *Stairway to the Mind* (New York: Springer-Verlag, 1995), 182, makes the same point: the dynamics of biological operations don't violate the laws of physics and chemistry, but they cannot be derived from them. They are independent and have their own proper laws.

2. Alfred North Whitehead, *Science and the Modern World* (New York: Macmillan, 1925), esp. 145–46, 156.

3. Robert Wright, *Three Scientists and Their Gods* (New York: Times Books, 1988), 24.

4. Fred Hapgood, *Up the Infinite Corridor: MIT and the Technical Imagination* (Menlo Park, Calif.: Addison-Wesley, 1993), 176. See also James Grier Miller, *Living Systems* (New York: McGraw-Hill, 1978), a prodigious volume, in which he enumerates nineteen critical subsystems essential for life, processing matter or energy or information, or all three (see esp. 511), and further identifies seven levels of organization that exhibit these subsystems (see p. 1).

This is an exhaustive study (eleven hundred pages) with fine distinctions, careful definitions, examples, illustrations. Begins with the cell, ends with societies and supranational systems.

5. See Stuart Kauffman, *At Home in the Universe: The Search for the Laws of Self-Organization and Complexity* (New York: Oxford University Press, 1995), 48, all of chapter 3, and 274.

6. Christian de Duve, *Vital Dust: Life as a Cosmic Imperative* (New York: Basic Books, 1995), 76, 78. William F. Loomis, *Four Billion Years: An Essay on the Evolution of Genes and Organisms* (Sunderland, Mass.: Sinauer, 1988), 45, 60.

7. De Duve, *Vital Dust,* 77. To see some of the creatures evolution has produced, you might want to look at the beautiful picture book *The Thread of Life: The Smithsonian Looks at Evolution,* by Roger Lewin (Washington: Smithsonian Books, 1982), 250 pages of large color illustrations, and easy but informative text.

8. See James E. Lovelock, *Gaia: A New Look at Life on Earth* (New York: Oxford University Press, 1979), 68–82. Lovelock is an atmospheric chemist and has developed a scenario of how the life forms covering Earth control the conditions that are important for their own survival, such as the amounts of methane, oxygen, carbon dioxide, and ammonia in the atmosphere. For instance, there has to be enough oxygen for the creatures that need it but not so much as to make forest fires flare all over the planet. This is regulated by the methane produced by bacteria, which is oxidized to carbon dioxide and water, some of it in the upper atmosphere where the water in turn breaks up into hydrogen which escapes and oxygen which descends to the lower atmosphere. A great deal of the methane is oxidized in the lower atmosphere. This uses up the excess oxygen and keeps the amount in the atmosphere right at 21 percent. See also Sorin Sonea and Maurice Panisset, *A New Bacteriology* (Boston: Jones Bartlett, 1983), chap. 4. What is "new" in this book is the suggestion that all the bacteria on the planet constitute a single superorganism united by a variety of paths for exchanging genes.

9. De Duve, *Vital Dust,* 79–82, 115–17.

10. Sonea and Panisset, *A New Bacteriology,* 32–43.

11. See Lawrence E. Joseph, *Gaia: The Growth of an Idea* (New York: St. Martin's Press, 1990), 37.

12. See Lynn Margolis, *Symbiosis in Cell Evolution* (San Francisco: Freeman, 1981). For getting inside the eukaryotic cell and understanding its workings with the help of very large-scale illustrations, see David S. Goodsell, *The Machinery of Life* (New York: Springer-Verlag, 1993).

13. Lest we think that this is unlikely or would take a long time, we can consider the case of a laboratory in Tennessee where, in 1967, cells of a certain kind of amoeba were invaded by a particular sort of bacterium. Initially this was an "infection" and should have been injurious to the amoebae. But somehow the hosts managed to tolerate the invaders and little by little got on better with them. Cooperation developed, and by 1976 the amoebae were no longer able to live without the bacteria, which shows that an endosymbiotic relationship resulting in a new kind of creature can happen and need not be a prolonged process.

See Elisabet Sahtouris, *Gaia: The Human Journey from Chaos to Cosmos* (New York: Pocket Books, 1989), 85.

14. This material is called "chromatin" (it shows as "colored" when stained). There are four different types of histones used in chromatin. Two of each kind form an "octamer" in a ball and the DNA is wound 1 ¾ turns around this ball and then goes on to the next octamer and wraps around it in the same way. A long piece of this material looks like a string of beads. See David Freifelder, *Molecular Biology* (Boston: Jones and Bartlett, 1983), 202–4, for drawings, diagrams, and electron micrographs of different levels of these structures.

15. De Duve, *Vital Dust*, 158. Also see Peter B. Moens, "Meiosis," *Encyclopedia of Human Biology*, vol. 4 (McLean, Va.: Academic Press, 1991), 953.

16. Scott F. Gilbert, *Developmental Biology*, 3d ed. (Sunderland, Mass.: Sinauer, 1991), 793–95, for discussion and diagrams of the whole process. For more detail, see Moens, "Meiosis," 949–56; this is quite readable and helpful.

17. Robert Jay Russell, *The Lemur's Legacy: The Evolution of Power, Sex, and Love* (New York: Putnam, 1993), 60.

18. De Duve, *Vital Dust*, 159.

19. Cf. Kauffman, *At Home in the Universe*, 182, and John H. Holland, *Hidden Order: How Adaptation Builds Complexity* (Reading, Mass.: Addison-Wesley, 1995), 66ff., 72.

20. Sahtouris (n. 13 above), 105; and Lynn Margolis and Dorian Sagan, *Micro-Cosmos* (New York: Summit, 1986), 188.

21. See William F. Loomis, *Four Billion Years: An Essay on the Evolution of Genes and Organisms* (Sunderland, Mass.: Sinauer, 1988), 181–82.

22. Christopher Wills, *The Wisdom of the Genes* (New York: Basic Books, 1989), 46, 48, 174, 176–77.

23. Edward O. Wilson, *The Diversity of Life* (Cambridge, Mass.: Harvard University Press, 1992), 38, 50, 52, 56, 69. For an interesting discussion of speciation and the ups and downs of species diversity, including the major extinctions and their probable causes, see John Terborgh, *Diversity and the Tropical Rain Forest* (New York: Scientific American Library, 1992), esp. 132. Pleasant text, many color photographs, maps, diagrams; attractive book.

24. Cf. Eric R. Pianka, *Evolutionary Ecology*, 4th ed. (New York: Harper-Collins, 1988), 176–79, on population cycles.

25. Wilson, *The Diversity of Life*, 29–31, 191. Pianka, *Evolutionary Ecology*, 56–57, shows maps of the continental masses at various geological times: Pangaea at 200 million years ago; Laurasia and Gondwana at 180 million; 70 million years ago North America was still joined to Europe, South America had separated from Africa, India was on its way from Antarctica to Asia, and Australia was still joined to Antarctica. Terborgh, 139ff., explains the "Milankovitch cycles," alterations in Earth's orbit, tilt of axis, etc., that cause these climatic changes.

26. Wilson's book is in large measure a documentation of the human threat to planetary life, a plea for attention to this, and an outline of actions that could be taken to preserve biodiversity. Terborgh also devotes considerable space to these topics. Likewise, de Duve, *Vital Dust*, 273ff.

27. De Duve, *Vital Dust*, 196–97.

28. For a chart of the forking development and discussion, see ibid., 202.

29. Lewis Wolpert, *The Triumph of the Embryo* (New York: Oxford, 1992), 115–17; 83–84, 88; 37–42. Easy, interesting, instructive.

30. See Pianka, *Evolutionary Ecology,* chap. 12 on "Predation and Parasitism," 271–303; predator escape tactics are discussed on 286ff., and "coevolution" starts on 298. Sometimes the presence of a predator in an ecological community is advantageous to its prey in the sense that if it were removed, other competitors would come in and crowd out the prey species (Wilson, *Diversity of Life,* 176).

31. Lovelock, *Gaia,* 72–73. See chap. 7, n. 8, p. 188 above.

32. Wilson, *The Diversity of Life,* 176–79.

33. Pianka, *Evolutionary Ecology,* 287, 292. See also Wills, *The Wisdom of the Genes,* 190–209, which lays out the mimicry behavior in detail, with illustrations and particular examples, as well as genetic explanations.

34. Richard Dawkins, *The Extended Phenotype* (New York: Oxford University Press, 1982), 238, 247.

35. De Duve, *Vital Dust,* 77. See also 85–86, 222–24, for discussion of this focusing by means of modular assembly of exons.

36. Wills, *The Wisdom of the Genes,* 169–79, 140–44. Gilbert, *Developmental Biology,* 230–32, 360–66, 593–911. Loomis, *Four Billion Years,* 241–42. If you get really interested, you might want to look at Klaus D. Elgert, *Immunology* (New York: Wiley-Liss, 1996), esp. 228–36 on "Complex Cooperative Interactions among Immune Cell Populations Lead to Antibody Production," embedded in a more extensive section entitled "The Development of an Immune Response Requires Cellular Cooperation." This "cooperative interaction" is a good example of our basic principles of Being.

37. De Duve, *Vital Dust,* 226.

38. Wilson, *The Diversity of Life,* 84–85.

39. Ibid., 86. Murray Gell-Mann, *The Quark and the Jaguar* (New York: Freeman, 1994), 260.

40. Kauffman, *At Home in the Universe,* 182–89.

41. De Duve, *Vital Dust,* 300, citing J. Monod, *Chance and Necessity,* trans. A. Wainhouse (New York: Knopf, 1971), 145–46. This is a famous book. Its thesis is summed up by David Layzer in *Cosmogenesis: The Growth of Order in the Universe* (New York: Oxford University Press, 1990), 198: "Evolution, in Monod's view, results from *imperfections* of the replicative mechanism that serves each species' essential project. It is a by-product of the universal entropic tendency toward disorder. Monod assigns the precise replication of genetic material to the realm of necessity. Errors in replication belong to the realm of chance. Evolution results from an interaction between the two realms." De Duve himself says of it: "In this book, which sparked major controversies when it first came out, a master of modern biology (who died in 1976) defends a stoically and romantically despairing existentialist view of the human condition. Somewhat outdated but still beautiful reading" (350).

42. Gell-Mann, *The Quark and the Jaguar,* 257.

Chapter Eight: The Self-Creating Universe: Pathway to Consciousness

1. See, e.g., Tilden Edwards, *Living Simply* (New York: Phoenix, 1977), 32: Eastern and Western spirituality have a shared original awareness of "the immensely spacious, compassionate, imageless image of God shining through us, revealing an indestructible unity through endlessly changing forms."

2. Cf. Henri Bergson, *The Two Sources of Morality and Religion,* trans. R. A. Audra, C. Brereton, W. H. Carter (Garden City, N.Y.: Doubleday Anchor, 1954), 255: this is the conclusion to which "the philosopher who holds to the mystical experience must come. Creation will appear to him as God undertaking to create creators."

3. Sorin Sonea and Maurice Panisset, *A New Bacteriology* (Boston: Jones & Bartlett, 1983), 30.

4. William C. Agosta, *Chemical Communication: The Language of Pheromones* (New York: Scientific American, 1992), 13, 22, 33, 84, 87–88, 95–96. For the other senses, see Shannon Brownless, with Traci Watson, "The Senses," *U.S. News and World Report* (January 13, 1997): 51–59.

5. Some of the factors affecting the passage of signals through the dendritic tree are: whether the original inputs were stimulating or inhibitory; whether their relay was delayed (or blocked) by varicosities or at junctions where subbranches join major branches; whether an impulse was passed by an OR gate (either one of the subbranches would do) or by an AND gate (both branches needed). For thorough but easy discussion, with illustrations, see Alwyn Scott, *Stairway to the Mind* (New York: Springer-Verlag, 1995), 56–69. Also see the very attractive dialogue format in William H. Calvin and George A. Ojemann, *Conversations with Neil's Brain: The Neural Nature of Thought and Language* (New York: Addison-Wesley, 1994), chap. 6, "The Personality of the Lowly Neuron."

6. As cited by Fritjof Capra, *The Web of Life: A New Scientific Understanding of Living Systems* (New York: Anchor, 1996), 280–85. Network dynamics of self-making systems; easy. For detail on immune system, see Scott F. Gilbert, *Developmental Biology,* 3d ed. (Sunderland, Mass.: Sinauer, 1991), 727ff.

7. William H. Calvin, *How Brains Think: Evolving Intelligence, Then and Now* (New York: Basic Books, 1996), 121.

8. Calvin and Ojemann, *Conversations,* 172, 174; and Scott, *Stairway to the Mind,* 84–94.

9. Scott, *Stairway to the Mind,* 81–83, 89.

10. Ibid., 169.

11. David Layzer, *Cosmogenesis: The Growth of Order in the Universe* (New York: Oxford University Press, 1990), 261, 239. Includes philosophy of mind and matter.

12. Gary Cziko, *Without Miracles: Universal Selection Theory and the Second Darwinian Revolution* (Cambridge, Mass.: MIT, 1995), 111–21.

13. Scott, *Stairway to the Mind,* 84, 88–90.

14. Michael C. Corballis, *The Lopsided Ape: Evolution of the Generative Mind* (New York: Oxford, 1991), 112–18, 311, 235; on "generativity": un-

limited constructions from limited parts. Cf. Derek Bickerton, *Language and Human Behavior* (Seattle: University of Washington, 1995) 66–68; very helpful.

15. Bickerton, *Language and Human Behavior*, 90–97, 105, 147; Index: "Secondary Representational System."

16. Ibid., 149, 151.

17. Daniel C. Dennett, *Consciousness Explained* (Boston: Little, Brown, 1991), 410; Calvin and Ojemann, *Conversations*, 138.

18. Bickerton, *Language and Human Behavior*, 152.

19. William F. Allman, *The Stone Age Present: How Evolution Has Shaped Modern Life — From Sex, Violence, and Language to Emotions, Morals, and Communities* (New York: Simon & Schuster, 1994), 19–21, 69. Cf. Corballis, *The Lopsided Age*, 113.

20. Scott, *Stairway to the Mind*, 138, citing Francis Crick, *The Astonishing Hypothesis: The Scientific Search for the Soul* (New York: Simon & Schuster, 1994).

21. See Calvin, *How Brains Think*, 104, where a "Darwin Machine" is defined as a process possessing six essential properties: a pattern; copies made of this pattern; pattern changes due to mutations, error, or reshuffling; copying competitions; variants selected by interaction with multifaceted environment; next generation from variants surviving to reproduce. See also p. 140, which mentions his book-length treatment of this idea, *The Cerebral Code: Thinking a Thought in the Mosaics of the Mind* (Cambridge, Mass.: MIT, 1996), and 216, 284–85.

22. Calvin and Ojemann, *Conversations*, 286, 138.

23. Roger W. Sperry, "Forebrain Commissurotomy and Conscious Awareness," *J. Med. Philos.*, 2:101–26, 1977. For more on Sperry's ideas, see Paul Davies, *The Cosmic Blueprint: New Discoveries in Nature's Creative Ability to Order the Universe* (New York: Simon & Schuster, 1988), 191–92.

24. Karl R. Popper and John C. Eccles, *The Self and Its Brain: An Argument for Interactionism* (Boston: Routledge & Kegan Paul, 1977), 362, italics his; see elaboration in Eccles's *How the Self Controls Its Brain*, 1994.

25. Dennett, *Consciousness Explained*, 416, 455.

26. Bickerton, *Language and Human Behavior*, 150–53; Scott, *Stairway to the Mind*, 163.

27. Scott, *Stairway to the Mind*, 164, 165, 170, 172.

28. David J. Chalmers, *The Conscious Mind: In Search of a Fundamental Theory* (New York: Oxford, 1996), 125 (cf. 11), 124, 245.

29. Ibid., 126, 127. His concept of "natural supervenience" is (roughly) de facto correlations between physical states and consciousness states. "This happens when the same clusters of [low-level (=physical)] properties ... are always accompanied by the same [high-level (=conscious experience)] properties, and when this correlation is not just coincidental but lawful: that is, when instantiating the [low-level] properties will always bring about the [high-level] properties" (37; cf. 33). This lawful correlation is spelled out in the "psychophysical laws" which Chalmers says are the foundation of his view.

30. Ibid., 299, 124, 125.

31. Layzer, *Cosmogenesis*, 260.

32. Popper and Eccles, *The Self and Its Brain*, 554.

33. Scott, *Stairway to the Mind*, 115–16. The Wigner quote is from "Are We Machines?" *Proceedings of the American Philosophical Society* 113 (1969): 95–101.

34. Ibid., 167. See also p. 132: "Consciousness is — for each of us — a fact of reality.... There is nothing strange about consciousness except that we don't understand it." I would add "in objective or materialist terms."

35. Roger Sperry: "The causal power attributed to subjective properties is *nothing mystical*" (cited in Scott, *Stairway to the Mind*, 119; original reference given in n. 23 above.)

Christopher Wills: "There is a good...conventional neo-Darwinian explanation...for why our evolution...has every appearance of being somehow directed toward a goal. There is *nothing mystical, magical, or theological* about this explanation" (*The Runaway Brain: The Evolution of Human Uniqueness* [New York: Basic Books, 1993], 79).

Franz Boas "rejected...reductive materialism...but he did not *succumb to mysticism* in his attempts to understand...social behavior" (Scott, *Stairway to the Mind*, 186).

Michael Corballis: The scenario of the appearance of language among humans by an evolution that "took perhaps tens of thousands of years to...realize its potential...seems to imply some arbitrary genetic reshuffle...[that] smacks of *the magical, even of the theological*" (*The Lopsided Age*, 163–64; he prefers an even more gradual development).

David Layzer: "The notion of emergence generally figures in mystical accounts of cosmic evolution" (*Cosmogenesis*, 263).

David Chalmers: "There is nothing *antiscientific or supernatural* about this view" (*The Conscious Mind*, 126).

Erich Harth: "It is...nonsensical to assert that introducing such elements as political philosophies...or a climate of opinion, means *resorting* to some kind of *mysticism*" ("Self-Referent Mechanisms as the Neural Basis of Consciousness," in *Toward a Science of Consciousness*, ed. Hameroff, Kaszniak, and Scott (Cambridge, Mass.: MIT, 1995), cited in Scott, *Stairway to the Mind*, 161–62).

I should say here that "mysticism" has nothing whatsoever to do with parapsychological or paraphysical phenomena, such as precognition or psychokinesis, much less with magic. It doesn't even have anything to do with the supernatural or (necessarily) with the theological. It has to do with unitary consciousness. A state of consciousness in which one grasps in a global way the unity of all that one knows — one's whole world — is sometimes called a "mystical" experience. But usually the term is restricted to the unmediated experience of ground-level consciousness as Ground of Being. This is primitive, irreducible, nonrelative, and formless, or unspecified. The experiencer generally claims that this Ground transcends any particular being for which it is the condition of possibility and that it is the foundation of the whole natural world. As a physicist might say that everything is a particular organization of energy but that energy as such transcends any particular form, so the mystic says the same, only generalizing even beyond "energy" to "being."

David Layzer, who uses emergence in the same way several of these other researchers do and says that "consciousness is radically contingent,...a brute fact that could not have been predicted [and has from the objective standpoint of natural science] no rhyme or reason is emergent in a metaphysical sense." He then asks, "Is this view of consciousness *mystical?*" and, relying on a dictionary definition of mysticism, admits that "consciousness is certainly a reality 'central to being and directly accessible by intuition.' " Nevertheless, it is the very "stuff of perception" and available to "intellectual apprehension" (*Cosmogenesis,* 265; emphasis added). For a similar tension in the behavior science community, see chap. 9, n. 10, p. 195 below.

36. Chalmers, *The Conscious Mind,* 295–301.

37. He uses Claude Shannon's concept of information (distinguished from a semantic concept of information) as a particular state selected from an array of alternatives. The alternatives have "differences" among them. Complex information can be built up by having more variation in the array or by combining the alternatives available. We are familiar with this sort of thing from all the mixing and matching examples we have seen in the formation of atoms, molecules, cycles, cells, genes, etc. See ibid., 278–80; also 111.

38. Ibid., 284, italics added lest you miss the distinction between "space" and "state." Notice that he assumes (remember his "psychophysical laws") that there is a correlative physical substrate.

39. Ibid., 154–55; see also 129.

40. Ibid., 304–5.

Chapter Nine: Theotokos: The Ecstasy of the Cosmos as God

1. Richard Dawkins, *The Selfish Gene* (New York: Oxford University Press, 1976), 206.

2. William H. Calvin, *The Cerebral Code: Thinking a Thought in the Mosaics of the Mind* (Cambridge, Mass.: MIT, 1996), 18–25, 82, 197. This book is about copying and selecting ideas in a single mind, in the brain. The "mosaics" are formed by Hebbian cell-assemblies that include enough information to replicate themselves and accumulate copies in their neighborhood. For an updated version of the Darwinian process, see William H. Calvin, "The Six Essentials? Minimal Requirements for the Darwinian Bootstrapping of Quality," *Journal of Memetics* (1997; see http://www.fmb.mmu.ac.uk/jom-emit/1997/vol1/calvin_wh.html). When no obstacle intervenes, the "process is capable of repeatedly bootstrapping quality."

3. Aaron Lynch, *Thought Contagion: How Belief Spreads through Society* (New York: Basic Books, 1996), 3–12. Christians may be interested in Lynch's list of memes advantageous to Christianity: every believer must gain converts; rewards for belief and punishments for unbelief are maximal (eternal heaven or hell — hence strong motive in the context of risk rather than of truth); this decision for Christ must be made soon because the end is near (either the end of the world or the end of the individual's life); all benefits are due to the Savior's suffering and death to win forgiveness of sin for believers, so the grateful believer will do whatever the Savior commands, especially adhering to the faith and spreading the faith; believers love one another and help one another, believers feel good and are secure in the company of fellow believers, proselytizing

is evidence of loving concern for the unbeliever's welfare. This is a partial list; see pp. 107–26. He does similar analyses of Judaism and Islam and of several minor sects, such as the Amish, Mormons, Shakers, 1–2, 130–32. He also treats social structure and custom, sex, health, social sciences, sport, crime, drugs, diets, firearms, pacifism. Interesting book. See also Richard Brodie, *Virus of the Mind: The New Science of the Meme* (Seattle: Integral, 1996). Popular level, everyday applications.

4. Lyall Watson, *Dark Nature: A Natural History of Evil* (New York: HarperCollins, 1995), 69, 249, 252, 205. For examples of rape, adultery, and desertion among fish, birds, insects, spiders, frogs, and turtles, see 177, 251. For recent national rapes (twenty thousand Chinese women by Japanese, 1937; tens of thousands of Italians by Moroccan mercenaries given license by the French, 1943; hundreds of thousands of Germans by Allied troops, 1945), 179–80. On the inevitability of war, 174, 176.

5. Ibid., 261, 277, 65.

6. See William H. Calvin, *How Brains Think* (New York: Basic Books, 1996), 63.

7. Dawkins, *The Selfish Gene*, 98–100. This line of thought received a significant input from Robert Trivers, "The Evolution of Reciprocal Altruism," *Quarterly Review of Biology* 46 (1971): 35–57.

8. Robert Axelrod, *The Evolution of Cooperation* (New York: Basic Books, 1984), esp. 92, 20–21, 46, 182. "In the Prisoner's Dilemma game, there are two players. Each has two choices, namely, cooperate or defect. Each must make the choice without knowing what the other will do. No matter what the other does, defection yields a higher payoff than cooperation. The dilemma is that if both defect, both do worse than if both had cooperated" (7–8). There is nothing mystical in this. Viruses and bacteria can discover and play by an advantage strategy (93–94), and the results can be accurately worked out by mathematics (see, e.g., 96–97).

9. Watson, *Dark Nature*, 82–83; cf. 85–86. Morality, justice, 81, 211.

10. Frans de Waal, *Good Natured: The Origins of Right and Wrong in Humans and Other Animals* (Cambridge, Mass.: Harvard University Press, 1996), 189–90; 24–26, 156, 174; see also, by the same author, *Peacemaking among Primates* (Cambridge, Mass.: Harvard University Press, 1989), 42, 40–61; 160–61, 210–11. By the way, just as the consciousness scientists are uneasy about being "mystical," so the behavior scientists, according to de Waal, are reluctant to use human words such as "love," "friend," "reconcile," to describe positive behavior in animals, although they seem not to have a parallel difficulty with human words for negative behavior, such as "greed," "spite," "murder." Reconciliation sealed with a kiss becomes "post-conflict interaction involving mouth-to-mouth contact" (18–19). Reminds me of an old joke about the Army defining a spade as a "manually operated earth-moving implement." De Waal quotes economist Robert Frank on the behavioral sciences: "The flint-eyed researcher fears no greater humiliation than to have called some action altruistic, only to have a more sophisticated colleague later demonstrate that it was self-serving. This fear surely helps account for the extraordinary volume of ink behavioral scientists have spent trying to unearth selfish motives for seem-

ingly self-sacrificing acts" (*Passions within Reason: The Strategic Role of the Emotions* [New York: Norton, 1988]).

11. John Leo, Universal Press Syndicate, piece carried in *Winston-Salem Journal*, Tuesday, February 4, 1997, A9 (editorial) under the title "Spare Us the Rodman Phenomenon" (referring to Dennis Rodman, *Bad As I Wanna Be*): "The assault on norms — all norms, any norms — is a standard feature of the recurring intellectual battles on campus. Here is the eminent sociologist Irving Louis Horowitz, writing about the severe damage done to the once-healthy field of sociology since the '60s: 'The key objective of ideological extremism from the outset has been the total repudiation of the normative character of the social system.... In the wonderful world without norms, there can be no deviance — only alternative lifestyles....' The iconic importance of Rodman [poster boy of 'the transgressive culture'] has something to do with ... an imperial self, a rebel with no stable identity, set in opposition to all known norms, rules, traditions, authority and mainstream values ... [symbol of] the anything-goes culture that surrounds us now." A similar piece appeared on June 12, 1996, by Donald Kaul (Tribune Media Services), concerned about "the success of Rodman's book ... that there are young people who want to be like Dennis when they grow up, if not sooner. It must be the case. Why else would shoe companies and others pay him enormous sums to hawk their goods?" Both columnists complete their pieces with other examples of such role models.

12. Dawkins, *The Selfish Gone*, 215.

13. See M. Scott Peck, M.D., *People of the Lie: The Hope for Healing Human Evil* (New York: Simon & Schuster, 1983).

14. See John 8:44 (Father of Lies); John 8:32 (truth will make you free); John 14:20 (you will know that I am in my Father, and you in me, and I in you).

15. Watson, *Dark Nature*, 281–82, quoting Annie Dillard, *Pilgrim at Tinker Creek* (New York: Harpers, 1974).

16. Song in honor of the Paschal Candle, Easter Vigil Liturgy in some liturgical churches.

17. Leviticus Rabbah 28:1.

18. Gershom Scholem, *Kabbalah* (Jerusalem: Keter, 1974; reprinted by Meridian, New York Times Books, 1978), 147.

19. Moshe Braun, *The Jewish Holy Days: Their Spiritual Significance* (Northvale, N.J.: Aronson, 1996), 397, 372–73, 403.

20. Tamid 32a.

21. See *The Bahir*, Jewish text of the first century, attributed to Rabbi Nehuniah (Northvale, N.J.: Aronson, 1995), 92–94: "God's purpose in creation was that He should give of His good to His handiwork. When that purpose is fulfilled through 'awakening from below,' God's purpose is fulfilled, and, as it were, He is 'elevated' " (94). Cf. John 16:28.

22. Lawrence Kushner, *The River of Light: Spirituality, Judaism, Consciousness* (Woodstock, Vt.: Jewish Lights, 1990), 139 (adapted).

Index of Names

INDEX OF SUBJECTS